The Case for
BARRY BONDS
in the Hall of Fame:

*The Untold and Forgotten Stories
of Baseball's Home Run King*

K. P. WEE

For more information contact:
Riverdale Avenue Books
5676 Riverdale Avenue
Riverdale, NY 10471.

www.riverdaleavebooks.com

Design by www.formatting4U.com
Cover by Scott Carpenter
Front cover photos reprinted with permission from the San Francisco Giants
©2020 S.F. Giants

Digital ISBN: 97826015814
Print ISBN: 015821

First Edition: April

For Jason Takefman, Rick Ambrozic, Rick Tanton and Nahyun L.

Table of Contents

Acknowledgments

This book wouldn't have been possible without Richard Perkins, who pitched the idea to me in early 2020 to write about Barry Bonds and perhaps reveal a side about him that many baseball fans haven't heard about. So, thank you to Richard, along with Lori Perkins at Riverdale Avenue Books, for giving me the opportunity to write this book.

I would also like to personally express my gratitude to Adrian Brijbassi, Tom Candiotti, John Cangelosi, Royce Clayton, J. P. Hoornstra, Dustan Mohr, Bob Nightengale, John Patterson and Ted Sobel for taking the time to share their thoughts. Thank you, too, to Steve Buechele, Bob Walk and Don Slaught for spending a few minutes to chat briefly about Barry while discussing another one of my projects. Many thanks to photography assistant Suzanna Mitchell and the San Francisco Giants for their cooperation in supplying the photos for this book. On a personal note, I'd like to single out the following individuals for their enthusiasm and/or encouragement during the course of writing this book: Rick Ambrozic, Michael McCormick, Terrell Renfro, Nahyun L., Jason Takefman, Rick Tanton (who was actually the first person who suggested that I write a book about Bonds to give Barry's side of the story, when he casually brought it up about five years before Richard Perkins did) and Brant Valach.

Finally, thank you, Barry Bonds, for providing baseball fans with your outstanding play every single season during your incredible 22-year career in the major leagues. Neither Barry nor his representatives responded to multiple requests to be interviewed for this book—but it's okay. Barry, who should already be in the Baseball Hall of Fame but, as of this writing, still isn't, entertained fans with his on-field performances from 1986 to 2007 in the big leagues. He doesn't owe me or anybody else anything beyond what he did on the diamond. That's the hard part which people sometimes don't realize; people assume that athletes should talk to you simply because you're doing a story. For me, it's not worth it to bother somebody if he or she doesn't wish to talk or cooperate. As a writer who understands you simply don't get everybody whom you would like to talk to, the solution is to write the story using secondary sources. Thank you to you, the reader, for understanding.

—K. P. Wee, Winter 2020

Introduction

For many baseball fans, there is nothing more to be said about Barry Bonds that hasn't been repeated ad nauseam. One of this book's objectives, though, is to share stories about Bonds that reveal another side of him which isn't always reported by the press. Another is to highlight many of the untold and forgotten stories of Bonds' life in baseball.

Let's start with what many already know. Readers who follow the sport know that Bonds, as of this writing, isn't in the Baseball Hall of Fame primarily because his candidacy has been marred by the BALCO scandal in which he was indicted for perjury and obstruction of justice on his grand jury testimony that he knowingly used performance-enhancing drugs, although the charges were later dismissed. Different Hall of Fame voters—in baseball, the ones who do the voting are Baseball Writers' Association of America (BBWAA) members with 10 years' membership or more who also have been actively covering MLB at any time in the 10 years preceding the election—have different standards, of course, and there is no uniformity to how they vote. Because they have different voting perspectives when it comes to players linked to or suspected of using performance-enhancing drugs, during every voting cycle since the 2013 ballot the debate has been whether two of the greatest players in the game's history are worthy of the sport's greatest honor.

One is seven-time Cy Young Award winner Roger Clemens, whose name was mentioned 82 times in the 2007 Mitchell Report on steroid use in baseball, in which former Yankees trainer Brian McNamee claimed that he injected Clemens with the anabolic steroid Winstrol during the 1998, 2000 and 2001 seasons. Clemens, who never failed a drug test during a career which saw him win 354 games, has furiously denied all charges. The other is Bonds, the seven-time National League MVP who tacitly admitted to limited and unintended steroid use—and the subject of this book. Both men played their final major-league seasons in 2007 and first became eligible for Cooperstown on the 2013 ballot. Both—the two, as pundits have said, are logically tied at the hip in their Hall of Fame chances—are, year-by-year, inching closer to the required 75% for entry to Cooperstown, but because players have a maximum of 10 years of eligibility (which was lowered from 15 years since the 2015 ballot), Clemens and Bonds appear on the BBWAA ballot for the final time in 2022. It's very possible neither would be elected to the Hall of Fame by the BBWAA and, after their names come off the ballot, their only shot at Cooperstown would be the Veterans Committee, whose Today's Game committee considers and votes for candidates who played in the 1988-present era.

Some pundits have opined that although Bonds and Clemens gained momentum starting in their fourth year on the ballot and have seen gradual increases in their voting percentage since then, they will likely come up short and not climb over the 75% threshold required for enshrinement by 2022, their final year of eligibility. Others have opined that the writers are trying to punish Bonds and Clemens by making them wait until their final year on the ballot, and then vote them in. When the announcement came from the Baseball Hall of Fame in January 2021 that nobody had been voted in for that year, pundits (for instance Bob Costas on MLB Network) wondered if it was the writers' way of ensuring that Bonds and Clemens would not receive the opportunity to share baseball's highest honor with the 2020 inductees—a group which included the universally-respected Derek Jeter and Marvin Miller—and sully the induction ceremony. (Jeter and Larry Walker had been elected by the BBWAA in January 2020, while Miller and Ted Simmons were elected by the Modern Baseball Era Committee in December 2019. Because of the COVID-19 pandemic, the 2020 induction ceremony was cancelled and rescheduled for July 2021.)

Below is a year-by-year progression of the Bonds and Clemens vote in their first nine years on the ballot, with both men having nearly identical voting percentages each year. The number of votes each player received are in parentheses.

Year	No. of ballots	Barry Bonds	Roger Clemens
2013	569	36.2% (206)	37.6% (214)
2014	571	34.7% (198)	35.4% (202)
2015	549	36.8% (202)	37.5% (206)
2016	440	44.3% (195)	45.2% (199)
2017	442	53.8% (238)	54.1% (239)
2018	422	56.4% (238)	57.3% (242)
2019	425	59.1% (251)	59.5% (253)
2020	397	60.7% (241)	61.0% (242)
2021	401	61.8% (248)	61.6% (247)

After the first three years of the voting, in which both players were stuck in the mid-30s, there was a surge to 44.3% and 45.2% for Bonds and Clemens, respectively, as the 2016 ballot saw a drop in the total number of ballots (with BBWAA members who'd been inactive for 10 years being purged), creating a younger and perhaps more forgiving voting electorate as it relates to players linked to PEDs. Another surge occurred in 2017, when former commissioner Bud Selig's election to the Hall made some writers feel like hypocrites to not vote for Bonds and Clemens—as Selig, selected by the Veterans Committee's Today's Game committee, oversaw the "Steroid Era" and helped owners profit mightily off of that era—and the induction of Mike Piazza (2016) and the inevitable inductions of Jeff Bagwell (2017) and Ivan Rodriguez (2017) led others to perhaps feel that if players suspected of using PEDs are already in Cooperstown, you might as well let the best of the best join them. "For the first time in the four years he has been on the Hall of Fame ballot, I voted for Barry Bonds. How could I in good faith not vote for Bonds," admitted Hall of Fame voter John Shea in 2016, "when I might be voting for other PED guys?" In their eighth year on the ballot in 2020, though, Bonds and Clemens were still on the outside looking in, falling 57 and 56 votes shy, respectively, of the 75% needed for induction into Cooperstown. Their penultimate year on the ballot resulted in 61.8% support for Bonds and 61.6% for Clemens, as the BBWAA did not elect anyone in 2021.

What has hurt Bonds and Clemens (and will hurt them in their final year on the ballot) is writers who, like ESPN's MLB analyst Jeff Passan, ESPN.com writer T. J. Quinn and others, have ended up (and will end up) deciding to give up their votes because of the hypocrisy of the voting process—even if they believe those two players belonged in Cooperstown. "Every year that Barry Bonds was eligible and I had a vote, I voted for him," Passan said in 2020. "And in fact, what the Hall of Fame did a few years ago in putting out a statement, essentially impugning performance-enhancing drug users and saying, 'We don't want them in our hallowed grounds,' when in fact, there already are performance-enhancing drug users in the Hall of Fame, made me stop voting. I did not want to participate in the hypocrisy. I did not want to go along with what I felt like was a rigged system... Barry Bonds is arguably the greatest hitter of all-time. If he's not the greatest, he's one of the two or three greatest. And because he is so good, no matter what he did, to me, he is a Hall of Famer."

* * *

This book isn't going to convince you of the author's position if it's different from yours. The purpose of this book is to share the lesser-known and lesser-remembered stories about Bonds, who simply wanted to be the greatest baseball player who ever lived—so that, one can reasonably conclude, he could receive the love and admiration of his father, Bobby Bonds.

If you already don't like Barry Bonds and view him as a movie villain, though, this book isn't going to change your mind about him and whether or not he belongs in the Hall of Fame. It's not going to change the minds of Hall of Fame voters who view him as a cheating jerk who was hell-bent on ruining the day of everybody around him every single day. But Barry Bonds, just like any other professional athlete in any era, is a human being and has flaws just like you and me. If you love sports and enjoy reading about sports, this book perhaps can give you a better understanding of Barry Bonds and the side of him we never really hear about. With an open mind, perhaps you may even come to a better understanding of the man and forgive him for mistakes made 20 or 30 years ago. When it comes to sports, unfortunately, athletes are often regarded as either heroes or villains, not as human beings. For fans who dislike—or even hate—Barry Bonds, the all-time home-run king is viewed as a villain. A cheater. A jerk who wasn't kind to the press or the fans. A choker in the playoffs. Despite his numbers and records, the haters say, Bonds doesn't deserve a plaque in Cooperstown.

Let's address the "cheating" argument. Bonds, according to the *San Francisco Chronicle*, testified to a grand jury in 2003 that he used a clear substance and a cream given to him by his trainer—who was indicted in a steroid-distribution ring—saying he didn't know they were steroids. In 2005, the *New York Daily News* reported that federal investigators warned Major League Baseball in 1995 or 1996 that many of its players—including Jose Canseco—were using steroids, but the leaders of the game didn't act on the information. Pundits have maintained that Mark McGwire and Sammy Sosa's 1998 home-run derby helped rescue baseball from the post-1994 players' strike doldrums. The game became more entertaining and more popular than ever, with attendance going well above what it was before the 1990s. "From Houston to Minnesota to Arizona, the St. Louis Cardinals and their powerful first baseman, on pace to smash Roger Maris' record of 61 set in 1961," noted *The Washington Post* in the middle of the 1998 season, referring to McGwire's home-run exploits, "are packing ballparks, boosting television ratings, selling food and merchandise, and even jump-starting the wheezing baseball card industry, where 1985 McGwire rookie cards have increased in price twentyfold from two years ago."

Looking at the situation objectively, how is it fair to place all of the blame on the game's doping scandal solely on Bonds? If many other players were using PEDs, which were not being tested for and weren't against the rules, and the players bashing all those home runs were being celebrated, one can reasonably conclude that a highly-competitive athlete in Bonds' situation would feel the need to keep up. And even understand it. As some who do understand it have argued, we're talking about ballplayers of a very specific era, who made their decisions based on the context of that era, and who still excelled against their peers, many of whom were also making those same decisions based on the context of that era. Now, if Hall of Fame voters judge players by their eras and whom they played against— and the Hall itself is ultimately a museum of baseball history—why shouldn't Barry Bonds, the greatest hitter of his era, be voted in?

Even if you feel the 1998 home-run derby—which saw both

McGwire and Sosa shatter the single-season record of 61 home runs—didn't "save baseball," Grant Brisbee noted in *The Athletic* in January 2020, you'll have to at least acknowledge that the game definitely prospered during the so-called "Steroid Era." Besides, PED use was part of baseball's culture at the time. "It's always been at least a little hyperbolic to suggest that the 1998 home-run chase saved baseball, but the sport is still benefiting to this day from the nationwide obsession with the sport," Brisbee argued. "The chase definitely helped pull baseball out of the post-strike quicksand that threatened to send attendance and revenues back to the '70s. The billion-dollar media deals still might have happened without the chase, but the pie might have been smaller. A smaller pie affects labor negotiations. There are all sorts of dominoes that could have fallen without steroids and PEDs, and a whole lot of them would have cost the owners money. It's revisionist history, then, to claim that Bonds (and McGwire and Sosa and Roger Clemens and …) were actively hurting the sport's reputation and the sanctity of the game back then. For a sport that loves its unwritten rules, the gatekeepers sure have a blind spot when it comes to the unwritten rule of 'Yeah, go for it. You'll be treated like a god' that was a part of baseball culture back in 1998." And the steroid era was a part of the sport, just like the dead-ball era and segregated era were part of baseball history. For fans who are upset about all the records being broken, all of those eras affected the statistics in the record books—just like expansion and extended seasons, the high mound and even pre-humidor Coors Field—but again, they were part of the game's history.

Even if you don't consider the Hall of Fame a museum, perhaps look at what sports are supposed to be. Countless fans consider sports a great escape from the stress of everyday life, a form of entertainment to distract them for a few hours every night. But really, professional baseball, like all pro sports, is a business. There are many things about professional sports that we may not like. But those things are part of the game. Just to give an example, we live in an era in which virtually everything contains names of corporate sponsors. Whether fans like it or not, the Fall Classic is officially known as the *World Series presented by YouTube TV*. In 2019, the Washington Nationals and St. Louis Cardinals competed in the *National League Championship Series presented by GEICO*. Look around the nation, and you'll see that countless ballparks, stadiums and arenas in every sport (even those used in college sports) have corporate naming rights deals. Yes, Los Angeles still has Dodger Stadium, but look around the major leagues and you'll see the names Guaranteed Rate Field or Truist Park or Progressive Field, just to name a few. San Francisco's Oracle Park used to be known as AT&T Park, while AT&T Stadium is the home of the NFL Dallas Cowboys and AT&T Center is home to the NBA San Antonio Spurs. There was once a Sleep Train Arena in the NBA. The Arizona Cardinals play at State Farm Stadium, previously known as the University of Phoenix Stadium, although the University of Phoenix has neither a football team nor even an actual, physical campus. As of this writing, the stadiums in Seattle include Lumen Field, the home of the NFL Seahawks and MLS Sounders, and T-Mobile Park, the home of baseball's Mariners. The NHL has a T-Mobile Arena, home of the Vegas Golden Knights. Whether you love them or not, corporate naming rights deals are part of the game. Just as the steroids were part of the game in the 1990s and early 2000s, when juiced players bashing baseballs out of the ballpark at rates never seen before put millions of butts in the seats, which put billions of dollars into the pockets of team owners. Sports, after all, is a business.

Likewise, professional athletes are entertainers. When sports fans watch a ballgame, they're looking to be entertained. In baseball, a ballplayer's job is to produce on the field. Bonds, with his home runs, entertained fans wanting to see hitters knock baseballs out of the park. If whatever his trainer gave him helped him entertain more and entertain longer, wasn't that what fans wanted to see? And even if Bonds was often unaccommodating when it came to media and fan requests, so what? Sure, kids collect their favorite baseball players' cards and have those heroes' posters plastered all over their walls at home—and fans of all ages across the nation proudly wear jerseys with the names of ballplayers they love—but, if you stop to think about it, major leaguers don't owe anybody anything other than their performances on the diamond. Athletes are expected to perform at the highest levels that they're capable of, and that's it. Although sports fans might like romanticizing them, athletes shouldn't be idolized or put on pedestals. We shouldn't hold athletes to a higher standard than we hold ourselves. Conversely, when an athlete does indeed do something nice, we shouldn't question the sincerity behind the gesture. It simply isn't fair that whenever Bonds did something kind, for instance, the gesture was often dismissed by critics as there being an agenda behind it.

There's also personality; some athletes are sociable and love to talk, while others don't. Some are wonderful people, while others aren't. Every baseball player is different. Just like people in regular society. Just like people working in non-sporting industries. Every individual is different. That's part of life. Besides, Barry Bonds is hardly the only athlete in the world to act unkindly to those seeking an autograph. He performed on the field and didn't owe anybody anything else.

He didn't perform in the playoffs, you say? Perhaps you're one of those who scoff at Barry Bonds because of his less-than-stellar postseason numbers. True, prior to 2002, Bonds might not have performed in October the way that he had during regular season play, but he's hardly alone among the all-time greats, as the annals of postseason baseball are filled with big names—superstars and Hall of Famers—with poor October stats (and, conversely, virtual unknowns who stun the baseball world by coming up big in postseason play). Not every superstar delivers in the postseason like a Reggie Jackson or a Derek Jeter, yet many of them aren't as heavily criticized as Bonds was.

Mike Trout, the best player in the game today, is a perfect example. In his first 10 seasons between 2011 and 2020, his Los Angeles Angels reached the postseason only once, a three-game sweep at the hands of Kansas City in the American League Division Series in 2014. (In that series, Trout batted only .083 with one hit in 12 at-bats.) In the case of Trout, the Angels' superstar center fielder is playing in an era which sees more teams than ever reach the postseason (with five teams per league qualifying every season), yet Los Angeles finished under .500 six times from 2011 and 2020. Trout, however, is hardly ever criticized for the Angels' failures. In Bonds' case, meanwhile, without Barry, the 1990-92 Pirates might not have reached the postseason three years in a row, the first NL team since the 1976-78 Phillies to capture three consecutive division crowns, in an era in which only division champions saw playoff baseball. Without Bonds, the Giants might not have finished first or second in the NL West 10 out of 12 seasons between 1993 and 2004, either.

When it comes to the Baseball Hall of Fame, Barry Bonds was the greatest player of his era and was an all-time great long before his name was ever linked to PEDs. Although many others were juicing in that same era, nobody approached the performance level of Barry Lamar Bonds. The Hall has already enshrined cheats, enablers, scoundrels, segregationists, suspected PED users and downright terrible people. Bud Selig, the man who presided over the "Steroid Era," has already been enshrined. For baseball writers to deny Bonds a Cooperstown enshrinement because he was the highest-profile player suspected of PED use during that so-called tainted era simply comes across as petty. Acknowledging Bonds as a Baseball Hall of Famer isn't putting him on a pedestal; it's simply recognizing him as an all-time great in the game of baseball and giving him a well-deserved place in the sport's museum. Put him in already.

Looking at Things from a Different Perspective

Barry has the best swing ever. It's hard for people who play the game every day to be so consistent. I've seen Barry maybe six times look bad at the plate in 10 years. That's amazing. His concentration is unreal, I mean unreal. You talk about a picture swing. He has a tailor-made swing. He can see the ball all the way to the plate. It's incredible. Hitters get in the zone for three weeks. But to do it for 10 years...

—Hall of Fame first baseman Orlando Cepeda,
as told to *The [Santa Rosa, CA] Press
Democrat*'s Lowell Cohn (2004)

Even if they dismiss the numbers, baseball fans know the figures: 73 home runs in a single season, 762 career home runs and seven National League Most Valuable Player awards. If the name of the player who achieved these milestones wasn't Barry Bonds, you'd look at how the man persevered and celebrate his accomplishments.

As a boy, Barry didn't always have his father, Bobby Bonds, present. But when Bobby was around, he wasn't always a loving father. "In interviews," writers Mark Fainaru-Wada and Lance Williams noted in their 2006 book *Game of Shadows*, "Bonds said that when he was a boy, he hadn't liked his father. He told friends that his father beat him and psychologically dominated his mother. He claimed his father had ignored his achievements and refused to attend his games and other school events. He said that in college he discouraged his father from coming to watch him play because he feared he would show up drunk." Unfortunately, when Bobby was arrested for drunken driving and resisting arrest in 1973, the Bondses had to deal not only with Bobby's problem but also with the media attention that followed Barry to school. Fans would use Bobby's drinking problem to taunt Barry, for instance, when he first played as a collegiate and professional baseball player. At one game, as the story goes, Barry would always remember hearing the fans chant "502, 502!"—with the three-digit number being the California police code for driving under the influence.

Having an estranged father at Barry's age couldn't have been easy. The claims Barry had made couldn't be dismissed, either, as Bobby Bonds, during his 14-year career in the big leagues from 1968 to 1981, was known for his standoffish and moody behavior along with his alcoholism as much as he was known for his talent on the field. Although Bobby electrified Giants fans with his combination of power and speed—he'd go on to achieve the rare feat of hitting at least 30 home runs and stealing 30-plus bases in the same season five times over his career, a major-league record, including twice in a San Francisco uniform—management grew worried about his drinking and attitude and finally sent him to the Yankees after the 1974 season. Bobby hit 32 homers with 30 stolen bases for the Yankees in 1975, but they moved him to the California Angels after the season. Even his 37 home runs and 41 steals for the Angels in 1977 weren't enough, as California traded him, too, and after that no club wanted him for more than one season. That was also the case in 1978, when Bobby homered 31 times and stole 43 bags while splitting time with the White Sox and Rangers; after that season, he wound up changing uniforms yet again. Given the unfair label of being an underachiever—expectations were enormously high after he'd been called "the new Willie Mays" early in his career—Bobby retired following the 1981 campaign after playing for seven different teams over a seven-year period in the second half of his career.

The way Bobby was treated, despite the All-Star caliber numbers he consistently put up along with his five 30-30 seasons, certainly made young Barry frustrated and troubled. All the bad press the elder Bonds received, one could reasonably argue, undoubtedly had an effect on Barry. He grew up, after all, being exposed to all these negative comments written about his father. And it wasn't just the press; the poor treatment toward Bobby came from all directions. "No one in baseball ever supported Bobby Bonds, [whether it was] the owner, the general manager, the press [or] the teammates," columnist Thomas Boswell of *The Washington Post* once explained. "Nobody in the game stood up for the father. So, what Barry learned about baseball was, 'Great talent matters, great scholarship about the game matters, but you can't count on anybody in this game to stand up for you—cuz they didn't stand up for my father.'" Childhood friend Bob McKercher once added, "It was like his dad wasn't wanted [when he was getting traded from team to team]… You see that, and it lingers. You see your dad go from San Francisco to New York to Anaheim to Texas to Cleveland to Chicago… that can take a toll on you."

If having an estranged father was the only difficulty Barry Bonds endured as a boy, that would be one thing. He then had to deal with all the negative publicity about his father. But that wasn't everything—there was even more. Even as a boy, Barry didn't have the support of his peers; he became aware of other kids talking behind his back and, thus, became guarded when people tried to get too close. At least that's the version the press gives. "No matter how much he excelled at baseball," wrote Fainaru-Wada and Williams in *Game of Shadows*, "he couldn't escape feeling that people discounted his achievements because of his father. Outstanding play was expected of him because of who he was. Other kids would rag on Barry or talk behind his back, saying that no coach would ever cut him from a team or bench him from a game because he was Bobby Bonds' son. As a result, when people tried to befriend or praise him, Barry became suspicious, doubting their sincerity. Were people nice to him because they liked him? Or was it because they wanted something from his famous dad? Was Barry playing ball because he wanted to? Or was baseball simply something everyone expected of Bobby Bonds' son?" None of that was imagined. "Bobby would come to the ballpark to pick him up, and all the kids would just hover around trying to get autographs, and I think this kind of affected Barry, who closed himself off at an early age from the kids around him," Mike Roza, a high school teammate of Barry's, once recalled.

Despite the ordeals he faced as a boy, Barry, who played every sport as a youth including football, basketball and hockey—he even did activities like water-skiing and ice-skating—and excelled in each one while growing up in an athletic community, developed a strong passion for the game of baseball, in particular, at an early age and wound up reaching the major leagues. Possessing world-class athletic skills that he was happy to show off, he wound up becoming a better baseball player than his father ever was. By the time he won his first

MVP Award in his fifth major-league season in 1990, he was even widely regarded as the best player in the game, one who could beat opposing teams with his bat, his glove and his legs.

Such an accomplishment is one that should be celebrated. If his name wasn't Barry Bonds, any baseball fan would applaud those achievements. So, why look at his story and scoff just because this man happens to be Barry Bonds? Why scoff the way his own father had done throughout a large portion of his playing career? "I never played against another team," Barry once recalled. "I played against my father and Willie [Mays]. Their approval, am I as good a ballplayer as they are? Did I get their acceptance?" Even after Barry had won multiple MVP awards, Bobby, as the Giants' hitting instructor, was hard on him during batting practice. "He'd call me an idiot," Barry remembered, revealing some of the emotional wounds he'd suffered. "'What the f— are you thinking about? Whaddya mean you can't get to it [the ball]? It's right in front of you! Can't you see?' I said, 'This dude is wacko.' I would do it [succeed] to shut him up. If he said I couldn't hit the ball over the left-field wall, I'd hit 20 and then I'd hand him the bat and walk away."

Well, the notion that Bonds closed himself off from other kids at a young age and that he became suspicious of others around him comes from the media. In the rare interviews Bonds himself has given, though, he has explained the fact that he'd always simply been an introverted and private person. Coming from an athletic community, he had plenty of friends as a child—and still remains close to them, to this day—just like any other boy in the neighborhood. Childhood friend Bob McKercher once recalled that Barry was like many other kids in the neighborhood. "We were into water-balloon fights, we played baseball, basketball [and] football. We loved music and liked to dance. We went to the movies. Every Friday night from sixth to eighth grade we went ice-skating. He was just a typical kid." When it came to baseball, Barry had a high IQ. But as an introvert, he couldn't explain batting tips in words—but he could only show others by swinging a bat. If he was asked to express in words how to be a good hitter, for instance, he felt more comfortable showing with his performance on the field than to break things down verbally.

Prior to his taking the job as a hitting coach with the Miami Marlins in 2016, Bonds was initially reluctant about taking on that role—how could he teach what he knew to other players, even if those skills came naturally to him, when he was an introvert?—but received strong encouragement from his mother, Pat, and his children to give it a try. "Baby steps," he would admit, explaining that he had to come out of his comfort zone in order to accept that role with the Marlins. And even if he wasn't good at explaining his knowledge verbally, others were looking at his attributes—in particular, his patience, discipline and consistency—and incorporating them to establish their own blueprint for how to succeed on the field. Even in other sports. In 2019, for instance, Dallas Cowboys quarterbacks coach Jon Kitna preached an approach called the "Barry Bonds mindset" to the team's quarterbacks. (Fittingly, this example is about the Cowboys, who, just like Barry Bonds, are either loved or hated by sports fans across the nation.) "You want to have a Barry Bonds mindset, which is he broke the record for home runs in a season," Kitna said in November 2019. "He also broke the records for walks in a season. That meant they weren't throwing him pitches to hit. But when he hit, he hit it out of the park. That's what we want to have as a quarterback: the discipline to say, 'That's not my pitch. Let's check it down.' But when it presents itself: Let's let it rip."

The fact that Barry, having an introverted personality, found it difficult to explain his skills in words doesn't make him a villain; it makes him similar to countless other individuals in countless other professions across the globe. A column by the *San Francisco Chronicle*'s Lowell Cohn in May 1993 perhaps best summed up Bonds' character as an introvert. Comparing Bonds to Michael Jordan, Cohn noted that "Air Jordan" loved the media spotlight, endorsed as many commercial products as he could and always seemed to want to be the center of attention. Barry, meanwhile, "disdains fame. He said that he feels uncomfortable that his shoe company wants to put up a Barry Bonds mural in San Francisco. He tries to avoid every interview the Giants ask him to perform." Cohn concluded, though, that Bonds' discomfort with fame actually made him seem more human and "more likable."

There are two sides to every story. Sports fans normally hear only the side—typically the negative side—reported in the newspapers. Why not try to hear the other side, the one which allows us to understand (and even appreciate) more why Barry acted the way he did? Besides, if his name wasn't Barry Bonds, many fans would applaud his accomplishments. So, why look at his story and scoff just because his name happens to be Barry Bonds?

* * *

Baseball fans know the numbers: 714, 755 and 762. Those are the career home-run totals of Babe Ruth, Hank Aaron and Barry Bonds, respectively. Although Bonds finished with the most home runs in the history of Major League Baseball—a number that stands atop all the record books—many media members and fans have chosen to call the number 762 "meaningless" or "not real" while producing their own definition of the "true" home-run champion.

Those who love Hank Aaron contend that the former Braves slugger is baseball's all-time home-run king. Others say it's Babe Ruth. Others say the answer is clearly Bonds. Since there isn't a consensus despite what the numbers say, some have come up with a solution. Take *Boston Globe*'s Bob Ryan, for instance. Every era in baseball, Ryan has argued, is different, and each era can be looked at separately. Bonds, for example, played in the Steroid Era. Ruth never played in a racially integrated league. Aaron played in an era in which amphetamines were pervasive—or, as many pundits have said, "handed out like candy."

Looking at Aaron specifically, just to illustrate why baseball fans view the idea of the "true" home-run champ differently, some aren't sure all of his home runs fall into the category of being legitimate. Aaron, according to some, not only played during a time in baseball in which amphetamines were ubiquitous, also played in an era which gave him another advantage. As Jay Jaffe once noted in *Sports Illustrated*, Aaron played under favorable conditions which included two rounds of expansion and diluted talent. Ninety-one of his 755 home runs, he wrote, came against the Astros and Mets, both of whom were established in 1962. Another 40 homers came against Montreal and San Diego, established in 1969. On a per plate appearance basis, added Jaffe, Aaron's home run rate rose by 10% against those teams relative to the rest of the majors. As if that wasn't enough, in 1966 Aaron's Braves moved from Milwaukee to Atlanta, "where Fulton County Stadium's 1,000-foot elevation was the highest in the majors until the Rockies joined the league in 1993," the *SI* scribe pointed out. In nine seasons at the ballpark known as "the Launching Pad," Aaron smacked 192 home runs, compared to 145 on the road. Although the discrepancy between long balls hit at home and ones hit on the road isn't unusual, the fact that Fulton County Stadium gave Aaron an advantage is a fact that cannot be ignored. (Many observers have opined that Willie Mays might have surpassed Ruth's home-run total of 714 if not for the dimensions and hurricane-force winds at Candlestick Park. Mays, whose 660 home runs are sixth all-time behind only Bonds, Aaron, Ruth, Alex Rodriguez and Albert Pujols as of this writing, played home games for 12 full seasons at Candlestick, where the incessant winds muted drives to left field by right-handed hitting sluggers, which cost him plenty of home runs.)

Ryan, the former *Boston Globe* writer, has a simple solution: Recognize that baseball, really, has three home-run champions: Babe Ruth, Hank Aaron and Barry Bonds, because the game has had three distinct home-run eras. As Ryan noted in 2017, the first home-run era occurred in an era where circumstances were completely different from today, with Negro League players barred from playing in the major leagues, with no night games and with no official "closers" (meaning Ruth could get four cracks at a possible tiring starter). In Ruth's case, specifically, his career with the Yankees began at the Polo Grounds, where it was 257 feet to the right-field foul pole. Yankee Stadium, with its 296-foot right-field distance, was constructed expressly for The Babe in 1923, added Ryan. When Jackie Robinson broke the color barrier in 1947, it was the start of a new era. After the Second World War, American GIs brought several things home with them from their foreign adventures, among them the habitual use of amphetamines, which spread quickly into baseball. Soon enough, the game entered the "Greenie Era," where amphetamines were pervasive and continued to be for decades. "Amphetamines were handed out like candy in every major-league locker room," Ryan continued. "They all took them. It was regarded as the only way to get through 162 games." In Aaron's case, he once admitted taking a "greenie" during the 1968 season when a teammate offered it to him—and he took it. "When that thing took hold, I thought I was having a heart attack," he wrote in his autobiography. Aaron, who also benefited from the Braves' move to

Atlanta, is the champion of this "Greenie Era," as Ryan put it. Finally, Bonds is the champion of the third era.

Some feel that if one wants to attach an asterisk to Bonds' numbers, there should be one next to Babe Ruth's, too. "Ruth's 714 home run record lacks the spit-shined purity his backers trumpet," Dave Zirin opined on TheNation.com in 2006. "The Sultan of Swat made his bones playing against only a select segment of the population because of the ban on players whose skin color ran brown to black. Ruth never had to hit against Negro League greats Satchel Paige or Lefty Mathis to amass the magic 714. Yet no asterisk for institutionalized racism mars the Babe's marks. Ruth also was a habitual user of a banned substance that was deemed unambiguously illegal by the federal government—a drug Ruth believed enhanced his performance: alcohol. Ruth was a star during the roaring prohibition 1920s, and as teammate Joe Dugan said, 'Babe would go day and night, broads and booze.'"

NBC Sports' Craig Calcaterra offers another solution: Take emotion out of it. Whether or not you were turned off by the controversy surrounding Bonds, whether you love Ruth or Aaron and hate Barry, the simple fact is that Barry Bonds has more home runs than anybody else in the history of Major League Baseball. Hank Aaron isn't "baseball's all-time home run leader," Calcaterra wrote in 2014. "Or its 'true' Home Run King or however people wish to characterize it. To say that is to go beyond expressing your enjoyment of his accomplishment and your appreciation of him as a player and claiming that those qualitative things—and whatever disdain one has for Barry Bonds—trump the actual record of history. The record of history—which is devoid of judgment and opinion—states that Barry Bonds hit more home runs than Hank Aaron did. Baseball recognizes this fact without qualification. We should as well. To do otherwise is to invite chaos, as each of us brings our own values and assumptions into an assessment of the records."

To prove his point, Calcaterra brought up other records that nobody is questioning even though those marks were attained under "unfair" conditions. For instance, nobody seems to care that the top five all-time pitching wins leaders—Cy Young (511), Walter Johnson (417), Pete Alexander (373), Christy Mathewson (373) and Pud Galvin (365)—had "ridiculous advantages" that Warren Spahn, sixth all-time with 363 victories, never had, which should render him the "True Wins Leader."

We could attempt to make these arguments with most records, added Calcaterra, but doing so "would be silly in most instances and would render the idea of an actual record book—the thing people who call Hank Aaron the True Home Run King say they are trying to protect—[an] utterly meaningless thing." Of course, it's perfectly fine to celebrate Hank Aaron, opined Calcaterra, and consider his career accomplishments more impressive than Bonds' if you feel that way. "But stop there. Don't claim that black is white. Don't claim that Hank Aaron is the real and true Home Run King. Because that's just nonsense."

Nikolai Bonds, Barry's son, put it this way in a 2015 interview with writer Jeff Pearlman: "There are so many reasons why he will always be the home-run king. But everybody is entitled to their own opinion. Here is mine. My dad's job was what exactly? To entertain. That's it. That's the first reason. Second is, as you said, he didn't break any rules of the game. So what did he do wrong? Third, Hank Aaron admitted to greenies. An enhancer. Babe Ruth drank during prohibition. Illegal. Ty Cobb beat a woman during a game. What we are talking about is someone who is enhancing his performance within the rules of the sport he plays to entertain the rest of this world … *and he is getting crucified for it.*

"It's like Michael Jackson. His entire life he entertained and wanted to be loved by the people. Once that was taken from him, what did he have left? My father did nothing wrong but play the game he loved to the best of his ability. So, is he wrong for that? … Everybody tries to say, 'You're a bad influence on the kids.' How? My dad isn't the one out there marketing steroids or putting them on the news. That's the media installing it into the minds of the people. If nobody ever said anything, people would continue to train. Continue to get education on substances that are good and bad for you. And continue to strive to be just like the greats who gave them hope and faith that they can be there, too.

"Really, think about it. We are talking about a record of a sport. Does it really matter all that much? If the world wants it, they can have it. The record doesn't bring happiness. It's a number. But if you strip my dad of it, everyone who did something that we don't agree with has to get [his or her] biggest achievement taken also. Now does it still matter that much?"

* * *

Baseball isn't life and death. It's a distraction, as all sports are. It's entertainment. If one forks out money to watch a baseball game at the ballpark, he or she wants to be entertained. It's no different from spending money to watch a movie or an opera. It's just a different form of entertainment.

Barry Bonds viewed baseball as a form of entertainment. He simply wanted to show up at the ballpark, gather his thoughts in the clubhouse, go out to play and entertain the fans, and then go home. What was wrong with that?

Besides, he was the best entertainer in the game. Wasn't that enough?

Regarding the part about Bonds being the best player in the game over the last century, that's not even a question. "I think outside of Babe Ruth, you could argue he's the greatest player who ever lived, certainly the greatest player of his generation, the most feared hitter, good outfielder, baserunner [and] everything," says *USA Today* writer Bob Nightengale when the topic of Bonds comes up. "There's nobody who really compares. During his time playing in the big leagues, nobody was even close to Bonds; [in his own era, Barry was the greatest] by far. Nobody else was even close. He's that great of a player. People can talk about Mike Trout and everybody else, but Bonds is the best."

Unfortunately, Bonds was known throughout his major-league career for being standoffish to both teammates and media, leading to more criticisms—from early in his career—than praises for his on-field accomplishments. "Some guys didn't care for him. They thought he was too standoffish, too into himself," Nightengale acknowledges. "He can certainly be perceived as a loner-type guy or aloof, but you go around baseball, a lot of stars are like that. And that's true in all sports, not just baseball."

Dustan Mohr, a former Giants outfielder, is also quick to defend Bonds, refuting the notion that Barry was "selfish," a label put on the all-time home-run champion by the press. "When you're talking about Barry Bonds, it's hard to put yourself in his shoes, I would think, because there's so many people who sort of want a piece of him every day," says Mohr, who played in San Francisco in 2004. "And I think it's easy to overlook the fact that he's human like the rest of us.

Sometimes he just doesn't have anything to say. Or maybe he's in a bad mood. He's like anybody else… I didn't see Barry as selfish. I think everybody has to have a certain level of that selfishness about them to get themselves ready. I think Barry was not selfish. He wanted to win as bad as anybody else. I think, really, it was others around him, at times, that created things that really weren't there. Maybe he didn't talk to them. I don't want to say jealousy, but maybe they resented him because of how good he was. I can't speak for him, but… I think that he just wanted everybody else to lift their game and take it as seriously as he did, but unfortunately, not everybody was always willing to do that. He was focused on making sure that he was going to be able to do his part, and perform up to his standard. People [might] think that's selfish… but I certainly didn't see it that way."

Mohr does have a point. It's difficult to imagine what Barry had to go through with requests every day. Ballplayers, perhaps especially the superstars, routinely have friends and family calling them up all the time for tickets. There's always media wanting a piece of them. Once you become famous, everybody wants a piece of you. The good people. The bad people. And because everybody is different, every player deals with game days differently. Kirk Gibson, just to give an oft-told example, was an intimidating player who wanted to win every single night, and he'd have his intense game face on when he arrived at the ballpark—and have that on until he left the stadium. That's how he was as an athlete, as a baseball player, as a competitor. In Los Angeles, left-hander Fernando Valenzuela, a pitching sensation for the Dodgers in the 1980s who drew large crowds from the city's Latino community every time he pitched and captured the interest of fans across the world (the craze surrounding him came to be known as "Fernandomania"), was known as a private individual who rarely gave interviews, not even in his native tongue. A former Mariners player once shared this story with the author about all the requests future Hall of Famer Randy Johnson dealt with. "When I played in Seattle," said the former Mariner, who requested anonymity, "there was one day when someone brought in 50 shopping bags of letters and cards for Randy to read and sign. *Fifty!* They were all over the floor and took up all the space." Indeed, ballplayers, in particular the superstars, receive so many requests that at times, it could be overwhelming.

Barry Bonds didn't trust the media to begin with because of how the press treated his father. Dealing with all those requests—ones from the media, in particular—wasn't part of playing baseball, Bonds decided early in his big-league career, because they weren't part of his job as an entertainer. Barry himself once said early in his career in Pittsburgh, "My job does not say, 'Walk in the locker room and kiss butt.' It says, 'Go to work.' I say hello sometimes, and sometimes I don't. I get to the ballpark and I'm going to be focused on what I have to do. But you know what they'll say? 'Hey, Barry, what's your problem? What's your attitude?' 'I don't have an attitude; I'm sitting here by myself. You got a problem with it?'"

When one looks at what he said more objectively, one could argue that Bonds had a point. In a separate interview two years later, he said, "I have a job to do and sometimes the media conflicts with my job. There's a lot of times I want to say I'm sorry for not being the type of person that you expect me to be. But I'm a straightforward person and I'm not going to B.S. you. If the media wanted to pay me what the Pirates pay me, I'll talk to them all day and all night."

Late in his career, when he was with the Giants, Bonds addressed his relationship with the media and again explained his point of view. He wasn't trying to be standoffish; he simply wanted to focus solely on the game when he took the field and couldn't afford to waste one ounce of his energy on other matters. "My family comes first, but then comes baseball. Everything else, the autographs, the media, the million questions, I can't worry about all of that stuff because that's really not the game." He didn't worry about what his teammates thought of him. He didn't worry about his public image. He was all about being a great baseball player on the field and absolutely nothing else. His performance on the field was supposed to be the only thing that mattered. "I'm a business-type player," he explained. "I want to give the fans their money's worth."

To understand his perspective, he believed he was an entertainer whose job was to produce on the field (which, obviously, he did quite well); when he was in the clubhouse, he didn't believe he needed to be "on stage" again to talk to reporters. In the clubhouse, he wanted to get his treatments or gather his thoughts in peace, not deal with 30 reporters asking him questions repeatedly. After all, hadn't his performance on the field—whether it was a big home run or fine defensive play or key stolen base—already done all the talking? "Why can't people just enjoy the show?" Barry once asked. "And then let the entertainer go home and get his rest, so he can put on another show?"

Rich Donnelly, a former Pirates coach who considers Barry a friend, once recalled a typical Bonds clubhouse interaction with the press. "I remember the time he hit a home run against the Mets at our place. We didn't have a real cafeteria. So, after the game, we'd come into the clubhouse and set the food on these equipment trunks while you ate. [Bonds] put his food down and then put his feet up," Donnelly told *The Athletic* in 2020, providing an insight into Bonds' point of view. "All these writers came in. He looked up at them and said, 'Hey, let me ask you—' I don't know what he said, 'jerks' or something. 'Do I come into your dining room at suppertime and bother you?' They all said, well, no. He says, 'Well, get the hell out of mine.'"

Years later, Bonds elaborated on his thoughts in an interview with Giants public address announcer Renel Brooks-Moon. "When I'm at the ballpark, I'm just trying to heal my legs. I'm just trying to go to work," he explained matter-of-factly in the 2019 conversation. "But when you have 30 reporters [at] your locker, by the time I take my shirt off, they're like, 'Barry, what do you think of this?' that is not the time to bother anyone. And, with us [athletes], it's just magnified. But I know you [the interviewer] or anyone else, [if people come to ask you a bunch of questions, you'd say] 'Boy, you come to my dressing room while I'm trying to get ready…' You know what I mean? … But in the sports world, the media [is there and] even when you're in your dressing room, you have to be 'on stage.' I really wasn't good at that. I couldn't separate the two. I don't have that mentality or that thought process in my head. My head is, 'I'm at work. Shhh! Leave me alone.' Like, I'm just programming myself all day [to say], 'What? What? Leave me alone.' I couldn't do two. I can't do both. I was never good at that. I don't blame the press. I know now that I'm retired, you're doing your job. You've got families to feed. You've got things to do. But at that time, I wasn't thinking like that. It was like, 'Why are you bothering me?' Then, it's like, 'Why are you saying nasty things about me and then you want to talk to me tomorrow. Why? I have other things to do. I have to play. I got to perform.'"

Bonds had also long felt that his lineage and stats received more attention than Barry Bonds the person. His father Bobby Bonds, after all, was a star player for 14 seasons in the big leagues and Willie Mays was his godfather, and Barry grew weary of all the comparisons to his father and of being referred to as Mays' godson. "I always dreamed of being someone like Michael Jordan, growing up in North Carolina; after a game, having someone asking me how I felt. No one ever asked that kind of question," Bonds once said during his big-league career. "My questions were always from someone wanting to know if I was going to go to the major leagues like my dad. If I thought I was going to be as good as my father was. Other athletes got to be themselves their whole lives. People have loved them for their whole lives. I never got to be loved for me."

Perhaps his father, Bobby Bonds, summed it up best when he affirmed early in Barry's career, "Barry just wants to play baseball. He's not pushing ballots for popularity." And it's fitting to bring Bobby into the discussion. It's been said that Barry inherited his personality from his father. In the 1970s, Bobby achieved things that no other leadoff man in the game's history had done—he was a combination of Lou Brock and Willie Mays, bringing power to the top of the lineup without sacrificing speed—yet he wound up becoming a baseball vagabond, playing for eight clubs. And not only was he not celebrated enough for his accomplishments, but he was criticized by the media as aloof and arrogant. He was portrayed as a chronic complainer. "Bobby Bonds," a former teammate once said, "was the most miserable person I ever knew inside or outside of baseball." After a 1970 season which saw Bobby hit .302 with 26 homers and 48 stolen bases, expectations were sky high, but when he didn't duplicate those numbers the next two seasons, he was branded a loner and a troublemaker. Three times he made the All-Star team, yet once a teammate said Bobby never stole a clutch base and wouldn't hit a cutoff man if he were King Kong. "What is potential?" Bobby, reflecting on the fact his accomplishments never seemed enough to the baseball world, once asked rhetorically, long after his playing career had ended. "Why do I have to live up to anybody's expectations? If you use that word, then nobody in this world has been a success, because he has failed somebody's expectations."

As many in the media have pointed out, Barry is very much like Bobby. As Bobby once said, "I would never say I was better than everybody else. But there was nothing on the field that anybody could do that I couldn't." Barry himself put it like this: "Tell me something I can't do, and I'll show you I can do it." In 1990, Barry became the first Pirate to ever hit at least 30 home runs and steal 30 or more bases in the same season, and only the second major-leaguer in history to produce at least 30 homers and steal 50-plus bases in the same campaign. He also became the only .300-100-100-30-50 man in baseball history: bat .300, drive in 100 runs, score 100 runs, hit 30 homers and steal 50 bases in a season.

It's not difficult to see why Bobby had such a strong influence on Barry. "Whenever we talk on the phone," Bobby once said, "Barry knows I've been there, I've stood 60 feet six inches from Bob Gibson and Don Drysdale. There's no situation that comes up for Barry that I haven't gone through myself at one time. The hitting aspect. The mental aspect. Any aspect." And, undoubtedly, the aspect with the media. Even the aspect with his team.

In fact, it came out later that after Barry had lost to the Pirates in salary arbitration for the second straight year prior to the 1991 season, Bobby told him before he went to spring training to be careful because the Pirates would set him up to make him look bad. During spring-training camp, Bonds had a highly publicized argument with Pirates manager Jim Leyland, which was caught on television cameras. Bobby Bonds later told *Playboy* magazine that he believed the Pirates had arranged the incident because the team wanted to make Barry look bad, perhaps to "alienate" fans and keep them on the ballclub's side in "battles over money." Barry himself was quoted in the same *Playboy* interview as saying, "It wasn't an accident. They set me up. Why would a microphone and TV crew be right there at that time? Just to stir up [expletive]. The funny thing is, my dad told me before I went to spring training, 'They're going to set you up when you get there.' He was right…"

You just have to wonder: What if Bobby had told him differently?

* * *

Those who criticize Bonds often point to the way he was often unpleasant with the media, something that has been well-documented. But, to understand Barry and why he acted that way, as some will insist, it's important to understand how he was raised. Jeff Pearlman, author of the 2006 biography on Bonds titled *Love Me, Hate Me*, determined that Barry learned at an early age that it was okay to abuse the privileges of stardom. "When people say, 'Look at Barry Bonds. He's a horrible guy,' I just say, 'What do you expect?' Look at how the guy was raised before you just say, 'Oh, he's a horrible human being.' Barry Bonds was raised watching his dad, watching Willie Mays, the way they treated people," Pearlman said on the ESPN2 documentary *Top 5 Reasons You Can't Blame Barry Bonds* in 2006. "The way if you want a cup of coffee, you could get a clubhouse guy to give it to you in five seconds. The way if you walk into a store and they say, 'Oh, Mr. Bonds, we'll give you 60% off that suit,' you say 80% and you'll get it. He learned from this very early age that athletic stardom comes with entitlement."

Numerous other stories about how poorly Bobby Bonds and Mays treated others have been printed over the years, and, as Pearlman suggested, it's easy to connect the dots and conclude that those acts influenced Barry. One particular story involved a man who found himself on a plane, sitting next to Mays. Although the man recognized Mays, he didn't want to bother him and kept quiet. During the flight, the man had to ask Mays for a small favor—not an autograph or a ticket request but the kind of little favor that one airline passenger asks of another—but, as the story goes, "The Say Hey Kid" supposedly responded with "fuck you." "[Barry] never had someone saying, 'You can't treat people that way.' It was just the opposite," added Pearlman on the same ESPN2 documentary. "It was, 'You should treat people that way. If you want to be great, treat people like dirt.' That's what he learned from his dad. That's what he learned from Willie Mays. There's no denying that."

USA Today's Bob Nightengale, when asked to discuss the topic, acknowledges that Bobby Bonds had a "big influence" on Barry. "[Barry] looked up to him. [Bobby] was his hitting coach," says Nightengale. "They talked often. I'm not saying they were best of friends. There was a period there when they weren't that close, but certainly [Bobby was] someone that he admired and respected. Just as he did Dusty Baker, who also grew up in Riverside. Bobby was very head strong. He never kissed up to anybody—media, management, anything like that. I'm sure that's where Barry got some of it from.

Barry's very head strong. Barry's a brilliant guy. He could have been CEO of a bunch of companies with his intelligence. [Regarding the way Bobby treated others,] I'm sure some of that rubbed off on Barry—the mannerisms and the way he conducted himself. [Barry learned,] 'You worry about yourself. Watch out. Some guy might be out to get you.' I'm sure Bobby had a strong influence on the way Barry reacted toward people."

In terms of Bonds' reaction toward the media specifically, Dustan Mohr, who played one season in San Francisco in 2004, acknowledges that Barry had sometimes spoken about why he was hard on the media. "I know for a fact that he was pretty cold to the media at times for a reason," Mohr recounts. "A large part of why he was, is because he didn't feel that the media was very fair to his father when he was playing. I think he had some alcohol problems, maybe. Or he had some problems off the field. I know that he didn't feel that they were very fair to him during his time playing. That was a large part of why Barry was sort of cold to them. And, of course, you have guys that want to interview Barry, and he probably doesn't have time. Or he's got to be doing something else. He says no, but people will take that personally. And they react and they write something bad. But a large part of it was he felt they treated his father poorly in the media when he had some issues while he was playing. I think probably a lot of people know that, maybe, but he did talk about that. Not often, but he did mention that a few times."

Barry didn't trust the media, writer Josh Suchon once explained, because of how Bobby was treated. "He … believes that … the press never gave his father a fair shake," Suchon said. "He always felt that from the time that he was in high school. So he distrusted the media before the media even started writing bad things about him. I think that's an important thing to understand in the Barry Bonds relationship with the media. … [When] he was still an up-and-coming player trying to establish himself… he had a quote that said, 'The media never did my father right. Why would I expect the media to do me right?' I think that's an important lesson to know about Barry."

There's also the way the media seemed to suggest whatever Barry did was never enough. In 2001, for instance, he homered three times in Colorado on September 9 to give him 63 dingers on the season. Everything in America went on hold two days later because of the 9/11 terrorist attacks, before the baseball season resumed a week later. When an emotional Bonds announced he would donate $10,000 per home run to United Way for the victims of the terrorist attacks, it wasn't enough in the eyes of some. An ESPN reporter instantly devalued the gesture by asking Barry why he didn't just give a lump sum. "That's just the way I feel in my heart," Bonds said. It was as though Bonds was often criticized for not opening up to the press, yet when he was ready to open up, he wasn't given the opportunity. But without trying to play psychologist, it would seem logical that questions like the one from the ESPN reporter perhaps gave him another reason to distrust the media; whatever he did, it was never enough.

Things could have been different for Barry, but it's also worth noting how he handled the media at the beginning of his big-league career. When he was first called up to Pittsburgh, as the story goes, he enjoyed talking to writers. But, as observers noted, things changed when he struggled at the plate—and when writers started calling him "Bobby." The Pittsburgh press, after all, was still replete with writers who'd recalled Bobby Bonds and the Giants-Pirates rivalry of the early 1970s. "I think there was a little bit of a chip on his shoulder about being confused with his father the first couple years," pitcher Bob Walk once recalled. "It was unbelievable how many people would call him Bobby Bonds. He wanted out of that desperately." Barry, who resented being called "Bobby," remembered it this way: "'Are you as good as your father?' they'd ask me."

For Pirates manager Jim Leyland, the media proved to be a distraction for Barry at the beginning of his big-league career. And when the skipper let Bonds know it, the outfielder took it to the extreme. "When I first came up," Bonds once said on *SportsCentury*, an ESPN documentary, "I was talking to the media too much, but I was hitting like .205 or something, and I did all the interviews, and Leyland said, 'If you don't concentrate and do things [you're] supposed to do, you're gonna sit down.' He said, 'You have to leave these reporters alone because these people are not your friends.' So I cut out the media." The Pittsburgh manager didn't refute those comments, at least not on the same *SportsCentury* episode. "I think sometimes they take advantage of that, and there are times you need some private moments," Leyland said in response.

Ted Sobel, a long-time L.A. sports radio personality, acknowledges that Bonds has a good side to him, but is otherwise the worst athlete he has ever dealt with. "Bobby Bonds was a damn good player. He was the first [player to have more than two] 30-30 [seasons, meaning 30 home runs and 30 stolen bases in the same season], and he did it five times. The only other guy who did it five times was Barry. Everybody talks about the Griffeys, but the Bondses, in that category, are untouchable," says Sobel, who encountered Barry on numerous occasions when the Giants played at Dodger Stadium. "Bobby Bonds was a great player. But 'chip' is the key word. Barry was a chip off the old block, and he was taught by Bobby to have a chip on his shoulder. He wanted Barry to be that way. I'm not going to say he wanted Barry to be a jerk, but he basically said, 'Look. Do whatever you need to do to get to wherever you need to go. And if you want to treat people like crap on the way, that's their problem, not yours.' A horrible attitude to have, but that's reality. It was all taught to him by his father. And Barry absolutely adored his father. He coached for the Giants for a while when Barry played there. Willie May is his godfather. It all stems from his father, and how he taught Barry to be and Barry just took it to the extreme. He was the biggest prick who ever lived in sports. He was impossible to deal with. I'd say—along with Will Clark, the former first baseman for the Giants, and Kevin Brown, who was a really good pitcher for a few years—Barry Bonds was the most rude, self-serving, disrespectful athlete I've ever dealt with. And the next level down, it ain't even close!

"I mean, he was really complicated, in many ways. Barry has a good side about him. He's one of these guys where he turns on his charm when he wants to turn on the charm, and certainly when the camera's on. But for a radio guy, there's no camera—at least not in those days. You'd say to his face, 'Barry, you got a quick second?' but he wouldn't even look at you. He was just the rudest person I've ever dealt with in sports, and it's not even close. From what I understand, he's got this incredibly charitable side to him—a guy whom I respect told me this—where he does things for the needy and for kids. He goes to hospitals. Nobody knows about it. He's not looking for press coverage. So, that's a nice thing about him. There are 18 parts to the brain, and one of his is good, at least.

"I think a lot of this stems from his father dealing with a lot of racial crap when he was younger. And he built up this wall, and basically said, 'Screw the world. They're treating me like this. I'm going to treat them how I need to treat them. I gotta advance and succeed—whatever it takes.' And I think that's where it all stems from. His dad went through a lot of crap. Barry grew up in nice areas after his father got to the major leagues. I think he lived in mostly white neighborhoods during a time when it wasn't necessarily [a common occurrence, and we're talking] in the late 1960s and early 1970s. He had a pretty good damn childhood. He was born in Riverside, which is not exactly a high-end neighborhood. But whatever his dad went through—and his father was 'almost' a superstar, 'almost' incredible, 'almost' a Hall of Famer, but never quite there—he just passed on to Barry: 'Look, you do whatever you need to do to be that guy, because you've got more talent than I do.' Every time I dealt with Barry, it was the most uncomfortable feeling…"

But Sobel does mention a point that few people talk about: The fact that Barry goes to hospitals and does things for kids and others.

Another Side of Barry We Never Hear About

You know, sometimes I think we analyze Barry too much. Sometimes I think we should just sit back and admire what Barry does on the field. That's the interesting Barry.

—Charlie Hayes, former Giants teammate,
as told to *SF Weekly*'s Benoit Denizet-Lewis (2000)

It's one of those heart-warming stories that don't seem to get told often enough. A baseball superstar, by far the greatest player of his era, visits a sick teen in a hospital, befriending him and hitting home runs against the boy's hometown team later that season.

No, this story isn't about Babe Ruth hitting three home runs in a World Series game for Johnny Sylvester, a young fan from New Jersey suffering from a spinal infection, in 1926.

It's about Barry Bonds and a 13-year-old leukemia patient named Anthony Lee Franklin, whose encounter with Bonds made headlines in 1997 when the San Francisco Giants left fielder visited him at the Children's Hospital in Oakland. Unlike the Ruth-Sylvester story, later featured—and embellished—in separate biographical films about Ruth and Lou Gehrig, the Bonds-Franklin relationship has virtually been forgotten in history.

Not that Bonds—whom, according to Bonds himself in a 1998 interview with *Baseball Weekly*, the media often portrayed "as some horrible person, a monster, like I'm an animal"—was seeking the attention to begin with. He was seeking to help Franklin beat his leukemia, a malignancy of the blood-forming tissues where a bone marrow transplant might be needed. That's what doctors believed at the time—that the boy would require a life-saving transplant. A match, however, would be a long shot. Franklin was an only child, with no siblings to donate marrow. When Bonds read about the story in the newspaper, he immediately wanted to help out. At the same time, Bonds was concerned about the need for bone marrow donors across the nation, especially in the African-American community, and wanted to do something about it.

* * *

When agent Dennis Gilbert first handed Barry Bonds an article from the *Oakland Tribune* in February 1997 featuring the plight of young Anthony Lee Franklin, who'd been diagnosed with leukemia weeks earlier and only days after his 13th birthday, the Giants left fielder didn't have to do anything. One might assume he wouldn't have cared because, after all, he had often been labeled a selfish and egotistical athlete by the media.

Instead, Bonds was touched enough by the story about the 13-year-old, a near straight-A student and a shortstop/pitcher on Oakland's Babe Ruth League national championship team, that he decided to get involved. Doing some online research on bone marrow, Bonds learned that African-Americans represented only seven percent of the bone marrow donors throughout the country. And upon seeing that less than four percent of those African-Americans who needed marrow transplants received them because there weren't enough donors in the pool to maximize the match potential, Bonds sought to help raise awareness about bone marrow donation. "When I found out that the percentage of African-Americans who donated [bone marrow and blood] was so low," he later told a reporter, "I was appalled. I wasn't a donor, either. I decided to go to the hospital and meet Lee Franklin and educate myself on this… I'm just a small part of this."

Certainly, Bonds' actions aren't things that an uncaring, selfish superstar would do, which reveal a side of him that the media rarely discusses. "Barry has two sides to him," Franklin, who received a Giants jacket and two autographed baseballs from Bonds during that hospital visit, said in 2001. "The side that gets his job done on the field that can be kind of mean, I guess, and the other side that is more friendly that me and his wife and family see."

Sportswriter Monte Poole, who was at Children's Hospital Oakland when Bonds first visited Franklin, later authored a reflection piece in the

[Walnut Creek, California] East Bay Times about the "unforgettable" visit. Franklin, Poole noted, was "overwhelmed by Bonds' gesture." Franklin himself would say that "Barry's a good friend, and I really appreciate what he is doing." Poole, meanwhile, added, "Think of it: Here was a boy fighting for his life and there is Barry Bonds, the man with the reputation for selfishness, in his hospital room, giggling and cracking jokes." During the visit, which lasted the better part of an hour, Bonds and Franklin talked and giggled, exchanging stories and promises. Bonds even gave him his home phone number and promised that Franklin would get on the field at a Giants game. "It was in that room, as Barry sat beside Lee's bed," continued Poole, "that the brawny superstar forged a bond with the kid who was waging a courageous battle against a wicked disease." The impact that the 13-year-old had on Bonds was clear, as the Giants superstar then drove to the nearby Alameda-Contra Costa County blood bank to donate two samples of his blood—which was all it took to register with the National Marrow Donor Program—to see if he would be a donor match with Franklin. "[Franklin] had everything going for him," he said. "He has a great family; he is a near straight-A student; and he is a great athlete. I thought, 'Why does it always have to happen to the good ones?'" As it turned out, Bonds wasn't a match, but he was still ready to donate if he was found to be a match for another leukemia victim.

Forget Bonds' home runs—he'd go on to bash 40 of them in 1997, including a pair against Franklin's hometown Oakland Athletics in the first year of interleague play, while stealing 37 bases, falling just short of a second consecutive 40-homer, 40-steal season— and exploits on the field for a moment. Forget about the fact that Bonds—who'd finish fifth in National League MVP voting that year, his seventh top-five finish over the previous eight seasons—led his San Francisco Giants to a surprising NL West division title that season. In 1997, a year in which he led the Giants to their first postseason appearance in eight years, Barry Bonds was finding time to make an even more significant difference off the field—a caring side of him which, unfortunately, has been all but forgotten. But if one said Bonds was a selfish human being, his actions at the hospital and blood bank certainly said the opposite.

And he didn't stop there.

He spoke before the United Way of the Bay Area board of

directors, voicing his concerns for the plight of African-Americans who required bone marrow transplants. Those who interacted with Bonds off the field when he was working with various charities certainly never saw the Giants slugger as a selfish individual; they recall a compassionate man wanting to make a difference in the lives of underprivileged kids. "A lot of what Barry does is under the radar of the cameras, because getting applauded for his work is not his goal," Eric McDonald, a senior vice president of the United Way of the Bay Area, recalled in 2000. "I have often heard about the side of Barry as portrayed by the media, but we have never seen it here. All we have seen is the side that absolutely loves kids and will devote time and money to help them." Bob Rose, former vice president of communications for the Giants who went on to become executive associate athletic director at the University of California at Berkeley, added in 2001: "I think Barry read about Lee and saw this young, bright, athletic kid who had everything going for him and just wanted to help. Barry was so impressed with Lee."

Shortly after his visits to the Children's Hospital and the blood bank, Bonds also launched the Barry Bonds Bone Marrow Campaign, a two-year drive to register at least 1,000 African-Americans and raise $250,000 for families whose loved ones had leukemia or a related blood disorder. What began as a local campaign in the Bay Area—Bonds, along with Franklin and Willie Purvis, his grandfather and guardian, first promoted it with an appearance at Allen Temple Baptist Church in Oakland in May of 1997—would transform into a national crusade when he made an announcement about his efforts that July at the All-Star Game in Cleveland. Teaming with the United Way, the Judie Davis Program, the Giants and Celebrate Life, Bonds would go on to see the campaign register 3,000 African-Americans as potential donors and raise $500,000 for families affected with leukemia and other blood diseases. "We as members of the African-American community must rise above the suspicions we have had of the medical profession in the past, because in this case, only we can help ourselves overcome this crisis of our own children finding donor matches," Bonds said then. "I just want to see Lee and other kids who are victimized by these diseases live long and productive lives."

As for Franklin, he went on to live a productive life for another nine years. He didn't require a donor because his body responded to chemotherapy, and for three years, ending in May 2000, he endured drug treatment and radiation. In 2001, doctors said his leukemia was in remission, and believed chances of its return were slim. He excelled, in the meantime, in athletics and in the classroom. Unfortunately, two years after his high school graduation, the leukemia recurred and Franklin, then playing baseball at the University of Arizona, returned to California to receive treatment. Although the cancer went into remission once again, Franklin was unable to return to baseball in Arizona. He went on to attend San Francisco State University in pursuit of a career in sports broadcasting until the cancer recurred for one final time in March of 2006. He died from complications related to the disease in November that year, losing his battle at the age of 22.

But as tragic as the story turned out, Bonds did make a positive difference in Franklin's life. Through his relationship with Bonds, Franklin attended numerous Giants games and the 1997 All-Star Game in Cleveland. He even joined Bonds on the field during a workout with the All-Stars, which allowed him to interact with future Hall of Famers such as Tony Gwynn and Ken Griffey, Jr. That particular experience was undoubtedly a once-in-a-lifetime moment for the 13-year-old, who six months earlier had thought he was going to die shortly after being diagnosed with the leukemia. "Barry is a very nice guy. He was there in my time of need," Franklin said in an interview in 2001, adding that the support of Bonds helped him walk out of the hospital the first time his illness went into remission. "When you get to know him one-on-one, he's a nice guy. If you get to know him, the armor is not there."

When asked by the press to discuss his friendship with Franklin, Bonds never made it about himself. "That's old news," he responded to a reporter when asked in 2001, before murmuring, "Straight-A student. He's doing real well." Bonds had a genuine friendship with the young man, but he never wanted to discuss it with the press. And, really, if one stopped to think about it, why should he discuss it? Looking at things from a different perspective, if, say, Bonds were the CEO of a random company and not a famous Major League Baseball player, would reporters be hounding him with tape recorders and notepads to discuss his personal friendships? Of course not. It would be intrusive.

For Bonds, launching the Barry Bonds Bone Marrow Campaign at the 1997 All-Star Game was to ensure that the campaign gained as much exposure as possible to assist Anthony Lee Franklin and other African-Americans who might require bone marrow transplants. "It's just being there for your brothers and sisters," Bonds said at the time. He befriended Franklin and the two became close friends. That should be the end of the story. Why would he need to answer questions by the media about all that? He wasn't doing any of that to seek attention.

But it's a story that certainly shouldn't be forgotten when it comes time to discuss the character of Barry Bonds. "I learned about Bonds that he is most comfortable revealing his vulnerability in the presence of children," sportswriter Monte Poole once said. "A lot of adults share this characteristic, but it seemed more pronounced in Barry's case, given his impenetrable facade. He clearly was affected by Lee. And by Lee's plight."

* * *

Those who don't know—and/or don't like—Barry Bonds will say that the friendship with Anthony Lee Franklin was a one-off, pointing to examples of his stiffing young fans who wanted his autograph. Those who do know him say that he's a much different person when dealing with children off the field.

Rich Donnelly, a coach with the Pirates when Bonds began his major-league career in Pittsburgh, once told a story that, again, shows a side of Barry that the media rarely talks about. Donnelly had a daughter, Amy, who passed away with a brain tumor in 1993 at the age of 17. "I remember one day when she was 15," Donnelly said, "and she was supposed to meet me at the car after the game, and she showed up late. And when I asked why, she said, 'I just had the nicest talk with Barry Bonds. He told me how I should be when I grow up, how I shouldn't use drugs, how I should go to school.'

"And I said, 'Are you sure you were talking to Barry Bonds?'"

What happened was that Bonds had stopped by the family lounge at Three Rivers Stadium and spent 15 minutes talking to Amy and her friend, telling them how to grow up to be good kids and not to let others steer them down the wrong path. He also warned them against sneaking around with ballplayers once she got older. "He was just about God back then," Donnelly said, "so they listened." Who says Barry Bonds wasn't a good role model to kids?

Donnelly added that when he told Bonds about his daughter's death, Barry cried. "He can be the meanest guy a writer's ever seen and he can be the warmest, most considerate guy, too. And you'll ask, 'Is he the same guy?' Yeah, he is. He's an enigma."

There are those who have suggested that Bonds was all about himself. Again, Donnelly has seen a completely different side of the superstar left fielder that has largely been ignored by the media.

During spring training in 1991 with the Pirates, Bonds was caught on TV cameras in the midst of a heated argument with manager Jim Leyland, an incident that was highly publicized because the media considered it to be newsworthy. The fact that Bonds, coming off his first National League MVP Award (he'd win seven of those by the time he finished his career), had expressed his displeasure with the team—coupled with the fact that Leyland had yelled at his superstar—was news, as far as reporters were concerned. (When Bonds reflected on the incident years later in a 2019 conversation with Giants public address announcer Renel Brooks-Moon, he offered his side of the story: coach Bill Virdon was yelling at him about something but Barry had no idea what that was about. Bonds, confused and not wanting to be yelled at, shouted back, and Leyland jumped in to protect his coach. Barry acknowledged that Leyland, as the manager of the ballclub, handled the situation properly and there was no hard feelings between the two men— Bonds and Leyland even spoke behind closed doors in the manager's office afterward—but unfortunately the screaming incident was caught on tape and the press had only their own version of the story.) Yet, nobody talked about a completely different incident which had occurred three months earlier, on a snowy day in December.

Donnelly, however, remembers that day well. Bonds had just been named the National League MVP weeks earlier, and Donnelly had arranged for him to appear at a baseball clinic at the high school in the tiny town of Wellsburg, West Virginia, near his hometown. (Wellsburg, according to the 2010 census, is a town of just under 3,000 people.) As it was snowing heavily that day, Donnelly anticipated that Bonds wouldn't be able to make the 45-mile drive from Pittsburgh, and the coach arrived at campus that morning ready to apologize on the MVP's behalf. Instead, he found that Bonds had beaten him there—Barry had trudged his way through a foot of snow to attend the off-season clinic and arrived early—and was already speaking to the group of kids, going over the importance of practice on the playing field. Later, when Donnelly handed Bonds the $500 check that he was promised for an hour of his time, Barry tore it up and stayed for the rest of the day. "Give the money back," Bonds told his coach. "This ain't right. These people can't afford me."

As for that more famous spring training incident, Leyland has suggested that the media blew the argument out of proportion. The well-publicized incident created the misconception the two didn't get along, but, in reality, the two men count each other as a close friend. "One of the biggest regrets I have in baseball is that people misunderstood, that it was like I originally made my name because I got into an argument with Barry Bonds," Leyland told the *St. Louis Post-Dispatch*'s Rick Hummel in 2005. "But that was the furthest thing from what it really was about... That was a family quarrel and it was over immediately. Barry Bonds and I have been very close friends. And we will be." The Barry Bonds he knows, Leyland added, is not the same as the one talked about in the press. "Has he brought some of this stuff on himself? There's no question about that. But, I know the side that sits with me when I see him, like in Pittsburgh he'll sit for 40 minutes and talk. Or I'll get something in the mail at Christmas... I like Barry Bonds. I'm in Barry Bonds' corner—and I always will be. That's just the way it is. I know the side of him that a lot of people don't know... All I can tell you is that Barry Bonds has treated me like a father and he busted his butt for me every day."

Donnelly, who spent 14 seasons on Leyland's coaching staff with three organizations (Pittsburgh, Florida and Colorado), adds that the shouting match between Bonds and Leyland created the misconception the two didn't get along—which is the furthest thing from the truth. "When he and Jim talk, it's a side of Barry you'll never see," Donnelly once said. "Barry's respect for Jim is unbelievable... Most players, after an incident like that, would have gotten turned off to the guy. But their relationship actually got stronger, because I think both of them respect each other for never backing down... I don't think people outside Pittsburgh understand the relationship the two of them have. Barry loves Jim, and Jim loves Barry. And they have a tremendous mutual respect for one another."

Donnelly isn't the only one who has witnessed the generosity

Barry shows to a friend and his willingness to do whatever is asked and more. Ashley Gilbert, the daughter of Bonds' one-time agent Dennis Gilbert, has also shared fond stories of Bonds' generosity. The week before Bonds visited Anthony Lee Franklin at the hospital in February of 1997, he made a surprise visit to Los Angeles after Ashley, then a high school freshman, asked him if he could appear at a fundraiser for the Agoura High School baseball team. Not only did Bonds attend, he stayed for hours signing autographs. He also refused to accept a high school baseball jersey until all the varsity players had signed it, and he gave an inspiring speech directing the teens to keep an eye on their goals. "Bonds was great," baseball coach Bruce Beck recalled. "He talked about growing up… He was cordial. He was accommodating. We gave him a jersey, and he asked the varsity team to sign it. He's going to hang it in his home." The event and an auction of Bonds' baseball and bat, per an article in the *Daily News of Los Angeles* reporting the story, raised nearly $17,500 for the team, with the funds being used to pay for uniform pants for the players as well as baseball equipment.

For Ashley, Bonds was like family. Her father, after all, often invited players he represented into the family home, and, in Dennis Gilbert's words, Ashley and Bonds were "special friends." "Ever since I was little," she told the paper, "he's been around. He stays with us all the time. He's a rad guy. He acts like he's my second father. He hangs out with me and my friends." Whenever he was in town, Ashley would ask him to take her friends and her to the movies, and Bonds would oblige. Her friends thought Bonds was cool. "They think he's really rad because he's nice," Ashley added. "He's always there."

Former Dodgers knuckleball pitcher Tom Candiotti recalls a kind gesture Bonds showed his oldest son, Brett, before a 1993 game at Candlestick Park, where, because of the bad blood between Los Angeles and San Francisco, Giants fans were known to shout obscenities at Dodger players—and, often, make inappropriate comments about their moms. According to Candiotti, his son still remembers that moment today. "We're playing the Giants in Candlestick and I brought my son Brett—he was seven or eight years old at the time—with me, to be one of the batboys for the Dodgers. So, at old Candlestick Park, you had to walk out of the locker room, down the right-field line. And I told him, 'When we get out there through those doors, there's gonna be a lot of screaming and there's gonna be a lot of yelling. You're gonna hear some words you're not used to hearing. Don't worry about it. They're just fans. Don't take it personal when they're yelling at me or whatever.'

"I don't think he knew what to expect. So, we walked through the doors and, sure enough, people are yelling at you [and] throwing stuff at you. Barry is playing catch on the right-field line there with some of the other Giants. Barry looks over, and he comes over and gives me a hug and says, 'Who's this?' So, I introduced him to my son, and Barry picked him up. And as soon as Barry came over, the crowd was just silent. They just stopped saying stuff and [throwing things]. But Barry just picked my son up, put him over his shoulder and just walked with me all the way to the Dodger dugout, and then dropped him off right in front of the dugout."

After that, Bonds went back to his spot in right field. "I thought that was, like, one of the coolest things a guy could do," continues Candiotti. "You know, he kind of recognized that there's a lot of swear words going on, a lot of stuff being thrown and all this stuff. And he immediately just shut it as he's walking over to me and then grabbed my son and walked him over. It was really, really, really a cool moment and, in fact, I know my son… will never, ever, forget that moment."

Giants first baseman J. T. Snow saw first-hand that Bonds treated teammates' kids well. "Barry loved kids, because they didn't want anything from him," Snow told writer Gwen Knapp in 2013, recalling an incident in the clubhouse when his son Shane climbed all over Bonds' deluxe leather recliner while eating chocolate. Bonds was furious when he saw the mess—until he learned who'd done it. "Barry just looked at him," continued Snow, "and said, 'That's all right,' and slapped him on the back."

That was typical of his personality with children, *San Francisco Chronicle* writer Glenn Dickey once wrote. Bonds was very loving with kids, noted Dickey, and was always active in children's charities during his time with the Giants. "When a young Giants batboy tripped trying to pick up Bonds' bat after he had drawn a near-intentional walk in [a 1998] game," added the *Chronicle* writer, "Bonds stopped and retraced his steps to help the young boy to his feet." Back in Pittsburgh, Bonds once lost to coach Rich Donnelly's son Bubba in a basketball game of

H-O-R-S-E; although Barry called the high-school-aged batboy a "little pipsqueak," he ended up buying Bubba dinner for a whole week.

There's also the story freelance sports photographer Scott Clark, a friend of Barry's, once shared with writer Jeff Pearlman. Following a game in New York in 1990, Bonds met up with Clark in Greenwich, Connecticut. That night, Clark's wife went into labor, and the three rushed to nearby Greenwich Hospital. "You can't get much whiter than Greenwich," the photographer recounted to Pearlman. "And a white guy and a black guy charge into the emergency room, both claiming to be the father. The looks in that place were pretty funny." Bonds stayed the night, signing autographs in the waiting room while anxiously awaiting the news. When baby Haley Clark was born the next morning, Bonds was euphoric. "You should see the Christmas basket he sends us every year—a small family could live in it," Clark said in 2006. "I wish people could see that Barry Bonds, because he does exist."

James Mims could relate to that side of Barry. A former baseball player at the University of Southern California, Mims started his own wristband company, M&N Bandit, in 1988. Two years earlier, Dusty Baker, then still playing for Oakland, had introduced Mims to Barry, and the two remained casual friends. One day, Mims and Bonds were talking when the topic of wristbands came up. "Do you need money?" Barry suddenly asked. Mims explained that he needed $5,000 to purchase some machinery—but that he wasn't asking Barry because he was trying to get a loan from other people. Bonds, though, interrupted him. "Five thousand? Pfft, that's nothing." He immediately wrote a $5,000 check and handed it to Mims, no strings attached. He even became one of Mims' first customers, and the wristbands, featuring the faces of players above the tagline "SAY NO TO DRUGS," soon exploded into a major-league fad. "He didn't know whether the product was going to fly," Mims later said. "But he took a chance on a young guy trying to make it. I'll never forget that."

* * *

Yet it isn't always about helping out a friend or a friend's kid. Sometimes, it could be a complete stranger. In 1999, a woman from Wisconsin by the name of Mergee Donovan, with the help of the Brewers, reached out to Bonds when her sick 12-year-old son,

Benjamin, was awaiting open-heart surgery. With the Giants in Milwaukee to play the Brewers, Mergee was hoping Bonds could fulfill her son's wish and say hello. The Brewers cautioned her that Bonds never honored such requests, but still, someone slipped a note in his locker at old County Stadium, asking if he might find time to try to cheer young Benjamin up. Next thing Mergee knew, Bonds invited her son to the following day's game and young Benjamin was hanging out with the Giants slugger. Barry befriended the Donovans, even sending a limousine for them when they visited San Francisco, and the family saw him multiple times over the years. Fast forward to eight years later, the year Bonds was chasing the all-time home-run record. Benjamin had recovered from the heart surgery, and the Donovans were at the ballpark when the Giants came to town, with Mergee presenting Barry with a bouquet of flowers prior to the game. Bonds, says Mergee, is a "wonderful man."

Another example of the other side of Bonds that has never been discussed enough was his genuine affection for super fan Marge Wallace, known to Giants fans and employees as "Ballpark Marge."

Born developmentally disabled, "Ballpark Marge" was raised in the Sonoma State Hospital, where she remained until her 31st birthday. Although details of her life are sketchy, in 1958—the same year the Giants left New York and the Polo Grounds for the Bay Area—Wallace also moved to San Francisco. She immediately became a regular at Giants games, arriving hours early before each game to greet the players. After the team moved from Seals Stadium to Candlestick Park, at some point the Giants began leaving a chair for "Ballpark Marge" outside the clubhouse door, where she would greet every player who ever came through.

When Bonds signed with the Giants in December 1992, he gazed into the audience at his introductory press conference and, upon spotting her, excitedly exclaimed, "Hey, there's Marge!" Bonds had already known Wallace when he was a youngster hanging out in the home clubhouse at Candlestick during the years his father, Bobby Bonds, was a star with the Giants. And then some 20 years later, Barry himself was a star with Wallace's favorite team, and he always treated her with the utmost respect. Each day without fail, according to observers, Barry would bend down to hug "Ballpark Marge" before entering the clubhouse, and ask how she was doing while gently touching her arm or shoulder. "Never when the TV cameras were on," C. W. Nevius, a columnist with the *San Francisco Chronicle*, once recalled. "It wasn't a formality with Barry. He was genuinely concerned for the woman's well-being."

Royce Clayton, teammates with Bonds from 1993 to 1995, remembers Marge Wallace and Barry's interactions with her. "She was the biggest Giants fan forever," Clayton says now. "Margie was somebody that was there when Bobby [Bonds] was around and when Willie [Mays] was around. So, Barry automatically had that respect for her. Loved her passion. He stopped [for Margie], which he wouldn't do in his [game-day] preparation as far as how he got to the ballpark, [focused on] what he did, just kept on moving, [and] walked to his car. Didn't sign a whole lot of autographs. But he stopped for Margie. That's just the type of person he is. I'm not saying it's for everybody. But when somebody touches his heart [the way Margie did], he had a big heart. Dude had a big heart. He was able to show that."

"Ballpark Marge," who followed the Giants to Pacific Bell Park (which, since 2019, has been known as Oracle Park and was also known as AT&T Park between 2006 and 2018) when the team left Candlestick, died of pneumonia at age 77 in June 2003. Bonds, according to *SFGate*, was her second favorite Giants player—just behind J. T. Snow, whom she thought was awfully cute.

* * *

Then, there is also the Bryan Stow story.

Stow, a Giants fan and a 42-year-old paramedic, was critically injured when he was brutally assaulted by two Dodgers fans in the Dodger Stadium parking lot following a San Francisco-Los Angeles game on Opening Day in 2011. The Santa Cruz, California, native sustained severe injuries to his skull and brain and was placed into a medically induced coma after the incident. He would spend months at the hospital and would be unable to even write his own name until late October that year.

Bonds, who'd played in his final big-league game four years earlier, was quick to offer his support to the family. "My father pays for Bryan Stow's kids to go to school," Nikolai Bonds, Barry's son, reminded writer Jeff Pearlman in 2015. Barry, added his son, helps more children and families than most athletes and entertainers, something that the media isn't aware of. "Not because he has to but because he chooses to."

According to Stow family attorney Thomas Girardi in an interview with NBC Bay Area KNTV several weeks following the assault, Bonds volunteered to pay for the college education of Stow's two children, Tyler (then 12 years of age) and Tabitha (then eight), by starting a college fund for the pair. But as ESPN.com called it, Bonds' gift was "one quiet gesture," as the home-run king was not seeking any attention for doing so. "It was extraordinary of Barry Bonds, I thought," Girardi told the Bay Area TV station. "He didn't say anything about it to the press. This was just a gift he gave the family because he knew that it was going to be pretty important to the kids." According to KNTV, Bonds spent an hour with Stow at Los Angeles County-University of Southern California Medical Center on April 22, and also left a signed baseball bat for Stow's children.

According to the Stows themselves, Bonds was very active in visiting Stow and also helping the family, even appearing in a video with the family later that year to make a public service announcement to encourage others to donate to help out the Stows. In a statement on the family's website, Bonds said, "Please join me, Barry Bonds, and my friends in our fundraising efforts to help provide Bryan's two wonderful children with the gift of a college education. Let's help Tabitha and Tyler fulfill all of their dreams by investing in their future. This is a great opportunity for us to continue to show our love and support for Bryan and his family."

The Stows aren't the only ones to benefit from Bonds' generosity. Following his playing career, Bonds has also paid visits to children's hospitals and donated to schools in San Francisco. He has spent afternoons hanging out with patients, families and hospital staff in children's hospitals and visited one-on-one with kids in their hospital rooms, which have been reported by local Bay Area newspapers. "Through Barry's generosity, our playroom has been completely renovated and is one of the most popular spaces in the hospital," Kimberly Scurr, an executive director of UCSF Benioff Children's Hospital in San Francisco, said in 2011. "A frequent visitor to the hospital, Barry has developed close ties with our kids, families and staff over the years, and has put smiles on the faces of many young patients." Giants fans, who have a love affair with the home-run king, have over the years gotten to see that side of Barry's personality, not just the headlines written by the national media.

Jim Leyland, his manager in Pittsburgh, has certainly seen that good side, too. "Underneath all that toughness, I know what a big heart is there," the former Pirates skipper reflected in 2020. "I know the things that Barry has done for kids and different [charities], things he did for people that a lot of people never knew about. I saw a side of Barry that some people to this day haven't seen."

* * *

Those are some of the forgotten or untold stories about Barry Bonds and his interactions with children and "Ballpark Marge." And Anthony Lee Franklin. And Bryan Stow and his family.

But those unconvinced about Barry's good side will refer back to the way Barry treated the press. L.A.-based sports radio reporter Ted Sobel, who was on the receiving end on numerous occasions, shares his experience. "Every time I dealt with Barry—I mean, every time—it was the most uncomfortable feeling, because he didn't want any part of you, and my job was to just get one or two 12-second soundbites," says Sobel. "And he [couldn't] care less about any of our jobs. If he was in the mood to talk, he'd talk. If he wasn't, he'd pretend like he wasn't even standing there. It was just unbelievable. I've dealt with [over] 100 superstars. None of them were like that. Some of them were egomaniacs, but they weren't even in the same universe as Barry Bonds. And you can look it up [in terms of finding stories about how he handled the press]. It's not anything unusual for me. It was anybody who covered him."

There's also, say critics, the matter of how he interacted with his teammates. Those unconvinced about Bonds' good side might ask, "What about the way he was with teammates in the clubhouse?" There are, of course, those who will say that he never, ever bothered to put an arm around another teammate to see how he was doing. Or he never offered to pay for anything. Or that he was all about himself. "He wasn't liked by his teammates," adds Sobel.

Yet, there are also those who will say the complete opposite.

Barry with Peers and Teammates

Well, it seems like everybody has a bad story about Barry Bonds. I had a chance to go to Japan with him to play on the American All-Star team. And he was awesome. He was a great teammate. He played the game hard and he played it the right way. ... I'm rooting for him.

> —Mike Sweeney, Kansas City Royals' five-time All-Star
> first baseman/DH, as told to *San Jose Mercury News*
> writer Daniel Brown (2007)

Critics of Barry Bonds will say that the superstar left fielder didn't have any friends on his teams. Stories are out there saying that a Giants teammate once said of Bonds that there was no player he respected more or wanted his own children to emulate less. There's one about a Pirates teammate once saying he'd rather lose without Barry than win with him. There's one about another teammate suggesting nobody on the team cared if he got drilled by an opposing pitcher. There are stories about teammates and observers who suggested he cared more about his own stats, pointing out, as an example, that his batting average suffered in 1989 because he'd spent the final weeks of the season trying to hit his 20th home run (he finished at 19). (There aren't enough stories, though, about how Barry understood that he sometimes got home-run happy and so he worked to develop the best batting eye the game had ever seen—so much so that he almost never swung at a bad pitch.) Or that he was stealing bases in the final month of 1996—running when the situation didn't warrant it or attempting to steal against strong-armed catchers like Florida's Charles Johnson or Pittsburgh's Jason Kendall—just so he could become the first National League player to ever hit 40 homers and steal 40 bases in the same season. Or that he was complaining about teammates fouling off a pitch when he had a base stolen.

Those who do know—and understand—Barry Bonds will tell you such comments do not reflect those of everybody in the clubhouse. John Wehner, a former Pirates utility man who worked out with Bonds for several winters in Pittsburgh, once said Barry could be funny and engaging, that he was a decent guy beneath the bluster and image. "He could be a miserable ass in the clubhouse at times, but I always thought he was a pretty good guy," Wehner said, adding Bonds' attitude was part of what made him a special player. "Sure, he's arrogant. But you've got to be arrogant in this game." Rich Donnelly, a coach in Pittsburgh when Bonds was a Pirate, added, "He's brash, bold, cocky… but that's why he's good. He knows he's good. He knows what he's going to do and does it. If you were that good, you'd be cocky, too."

But, according to Donnelly, Barry was a different person around people he knew and trusted, around family and friends, than he was around people he didn't trust or believed might be a threat, such as members of the media. "He's a sheep in wolves' clothing," Donnelly said. "He'll do anything for a friend. He projects an image of being brash and cocky, but he's not that kind of guy. He's quiet. He talks about his family all the time." Former Pirates manager Jim Leyland and third baseman/right fielder Bobby Bonilla, meanwhile, have said in interviews over the years that Bonds is a caring, thoughtful person and true friend. "Barry Bonds is a great friend of mine," Leyland once said, years after both had left Pittsburgh. "We've had a lot of great times together. We've shared a lot of great moments and a lot of heartbreaking moments. And I always enjoy seeing him." *The Palm Beach Post*'s Dan Graziano once illustrated that friendship between Bonds and Leyland with this example during the 1997 season, when the former Pirates skipper was managing the Marlins. If you showed up early at Candlestick Park for a Marlins-Giants game, "you would have seen the National League's most feared hitter standing by the batting cage, laughing, joking and talking with the opposing manager. And [if] you stuck around late, you would have seen Bonds take his kids into the Marlins' clubhouse to meet Leyland, greeting the Marlins skipper with a wide-smiling, 'Hey, dude.'" Every time they were in the same town, added Graziano, Bonds went to visit Leyland and "it's always as if they've never been apart."

Shame on those who say Barry didn't have any friends on his teams, adds former teammate John Cangelosi. "Barry Bonds is a really good friend of mine," says Cangelosi, an outfielder who played with Bonds in Pittsburgh from 1987 to 1990. "We became very close my first year in Pittsburgh. I couldn't make his wedding one year—because I'd just had a newborn—and he couldn't make my wedding. He ended up picking me up at my mom's house. He and Bobby Bonilla came in. Barry said, 'Let's go buy motorcycles!' I'm like, 'What?' But Barry took me to a nearby dealer and purchased motorcycles for me and my wife [as wedding gifts]. I'd never owned a motorcycle, let alone bought one. Within 10 minutes, I'm on the highway, driving a motorcycle with Barry Bonds."

Another time, a friend named Frank Castro was holding a baseball card show, and Cangelosi convinced Barry to waive his fee and appear for free. "I was at the show, and he was phenomenal," says Cangelosi. "This is the kind of guy he was. He was very generous. He was a very good teammate. I don't have anything bad to say about him. It's just that what he did with the press is the reason why he's here now. When you don't take the time with the press—and again, it's not for me to say, but—that's why he's in this predicament. He said what he wanted to say, and Barry was Barry. But as far as [being] a teammate, [he was] a genuine person [and a] great guy. Those people that are saying [otherwise] probably don't even know [Barry]. Some guys are good with the press, and some guys didn't like the press. You can't hold that against the guy. [Focus instead on] what he did on the field."

Bonds didn't just show his generosity in Pittsburgh. A decade later, he also bought a Mercedes for Giants teammate Shawon Dunston following the 2001 season after losing a bet with the reserve outfielder, who'd predicted that Barry would break Mark McGwire's single-season record of 70 home runs that year. After Bonds finished with 73, Dunston joked about collecting on the wager, never expecting him to follow through. "But he kept his end," Dunston told sportswriter Gwen Knapp in 2013. "He called me 10 days later. 'Come meet me in Redwood City to get your car.'" To Dunston, the Mercedes, a brand-new, fully loaded, black CL 500, was a keepsake more than a vehicle. "It has 58,000 miles on it. It's my baby. I'll never trade it in."

Former Giants shortstop Royce Clayton has a similar story. Clayton, who'd debuted in the big leagues as a September call-up in

1991, was in his first full season in 1993. He entered that season with a .216 career batting average in 107 games, but Bonds had faith in him as the Giants' starting shortstop, pushing the 23-year-old by betting him he couldn't bat .280. "When he made that bet with me," laughs Clayton now when reminded about that wager, "it was like a big brother just challenging me, like, 'Hey man, I don't think you can do this. Show me something.' And that was the challenge he brought to me personally every single day, and I think he had that with everybody. But at the end of the season, we had to win that game against the Dodgers, and we came up short. It was a tough pill to swallow. I came into the clubhouse, feeling dejected. I couldn't believe it. It was my first experience of being in that type of atmosphere, a playoff run, coming up short by one game. It was heartbreaking."

The Giants were eliminated on the final day of the 1993 season, with Clayton finishing at .282 in 153 games, but Bonds didn't forget the wager. "After the game, the last thing on my mind was that bet that I had with Barry," continues Clayton, "but Barry walked up to me and handed me the money. He said that he was proud of me and said congratulations. It just spoke volumes to me about what this type of dude he was. I'd literally forgotten about it. It's just something that he wanted to make sure [that I knew] he was proud of me. It meant a lot to me in the fact that my big brother was proud of me for the way I went out there and held [the starting shortstop position] down, just did my part as a 23-year-old shortstop trying to find my way."

As far as the perception that Bonds cared only about his own stats, not team victories, Cangelosi says it's all hogwash. "I totally disagree," Cangelosi says emphatically. "Barry Bonds—I played with him for four years—was a great teammate. He gets a bad rep from the press. I had conversations with him about it. I'm like, 'Dude. You're on top now. Just treat them a little nicer.' But as far as teammates and playing to win, hell yeah. Baseball is an individual sport to begin with. He was a great team player. When a guy like Barry Bonds goes out there and misses only one or two games a year—and he's got 500 [at-bats] or 600 [plate appearances] and he's playing every day—that's a great teammate. You know what I mean?" Indeed. Between 1989 and 1998—when he won three of his seven career Most Valuable Player awards and finished in the top five in MVP voting seven times—Barry missed an average of only seven games per season. After he left Pittsburgh for the Bay Area, Bonds averaged 142 games a year in his first 12 seasons with the Giants from 1993 to 2004. "So, I've got nothing bad to say about Barry, and shame on the guys that do," continues Cangelosi, "because there's a lot of worse teammates that I played with. Barry told you like it was."

To illustrate that last point, let's say you asked another player for a favor. That player might agree to help you—but then flake out. Barry, on the other hand, would simply say no—perhaps not in a friendly way but, at the very least, he'd be straight with you—when he didn't want to do it at all. (According to long-time Pirates beat writer John Perrotto in Jeff Pearlman's *Love Me, Hate Me*, Bobby Bonilla once told him something along these lines: "If you ask, 'Hey, pick me up tomorrow at three,' Barry's the kind of guy who'll tell you to go fuck yourself. I'm the type who'll promise you I'll be there, then not show up.") "Barry told you like it was, and some people don't like that," adds Cangelosi, who is friends with both Bonds and Bonilla. "And I like that character about him. To me, he was a great teammate. A great friend. I enjoyed watching him play."

An example of Bonds not being always about his own stats came in April 2004 in San Francisco, when he took himself out of a game against San Diego and fell just short of tying the major-league record for most consecutive games (eight) with at least a home run, a mark set by Dale Long in 1956 (and matched by Don Mattingly in 1987 and Ken Griffey, Jr. in 1993). With the game out of reach—the Giants trailed 9-0 in a game they would lose 11-0—Bonds, who'd already homered in each of his previous seven games (with nine round-trippers among his first 19 hits while batting .500 for the season), asked to be taken out in the eighth inning, even though he had one more plate appearance left in the contest with a shot to tie the mark. So close to the record, he opted not to go for it—hardly the actions of someone who was worried only about his own numbers.

Some might be critical of the way that Bonds had a major say in whether or not he took the field on any given day—there were stories in the newspapers about clashes between Barry and long-time Giants skipper Dusty Baker, who managed in San Francisco from 1993 to 2002, about when he should or shouldn't be in the lineup—but as Felipe Alou, the Giants' manager from 2003 to 2006, once said, he deferred to

Barry when writing out the lineup card, a Hall-of-Fame-caliber courtesy that he'd learned when playing against Pirates Hall of Famer Roberto Clemente. "Roberto told me, 'I have the advantage on you because you play when the manager writes your name on the lineup, and I play when I feel good. If I don't feel good, I don't play because I'm not going to help my team.' So when Barry Bonds tells me, 'Hey, Skip, I'll embarrass myself and the team,' I don't play Barry Bonds," Alou explained. "And there are some days I believe I should give him a day off, but he says, 'No, no, no, I feel good,' and he goes out and shows me." (As for Bonds himself, he recalled in 2019 that in his Pittsburgh days in the early 1990s, Jim Leyland allowed him, Andy Van Slyke and Bobby Bonilla—the star players on the team—to pick their own off-days, and those off-days allowed those stars to stay rested and healthy during the course of a long season, which in turn helped them to be at their peak and stay productive when they did return to the lineup.)

As far as the myth that Bonds didn't have friends in the game, that's simply not true. Tom Candiotti, a knuckleball pitcher who pitched in the major leagues from 1983 to 1999, never played with Bonds, and he's quick to say he has no first-hand knowledge of how Barry treated teammates. Still, Candiotti saw how Bonds interacted with the knuckleballer's mother, treating her like family. Off the field, Bonds always treated Candiotti like a buddy, even if some of their interactions involved trash talk. Candiotti recalls one particular incident from July 19, 1996, fondly, even laughing as he recounts the story.

"Me and Barry always had this thing going back and forth where he thinks he'll hit a home run off me. [By 1996] we'd faced each other quite a bit, and he still hadn't hit a home run. We were playing at Candlestick Park, and he hit a bullet. It was so hard that it was, honestly, 15 feet off the ground all the way. At old Candlestick Park, the bleachers kind of overhauled almost the fence in right-center field where the ball was hit. There was just a little bit of a concrete wall underneath the bleachers, and [the ball] hit that, [which meant it was] clearly a home run. It came right back out on the field. It ricocheted back. The umpire [Wally Bell] calls it a double. I saw it was a home run. I think everybody but the umpire knew it was a home run. Even Barry, when he gets to second base, starts arguing with the umpire. Dusty Baker comes running out of the dugout, and Barry starts yelling, 'Tell the guy it's a home run!' I'm on the pitcher's mound, and Barry finally looks over at me. He starts pointing at me, and says, 'Hey, you know that was a home run! That was a home run!' I just put my glove over my mouth and held two fingers up.

"He waited for me when the game was over. He waited for me in the family area. I had a lot of family there at that time, because that's where I lived. As I came walking out, he's standing there with his arm around my mom and telling me, 'You know that was a fucking home run!' He was still upset over it, and my mom was a huge Giants fan. She was agreeing with him, and Barry goes, 'See? Listen to your mom! Listen to your mom! She says it's a home run!' It was pretty funny. Then we hugged each other. And he met my family. He was super gracious.

"Those are some of the stories that I have with Barry that don't get written about. People only know all the [negative] stuff. And look, I was never a teammate with him or anything like that, but our bond started because I was, really, friends with his dad and respected his dad. I think his dad, in turn, liked me a lot. I think that's why we kind of started our bond together, no pun intended. That's what kind of started it. And it continues even to this day. Even if I saw Barry today, we'd give each other a hug. That's how kind of close we were that way. But, again, like I said, I was never a teammate."

A year later, in another Giants-Dodgers game in San Francisco on June 22, 1997, with both teams battling for first place, Bonds homered off Chan Ho Park to put the Giants ahead early. In the eighth inning, Bonds singled off Mark Guthrie and was on first base, and then took off for second to try and put himself in scoring position. Although the throw was on target, Bonds appeared to, according to video replays, beat the tag by shortstop Greg Gagne. Second-base umpire Jerry Crawford, however, called him out. Bonds, stunned at the erroneous call, argued briefly before walking off the field, yet the camera crew caught him laughing with Crawford moments later when he returned to his position in left field for the next half inning. Bonds, in fact, put his arm around Crawford, who was smiling too, and gave the veteran umpire a playful hug. That's certainly a side of Bonds that isn't discussed much about either.

For Barry, baseball was pure and simple entertainment, and all he wanted was to enjoy being on the field. "You fail seven out of 10 times," he once said, referring to the baseball standard of success, a

.300 average. "I try to deliver 30%, with 100% effort. If I was in any other business—basketball, accounting or the stock market—30% and I'd be out of a job. That's why you'll never see me get mad out there. I'm too grateful." Broadcaster and Hall of Famer Joe Morgan, who was in the booth the day of the exchange between Bonds and Crawford, immediately recalled another incident from the early 1990s when Barry was called out on a third strike at the plate. "He argued with the umpire and he got kicked out of the game. He went inside, he saw it on instant replay and he saw that the umpire made a good call. He went into the umpires' room after the game and apologized," Morgan recounted during that 1997 broadcast, further illustrating the fact that Bonds was respectful toward umpires—even when calls went against him. That's certainly not the behavior of a man who cared only about his own stats.

Three months after the Crawford incident when the Giants defeated the visiting Padres in the final week of the season to capture the division title, Bonds was hugging teammates and celebrating with them on the field, and then ran to the dugout and climbed on top of it, where he started high-fiving Giants fans standing in the first-row seats. After receiving several hugs from those in the first row of seats, Bonds remained out there and continued running along the top of the dugout, passionately high-fiving as many fans as he could and exhorting the rest of the crowd to stand up and celebrate. He then clapped his hands before doing more fist pumps and hugging even more fans while the rest of the Giants players had already headed into the clubhouse for the celebration party inside. "Who says Barry Bonds doesn't care?" FOX announcer Thom Brennaman asked rhetorically as that scene was shown on the game telecast. "Bonds so often maligned as being a player who, at times, is extremely moody, doesn't care about the fans… Well, he's hugging them in San Francisco… Look at Bonds! Who would've believed this?"

But who could blame him? That was the first division title for the Giants in the Bonds era, and it had come following the disastrous 1995-96 seasons. Again, looking at the way Bonds passionately jumped on top of the dugout to celebrate with the fans, if you didn't see the name on the back of that uniform or saw his face, you would have concluded that this player definitely cared about winning and had a special connection with his hometown fans. When highlight reels of Bonds are normally shown, though, this particular clip of his celebration with the fans in San Francisco from that September 1997 afternoon is hardly ever shown, if at all.

* * *

MLB reporter J. P. Hoornstra didn't cover Barry Bonds as a journalist early in the all-time home-run champion's career—when, according to those who covered him, he was at his surliest—or during his record-breaking 2001 season. Hoornstra wasn't around during the period when, as another scribe noted, one day Bonds "would light up media hordes with a million-watt smile, the next his glare would chop them into bloodless bits." But Hoornstra was around between 2003 and 2006, and from his own observations during those seasons, he never saw Barry go out of his way to be unkind to anybody. "Anybody who says that Bonds didn't treat any of his teammates well or he treated teammates well only based on their importance to him and helping him win," Hoornstra says, "I wouldn't consider that true based on my own experiences as a reporter. I don't remember any players telling me anything negative about Bonds as a teammate off the record, but I'm sure that's out there if you want to find it."

Hoornstra does remember Bonds interacting well with former Giants outfielder Dustan Mohr. "[He] was a guy, one of the better players on that Giants team in 2004, a reserve outfielder who was on the Twins and then he went to the Giants. He was a backup, backup outfielder. He was mostly out there for his glove. He was one of the better hitters on that Giants team, but that wasn't a very good Giants team outside of Barry Bonds and a couple of other guys. Barry would have Dustan Mohr sitting across the table from him in front of his locker playing cards. I remember talking to Dustan about it one day. He'd heard stories about Bonds as a teammate. He just didn't find them to be true. He was probably one of the 20th to 25th best players on the team, so Barry didn't have a reason to go out of his own way to treat this guy well. They totally got along, as far as Dustan Mohr was willing to share with me—and as far as I could see as a reporter there in the clubhouse."

When asked about his relationship with Barry, Mohr remembers Bonds befriended him early on. "It was spring training that year. In

Scottsdale, the cages were behind the right-field wall. He, Michael Tucker and I were down there hitting. It was kind of a rainy day. The field's got a tarp on it. We're walking back to our clubhouse, which is under the first-base dugout. There's media in the entire dugout, and it's totally full. We were just having some normal talk, and I said, 'Hey, B. Hang on a sec. Would you mind carrying my bat in? All these guys are waiting on me to do some media stuff.' And he looked at me like I was crazy because I'd known him for only two weeks by then."

Mohr laughs as he reminisces about that 2004 season with Barry. "He'd say, 'How many home runs have you got?' And I'd say, 'I've got a better arm than you do.' That was the only thing I could do better. And he had a really accurate arm, but it wasn't like it was super strong. I mean, it wasn't Johnny Damon. But it wasn't like a bullet. It wasn't like Vlad Guerrero-strong. He was really accurate, which is something he talked about a lot—the importance of being accurate over velocity because velocity means nothing if you don't know where you were throwing it." (Speaking of Bonds' throwing arm, one aspect of his career that hasn't been recognized was how hard he worked to improve: He knew, for instance, that his arm wasn't the strongest and so he trained himself to charge balls harder than anyone else in the game.)

Ah, yes, the Giants clubhouse, which Hoornstra brings up. And trash talking, which Mohr mentions.

* * *

Trash talking is—and has always been—a big part of sports. That extends to trash talking among teammates. Michael Jordan, arguably the greatest player in NBA history, was an example. There have been published stories stating Jordan allegedly ruined Chicago Bulls teammate Rodney McCray's career, always being in the small forward's face in practice in 1993 and screaming, "You're a loser! You've always been a loser!" A newcomer to the Bulls for the 1992-93 season, McCray won an NBA championship ring with Chicago that season but never played in the league again. With respect to that rough treatment of McCray, though, Jordan fans will chalk it up simply to Air Jordan's extreme competitiveness.

There was a famous story about Bonds walking into a meeting of

Giants pitchers that same year in 1993—early in his first season in San Francisco—and pointing at the ones he'd previously homered off, saying, "I got you, and I got you, and you." Yet the press will take that story and use it as further evidence of Bonds' arrogance. (Sports journalist Glenn Dickey, though, once pointed out in the *San Francisco Chronicle* that Bonds, always a student of the game, would sit in on those pitchers' meetings because he wanted to learn how they were pitching hitters, so he could position himself accordingly in the field.) To those who understand Bonds, that sort of trash talk, as far as they're concerned, wasn't meant to be malicious. Knuckleball pitcher Tom Candiotti, who was never a teammate but faced Barry countless times between 1992 and 1998 when both were in the National League and during interleague play, says Bonds always trashed talked with him, going back to the days when both reached the majors in the mid-1980s. For Candiotti—who allowed only two homers to Bonds in 68 career plate-appearances, with the all-time home-run king going homerless in the first 64 of them—it was no big deal and he always enjoyed the back-and-forth with Barry.

Dustan Mohr, at times, also heard trash talk from Bonds when the two were teammates. "Barry would throw comments out, sometimes," says Mohr, "because he could. I mean, you're talking a little trash to him, he could drop it on you. 'How many home runs you've got?' He could say stuff like that. But I think people just took it differently from him because of envy, jealousy, a little bit." Mohr even discusses another thing that irked some Giants teammates and critics: Bonds' entire wing in the clubhouse at Pac Bell Park. "He had his own row of lockers, and a TV and a recliner. And it bothered some guys. It did. But I don't know why. I never heard a good reason why it mattered."

And to say that Bonds never let teammates enter his side of the clubhouse isn't accurate, either. Yes, the fact that—after the team's move from Candlestick Park to Pac Bell—Barry had claimed that whole wall for himself, his $3,000 recliner, his 27-inch television and his own cast of helpers is well-documented (with one of those lockers for his son, Nikolai, who often worked as a ball boy during the summer), but what isn't widely known is the following story. One year, Giants outfielder Marvin Benard, who spent his entire nine-year big-league career in San Francisco (1995-2003), couldn't pull out of a slump and figured he'd take his belongings and move them into a stall into a locker on Bonds' side of the clubhouse, hoping proximity to Barry's greatness would change his luck. "Everybody was freaking out: *Barry's going to go off on you*," Benard told writer Gwen Knapp in 2013. "He had to protect his image, so when he came out and saw me, he started screaming, trying to kick the chair... Then when we were between ourselves, he says, 'Hey man, it's cool. I just had to do that.'" Benard stayed in the locker the rest of that season. "He never did tell me to get out," he added.

For critics, Bonds and his wing in the clubhouse symbolized his isolation from the rest of the teammates. But for Barry, he had his own side of the story. The recliner was good for both himself and the Giants; because he had a bad back, elevating his feet in the recliner helped. Besides, part of Barry's routine was taking a nap before games, and lying quietly with his eyes closed, relaxed and calm, was how he prepared for games. At Candlestick, Bonds used to sleep on a training table, but that inconvenienced the rest of the team because the club had only two training tables, meaning if Barry occupied one of them, there wasn't room for players who needed trainer Mark Letendre's attention. But with the recliner in the clubhouse, Bonds believed it was his way of accommodating the ballclub.

And, with Barry being the centerpiece of the franchise—Bonds was the player, after all, who saved San Francisco baseball, with his December 1992 free-agent signing making the Giants relevant again (which lifted the franchise's profile and stimulated the public's approval in a 1996 vote to build Pac Bell Park, following four failed ballpark ballot measures)—was it that big a deal if he had his own wing in the locker room? For Dustan Mohr, it really wasn't. "The locker room was plenty big," Mohr says now, laughing. "I mean, it was fine. It wasn't like it was that big a deal. He had his whole wing. He did. It was, like, four or five lockers. But it was fine. It was no big deal, really. It's just a locker room. That guy is so good, if he wants to have that, let him have it. So what? That's the way I viewed it."

To say that Bonds saved San Francisco baseball wouldn't be hyperbole. Although the Giants won the pennant in 1989, interest in baseball in San Francisco steadily declined over the next three years, with home attendance at Candlestick Park dropping to 1.56 million in 1992. San Francisco was on the verge of losing Major League

Baseball when then-owner Bob Lurie agreed to sell the club to a group from St. Petersburg, Florida, before a group led by Peter Magowan jumped in and bought the team and signed Bonds that December. Bonds' presence helped home attendance jump to 2.6 million in 1993, and he continued to increase the value of the Giants franchise significantly as his presence helped attract more than three million fans season after season after the club moved in 2000 to Pac Bell Park, a state-of-the-art ballpark which many pundits believe would not have been built without Barry on the roster. And while the NFL's 49ers were still No. 1 for Bay Area sports fans, San Francisco had become "also a baseball town now," Magowan said in 2007, "and I trace a lot of that to Barry." According to *Forbes Magazine*, the Giants were worth an estimated $459 million in 2007—Bonds' final year in the big leagues—making them the seventh-most valuable franchise in the majors; Magowan's group had originally bought the team for $100 million. Bonds "made the organization a whole bunch of money" and "paid a lot of bills for a lot of people," former Giants manager Dusty Baker said during Barry's last major-league season.

Superstar catcher Mike Piazza, who was once asked to comment on Bonds' locker-room setup, didn't think it was a big deal, either. Piazza, then with the Mets, told the *New York Daily News* in 2001, "Barry Bonds may be different, but if he's getting results, I don't care. The locker room stuff, I think that's so overrated. You don't have to be the best of friends with everybody in the locker room. You don't have to take guys out to dinner. Don't get me wrong. I think it's good when you have good guys on a team, but it's sort of a bonus. There's nothing Barry Bonds can't do on a baseball field, so as far as I'm concerned, I want him on my team... How can you criticize a guy who's carrying you to the playoffs?"

Besides, Bonds was hardly the only player with multiple lockers in a major-league clubhouse, yet fingers aren't pointed at others. When it happens with other major-leaguers, their antics are generally interpreted as being humorous. Take three-time All-Star and 2001 American League RBI leader Bret Boone, for instance. Former sports reporter Erick Walker once wrote a column reminiscing his days covering the Mariners, mentioning a story about the Seattle second baseman fondly. "Then there was the time," Walker wrote in 2011, "Bret Boone declined the most basic of questions two consecutive days before finally relenting on the third day with 'OK, I'll answer your questions now.' I will remember Boone most for the space he took up in the locker room. He took up three locker stalls—one for him, another with a nameplate above that read 'Boone's friend' and a third with a nameplate that read 'Boone's friend's friend' that was scattered with about 100 bats."

If such a story sounds amusing when it involves any other major-leaguer, why is there that much outrage if the player referenced was Barry Bonds?

* * *

While the press has talked about the locker-room setup in San Francisco to portray him as being selfish and pampered, what has rarely been talked about is the way Bonds took care of some of his teammates, actions which show a generous side of him. Ted Power, a veteran relief pitcher who joined the Pirates as a free agent in 1990, had heard negative things about Bonds prior to arriving in Pittsburgh. But during one of the first days of spring training, as the right-hander recalled years later to writer Jeff Pearlman, in the midst of a brief conversation Bonds asked Power where he was staying in Bradenton, the Pirates' spring-training home. When Power answered he was staying in the team motel, Bonds stopped the conversation and said, "Absolutely no way. My wife and kids are leaving in four days. Why don't you move into my apartment with me?" The 35-year-old veteran pitcher accepted, but on the condition that he pay rent. Bonds, however, wouldn't hear of it. "Screw that," he said. "If you wanna buy groceries, buy groceries. If you don't, don't. Just relax and make yourself at home."

This is a side of Barry Bonds, who seemed to have a soft spot for journeyman players or grinders who worked hard every day to stay in the majors, that many fans have never heard of. Power was a veteran right-hander who pitched in middle relief; he'd already played for five teams over his first nine big-league seasons—he would play for a total of eight clubs over a 13-year career—and would never be confused for a superstar player. Yet Bonds, in that particular instance, had Power's back.

For John Patterson, that particular story doesn't come as a surprise. The utility second baseman, who played for parts of four seasons in the majors with San Francisco (1992 to 1995), gained temporary folk-hero fame when, as a September rookie call-up in 1993, in his first at-bat of the season he hit a pinch-hit, ninth-inning homer—his first major-league home run—off Mark Wohlers to give the Giants a 3-2 win in Atlanta on September 1. As Patterson recalls now, Bonds took care of him in San Francisco by pulling him aside often to give him tips on hitting. "I remember the scene in the whole locker room afterwards, because we were in the pennant race," he says, stressing the fact that, as a major-league player, he was essentially at the bottom of the totem pole. "I remember we had a team meeting, [where the players decided] I was going to get a full [playoff] share. I thought that was really cool. For me, that was a lot of money back then. I had the pompoms on the whole September. That year I'd been on the disabled list for most of the season with a sore shoulder, so I couldn't make the throws from second base. But I could pinch-hit, and I could pinch-run. I was rooting hard for those guys."

Sure, Patterson acknowledges, Barry clashed with some teammates, but Bonds was always great with him. "Will Clark was our leader in San Francisco, our best player, until we got Barry. [It's] just [that] their cultures were completely different; you go from hearing country music after you win to hearing hip-hop after you win. It's a different locker room. As great as Will was, I see why they [allowed Clark to leave via free agency and sign with the Texas Rangers], to keep Barry. The cultures just clashed. Someone had to be the alpha dog, and that's Barry for sure. He was a great teammate, as far as on the field. On the field, you couldn't ask for a better teammate. Most times if I was playing—I was a utility guy, but if I was starting on a given day it's because they wanted to give [starting second baseman] Robby [Thompson] a day off—I would usually hit [number] two [in the batting order]. Barry would hit three. He would always take me aside, tell me what [pitches the opposing pitcher] had, how he's probably going to pitch you and his tendencies. He didn't have to do that. I mean, this guy's the MVP of the league. But he'd always share any information he had to help me out. At times he was pretty good with his time if he had it." Unprompted, Patterson adds: "And I'll go on the record and say this. I know for a fact that the years I was there, about this whole steroid thing and whatever, I guarantee you he was not taking that stuff during the years I was there, because he kinda talked shit on guys who did. I know those years he was not using that stuff, for sure. And he was still the best player in baseball. He was still a 40-40 guy [40 home runs and 40 stolen bases in the same season]—a legit 40-40 guy."

John Cangelosi, meanwhile, shares two stories of how Bonds took care of him, too. "Barry Bonds is misunderstood," he says. "He really is a good guy. He was a really good teammate. He definitely had my back in a lot of situations." There were two which came to mind, with the first one coming in 1989, when both outfielders were still teammates in Pittsburgh. "I was on the fence of maybe being sent down [to Triple-A] or not making the [big-league] club for a little bit. [Manager Jim] Leyland, I guess, was talking to Barry, Bobby Bonilla and a few other guys. Barry stood up for me and said, 'No, you know what? We got him. Let's keep Cangy. He's part of this team. He's been with us for a while...' That was one occasion where he stood up for me."

Fast forward a half dozen years later, when Cangelosi had just been called up by the Houston Astros from Triple-A Tucson to fill a roster spot which became vacant when outfielder Phil Plantier went on the disabled list. Unfortunately, the Astros had strict rules about Cangelosi's living accommodations. "At the time, I had two little kids; my son was probably five or six months old, and my daughter was almost two. I had an apartment in Tucson and then I got called up. I ended up staying in Houston longer than they expected. We'd go on the road, and my family would have to fly back to Tucson. Every homestand, they'd fly back to Houston. We'd have to stay in a hotel room because I wasn't allowed to get an apartment yet because they didn't know if I was gonna stay or not."

But by late July, Cangelosi was still on the team and his situation hadn't changed. "Barry Bonds comes into town with the Giants," Cangelosi continues. "I'd been up for [over] a month now, and I'm [playing] well. It was getting very expensive for me, paying for the hotel and paying for the apartment in Tucson. Just a lot of stress with not having a place to live, with two young kids. Then, I was talking to Barry. '[Astros general manager] Bob Watson doesn't wanna let me get an apartment. I don't know what his deal is...'

"After batting practice, Barry Bonds goes into Bob Watson's office and says, 'Hey man, Cangy's on this team! Get him an apartment! Let him frickin' bring his family here... Look, he's on the roster!' I swear to God, after the game Watson calls me into his office to say, 'All right, Cangy. Go ahead. You can get an apartment. You're good to go.' That was really nice of Barry." Perhaps with a load off his shoulders after hearing Watson's news, Cangelosi was able to relax and focus at the plate. In that four-game series, he hit safely in each contest and batted .643, helping Houston take three of four against San Francisco. "Barry was really, really good to me," adds Cangelosi. "We're still friends today."

Dustan Mohr, like Cangelosi and Patterson, vouches for Bonds. "I'm pretty much a nobody, but Barry and I did have a good relationship," Mohr, who played for five teams in parts of seven major-league seasons, says today. "I was devastated when they didn't bring me back [after the 2004 season]."

* * *

Like several other teammates, Dustan Mohr discusses qualities about Bonds that aren't appreciated enough by the press: Barry's baseball intelligence and the way he went about studying opponents' tendencies, which Mohr saw first-hand. "He sat behind me on the plane. We had a lot of good conversations. In the clubhouse, too. I was on the opposite side. I was right next to J. T. Snow, who was probably my best friend on the team. Every now and again, Barry would look at me and he'd gesture me to come over. I'd walk over there and he had a stool that was over there. I'd sit down. He'd just start talking baseball. He was sitting in his recliner. He had his guys—his care team, I guess you'd call them—that rub his legs, help him work out, stretch, do all those things.

"But he was always watching the opponent that we were going to play in the next series. So, he was always watching the team that we were gonna be playing next, because he'd already watched the team that we were currently playing." And Bonds, in looking ahead at the Giants' next opponents, also had a habit of preparing extra against pitchers he had trouble with and was likely to face in those upcoming series. As an example, in May 2006, on the verge of surpassing Babe Ruth for No. 2 on the career home-run list, Bonds knew, with Colorado on the schedule, he'd likely have to deal with Rockies starter Byung-Hyun Kim. A submarine right-hander, Kim was a side-arm and under-arm hard thrower who'd held him hitless in 14 career plate appearances. Thus, Bonds spent a whole week hitting off side-arm pitching to get extra ready for Kim and indeed homered off the Rockies submariner on May 28 for No. 715 to surpass Ruth.

Oftentimes, of course, Bonds made it look easy. "We'd have these Saturday morning games, and a lot of the time Barry wouldn't take any B.P. or even hit in the cage," Giants reliever Aaron Fultz once told sportswriter Jeff Pearlman. "But it seemed like every time he stepped in for that first at-bat in the game, he'd hit a home run. That's like running a marathon without warming up." Rich Donnelly and Jim Leyland, who coached and managed Bonds in Pittsburgh, respectively, have offered similar recollections. They recalled that in Bonds' younger years with the Pirates, Barry would sleep on a couch in Leyland's office before games, trudge to the field before the first pitch, without stretching or warming up, and smack a first-inning homer. "He'll wake up about 7:25 for a 7:35 game, walk out, play the first inning and hit the first pitch he sees 400 feet," Donnelly recalled. "The game is easy for him. He's playing with the best players in the world, and he looks like that one 12-year-old in Little League who's better than everyone else." Donnelly also recalled a game in mid-May 2000, when Bonds suffered a sprained joint in his lower back during an at-bat. He fell to the ground in pain and eventually rode off the field on a cart. "That was against us," Donnelly, then a coach with the Rockies, remembered. "Guys were saying, 'Well, he's done.' And I said, 'No, he'll be back.'" His old coach was right; Bonds missed four games, then returned to the Giants' lineup and hit a home run.

But special athletes do that. Hockey Hall of Famer Mario Lemieux of the Pittsburgh Penguins, for instance, was such a dominant player that he could miss two weeks of action because of a significant injury, not play or practice during that time but simply do some stretching, and then return to the ice and look like he had never missed a beat—as he did against the Boston Bruins in the 1992 Stanley Cup semifinals. (Lemieux, who'd suffered a broken hand after being slashed by New York Rangers forward Adam Graves, scored two goals in that contest against Boston, and then tallied seven goals and 12 points over the next six games—all Pittsburgh victories—as the Penguins won the Stanley Cup.) Bonds was a player like that in baseball.

Either way, he was always prepared, even if it didn't seem like he was. "But he was always watching the opponent that we were going to play next," adds Dustan Mohr, continuing his recollection of his interactions with Bonds in the Giants' clubhouse. "And we'd just start talking baseball. I think one thing that doesn't get talked about is how smart he is. His baseball IQ is so high." Indeed. Bonds being the smartest player on the field—he had the ability to instantly analyze a situation and then take action—is something that isn't discussed enough in the press. Other journalists might glowingly drop comments about how, say, Yogi Berra once made an unassisted double play at the catching position or how other legends made outstanding plays to help their teams win ballgames. Bonds' athletic intelligence, meanwhile, isn't discussed much even though there are many such examples. He exhibited that in a 1996 game in Houston, for instance, in the 10th inning of a tie game, with himself on first base, Steve Decker on third and Matt Williams at the plate. When Astros pitcher Todd Jones threw a ball to the screen behind home plate, Decker didn't score. Bonds, who'd gone halfway to second, realized that if he left first base open, Williams would surely be intentionally walked. So, Bonds ran back to first, beating the throw with a slide. Williams followed with a two-run double and the Giants won 3-1.

Giants broadcaster Mike Krukow once recalled how Bonds used to play Tony Gwynn, one of the best left-handed hitters in major-league history, in the field—as *The [Santa Rosa, CA] Press Democrat* called it, "like he was some pitcher who couldn't get the bat around"—another example of Barry's baseball intelligence. "He knew with the speed of Bill Swift's sinker or the speed of John Burkett's sinker and with Gwynn's swing type, he had to hit the ball down there," Krukow told the *Press Democrat*'s Jeff Fletcher. "[Gwynn] couldn't pull the ball or he couldn't drive the ball in the gap. [Bonds] knew that if he tried to do that, he'd have to alter his swing. So the guy in left field has affected the guy at the plate, just by the way he's positioned himself. That is a smart sucker right there."

Ron Wotus, a Giants coach since 1998, once recalled that Bonds did little things that players of his generation often ignored, such as watching an opposing pitcher in the bullpen, before the pitcher had even gotten into the game. Barry, Wotus added, didn't go over scouting reports on how to position himself against hitters; defensively, Bonds had instincts. "I believe it's just from being out here and watching the game," the coach said. "Everybody talks about his talent, but he's real sharp. He picks things up that other players miss."

Regarding that last statement, former teammates and other coaches would agree. John Wehner, a former Pirates utility man who worked out with Bonds for several off-seasons in Pittsburgh, watched him up close and personal for years. "I would say he's the best player I've ever seen," Wehner once said. "He knows and sees things about the game that other people just don't know or see or think about. He may not look it, he may not act it, but I think he's somehow always preparing for the game. How he's doing it, I don't know."

An example that exemplifies the fact that Bonds knows and sees things about the game that others just don't know or see came late in the 1995 season in San Francisco. John Patterson, the Giants' utility second baseman, was sitting in the dugout, watching Colorado Rockies reliever Curtis Leskanic throw his arm-up pitches. On that particular evening, Leskanic's fastballs and sliders were so nasty that Patterson wondered out loud how anybody could hit the Rockies right-hander. Bonds, though, told Patterson, "Look. When Leskanic turns his glove, he's throwing a slider. When he comes in straight, it's a fastball." Patterson, along with Royce Clayton, and even manager Dusty Baker and other players including Matt Williams, spent the rest of the game studying Leskanic. But none of them were able to pick up what Bonds saw. When told they didn't believe him, Barry said, "Okay. Fastball." Sure enough, Leskanic threw a fastball. "Another fastball." And, indeed, another fastball was thrown. "Slider." He was right. Slider. "Another fastball." Right again. Another fastball.

"It was amazing," Patterson recalls. He was picking up [Leskanic's] pitches. It was Dusty, Robby [Thompson], myself and Barry, and I think Matty was there. Leskanic would put his hand up. We're all watching it. Barry goes, 'Yeah, he's tipping his pitches. Can't you see?' We watched the next two pitches but we didn't see anything. Dusty goes, 'Barry, what are you looking at?' Barry says, 'See, curveball!' Then, 'Fastball. Fastball. Curveball.' He turns to me and he's frustrated, because he's trying to share this but no one else is picking it up."

As it turned out, Bonds correctly predicted every pitch throughout Leskanic's two-inning stint, with everybody in the dugout looking at Bonds and wondering, "How on earth does he do that?" That wasn't the only time Barry shared his predictions with Patterson, as the former infielder recalls. Another night, just before Bonds was preparing to walk to the on-deck circle, he predicted to Patterson the pitch-by-pitch sequence of that at-bat—and where the last pitch was going to land. "Barry not only told me that he was going to take the pitcher deep, but he even predicted what pitches the guy was going to throw him during that at-bat—and which pitch he was going to hit out of the park!" Patterson recalls now. "Barry goes, 'First pitch, he's gonna skip something in the dirt. Then he's probably gonna throw a backdoor slider. Then, he's gonna throw a fastball and I'm taking him deep.' I kid you not. In that order, that's what happened. It was the most amazing thing I'd ever seen in baseball, ever. It happened exactly the way he'd told me. It was mind-boggling. When he got back to the dugout, he said, 'Told ya!' He sure as hell did!"

Rich Donnelly has told similar stories about Bonds sharing predictions of the exact pitches he was going to hit. "He would come in the dugout after he popped up and go, 'Richie, if that guy throws me a slider again, I'm gonna hit it in the second deck,'" the former Pirates coach recalled in 2020. "The next time up, the guy threw him a slider, and he hit it to the second deck. He was amazing. When he got real good stealing bases, he would do whatever he wanted. He would tell you what he was going to do. And do it." Dusty Baker, who managed Bonds in San Francisco for 10 years, has acknowledged in the past that Barry saw things others couldn't. "This guy can see things that only a couple of players that I've played with have seen: Hank Aaron and Reggie Smith," Baker, who enjoyed a 19-year player career with four teams, said in 2015. "They see things. What's obvious to them is invisible to others."

Add Bobby Bonds to that list, as Barry's father apparently had similar skills. When Bobby was acquired by the Cubs in June 1981, he pulled right-hander Mike Krukow aside one day and proceeded to spell out his new teammate's quirks as a pitcher. "He says, 'I know when you're throwing a curveball, and I know when you're throwing to first base,'" Krukow, who later won 20 games with the Giants in 1986 and has been a Giants broadcaster since 1990, recalled in 2013. "'Curveball, you look in to get your sign, and for whatever reason, you blink.' And when I was going to throw to first, I'd always dip my chin." As for Barry, Krukow confirmed he had his father's skills. "He sees a lot of things that other players don't see," Krukow said of Barry, "and it always blew his mind that nobody else saw what he saw."

As Barry himself explained years later, he watched all pitchers and studied each pitcher's body language. And because he'd seen the same opposing pitchers so many times, he could sense, by watching their demeanor and patterns, what they were going to throw. It was similar to the way, in an earlier generation, Red Sox legend Ted Williams could read what pitchers were thinking.

"Barry watched a game with a focus that was really different from most people," says Mohr. "He was paying attention to everything. And he loved talking about baseball. He'd just start talking. I wouldn't even say a word. He'd just start talking. I would think any player would want to sit next to him and just listen to him talk baseball because he knew what he was talking about." And when Bonds didn't have the answers, he tried to find out. Early in his career, when he didn't hit for average, he sought out good hitters for advice. "Tony Gwynn helped me the most," Barry himself said in a 1998 interview with the *San Francisco Chronicle*. "I regard Gwynn as the best pure hitter, and he taught me a lot about discipline at the plate."

Even Bobby Bonilla, his best friend in the game, taught him Major League Baseball's unwritten rules when he wasn't fully aware of them—bunting for a hit when your team was ahead by 10 runs was a breach of etiquette in pro baseball, for instance, but was something routinely done in college baseball—as Bonds recalled in a 2019 interview with Giants public address announcer Renel Brooks-Moon. By the middle of his career, he had the science of hitting perfected—by picking up knowledge from other superstars. "There's a science to [hitting], and it does work. And you CAN perfect it, to YOUR ability," Bonds once explained. "And your ability can look really, really good. It's just realizing who you are, because you have so many different tools [and] you can perfect your tools to be really, really good... I try to tell people [that] took a little bit from Tony Gwynn. I took a little bit from Willie [Mays]. I took a little bit from Hank Aaron. I stole a little bit from Pete Rose. I took a little bit from Cal Ripken... and then I customized it to what Barry Bonds is."

On the other hand, Bonds, as it's been well-documented, didn't always share tips with teammates. (Again, it should be noted that as Bonds himself has admitted, although he knew the game inside and out, as an introvert and socially awkward person, he struggled with communicating and expressing his thoughts.) But consider the role models he had in the game: During the days when Willie Mays and

Bobby Bonds were with the Giants, they never shared secrets. That's how the game was back then. Hanging around Mays and Bobby Bonds all the time as a young boy, Barry saw that particular culture. And that mindset stuck with him. Mike Krukow, the long-time Giants broadcaster who played in San Francisco between 1983 and 1989, understands that thought process. "The mindset of that generation was survival," Krukow once told writer Jeff Pearlman, referring to the days when Mays was still playing. "That was the era when players worked 12 months per year because they weren't making enough money. So you never showed your hand, because you never wanted to risk your place in the game." If you found out your teammate had a weakness, Krukow added, the last thing you'd do is tell him. "You kept it locked up for future information." Bob Nightengale of *USA Today* remembers Barry telling him his views on the matter. "I remember talking to him. A lot of times he didn't want to share his wisdom," Nightengale says now. "And he said the reason why is people get traded and everything else. He didn't want to be telling a pitcher what to do or a hitter what to do when you might be facing him two years later. He said that was the reason for not always sharing his knowledge."

But to suggest that Barry Bonds never shared secrets with teammates would be an inaccurate portrayal of the man, as far as players such as Dustan Mohr, John Patterson and Royce Clayton are concerned. As Patterson says, Bonds would always share any information he had with him to help him out. "He had, first of all, the physical ability as a player," Patterson says now. "He's definitely the best player I've ever seen in my life—one of the best players to ever play. But more importantly, his baseball IQ was ridiculous. When you combine all of that, he was just a special player. He's very smart. Always willing to share. He'd share tips and things. I didn't have a problem with him as a teammate on the field, ever. He always wanted to win. He put winning first. He was clutch. He was just a great player."

There were other instances in which Bonds offered help to teammates, on his own volition. In his record-breaking 2001 season, for instance, he took a rookie outfielder named Jalal Leach, who had a locker next to him during spring training that year, under his wing. Whenever he saw Leach in the batting cage, Bonds would adjust his hands or lift his elbow. He'd even explain the thoughts of an opposing pitcher. One day, the Giants were facing Colorado in a spring-training game, and the Rockies "had a starter who owned me with fastballs," Leach later recalled to sportswriter Jeff Pearlman. As the rookie went up to the plate, Bonds told him, "Just go up there and sit on the slider." Leach, though, ignored the advice and swung at a fastball, grounding weakly to third for an easy out.

Another game, as Leach went to the plate for his first at-bat, Bonds told him, "This guy's going to throw you a first-pitch fastball." The rookie instead went up looking for a breaking ball and popped out. Next time up, Bonds grabbed him. "I'm telling you, he's going to throw you another first-pitch fastball!" Looking for the fastball this time, Leach lined a double into the gap. "See, I told you," Bonds told him afterward. "You have to look at the situation. Look at who's coming up behind you. What the score is. Where the runners are on base. Situational hitting."

The following year, when San Francisco reached the only World Series of Barry's career, he was regularly sharing tips with teammates. "He wanted that ring," Shawon Dunston recounted in a 2013 interview with writer Gwen Knapp. "He started taking us aside and telling us things, especially during batting practice." The Giants in 2002, Knapp added, "had a genuine mentor" in Bonds. Alas, even when Bonds was sharing tips, it didn't always help because his teammates weren't as great a player as he was. First baseman J. T. Snow once recalled a night when Bonds was studying a reliever as he warmed up, comparing the way Barry noticed the pitcher's vulnerability to the way a cat homed in on a wounded bird. "He couldn't throw his slider, it was all over the place and Barry looks at me and says, 'You think he's going to throw me that slider, when he can't get it over the plate when no one's up there?'" Snow recalled. "And he was right. The guy couldn't throw him a slider, because he didn't have confidence in it. Barry said, 'I'm not even going to look for that pitch.'" Unfortunately, as Snow also acknowledged, the information didn't help J. T. himself. "I still had to look for [the slider], because I wasn't the hitter Barry was."

Batting tips or advice on baseball wasn't the only thing Bonds shared with teammates. Left-hander Kirk Rueter shares this anecdote whenever he is asked what it was like to play with Barry: When Rueter and wife Karla wanted to start a family in 1999, their stalled fertility became a running joke in the Giants clubhouse. On a road trip that summer when families were invited to go along, Bonds approached the couple on the team plane and kicked Rueter out of his seat. "Go back and play cards or whatever you do," Barry told the pitcher. "I'll talk to Karla." Said Rueter years later, laughing throughout as he was recounting the incident: "That whole trip, he sat there with her, and they were just talking, and he was telling her how to get pregnant and what I had to do. She got off the plane, and she was laughing. She said, 'I think Barry's going to take credit if we get pregnant, after all the things he was telling me.'" Rueter, who wound up having two daughters with Karla, added, "Barry was always great to me."

Those are examples of the way Bonds helped his teammates, although they often went unreported. Mohr shares another one. "We were in Cincinnati," Mohr recounts. "I wasn't swinging great at that time. Barry comes over and says, 'Hey, come out with me.' We go to the cage. That was underneath, and there was nobody in there. It was just him and me. He was behind the L-screen, throwing me batting practice, helping me get back on track. That, in and of itself, is a story that most people will never know, except for the ones that I tell. So, for anybody to say that he was just about himself, that's a pretty good example right there that he wasn't—because I wasn't anybody special on the team. I mean, I wasn't Ray [Durham] or J. T. [Snow] or [Marquis] Grissom or Edgardo [Alfonzo], or anybody like that. I wasn't anybody like that. I was just the fourth outfielder. And he was taking me, trying to help me so that when I do get in—I rotated in all three outfield positions—I could [contribute off the bench].

"That game, I went in to pinch hit, and I hit a home run off Danny Graves. So, that's kind of beside the point. I mean, he helped me. Obviously, I hit a home run. But he didn't have to take me down there. And he offered. I didn't ask. He came over and tapped me on the shoulder and said, 'Hey, come out here with me.' He walked me to the cage and said, 'Hey, let's get this ironed out real quick.' He got behind the L-screen and actually threw to me in the cage. Because of things like that, it'll be really hard for me to buy into the whole 'he's selfish and really wasn't a team guy' type of comments, because that certainly is not something that a selfish guy would do. Nobody else on the team did that for me."

Mohr wasn't around two years later, when Bonds again

demonstrated he was a team guy by participating in a 2006 spring-training spoof of the reality competition series *American Idol*. Prior to a spring workout in Scottsdale, Arizona, Bonds dressed in drag portraying *American Idol* judge Paula Abdul—he wore a blonde wig and had what looked like an oversized black Giants T-shirt wrapped around his body like a halter top—to judge "Giants Idol," the Giants' spin-off of the hit reality program, where prospects in their first big-league camp had to sing in front of the judges. Impersonating Abdul, Bonds entertained and delighted a small gathering of fans and Giants teammates, as part of a fundraising event which also served to promote team chemistry. After pitching prospect Brian Wilson dressed as Billy Idol and belted out "White Wedding," Bonds raised his voice two octaves and cooed, "Call me." When Bonds, with his giant smile and in his drag outfit, sashayed up the clubhouse steps and onto the field, jaws dropped. "That floored me," catcher Mike Matheny said that afternoon. "If I were a betting man, when I originally heard about it, I would have wagered he was not going to be out there. I wouldn't have done it. I couldn't have done it." Bonds, meanwhile, said he did it simply because he was asked. Added Matheny: "For him to do that means a lot to the guys in here. It puts him on our level. It was a huge step."

Critics would highlight the negative qualities of Bonds, though, without mentioning the good deeds he'd done. Mohr is one who believes Barry was always held to an "unfair standard" simply because he was Barry Bonds. Others who consider Barry to be a friend believe the same. Part of it, Mohr believes, is because some guys took it personally when Barry wasn't always in a chatty mood. "You could tell, when he got to the ballpark, what kind of a mood he was in," Mohr explains. "I could, anyway. You could tell if he wanted to talk or not. And there were times when I'd say, 'Hey, what's up, B.?' and he just wouldn't say anything. He'd just keep going like he didn't know you. Some guys would be like, 'I'm his teammate. Why wouldn't he even say hi?' But if you really step back and think about it, is it that big a deal?

"People have lives outside of the field. Sometimes, guys [are preoccupied with their] thoughts and maybe they're not really paying attention. Maybe he heard me say 'What's up?' or he didn't hear me say 'What's up?' And I think that people would react, because of that, to him differently than they would to somebody else. He didn't necessarily open up to people. He's just not that kind of personality.

But I think there can really be two ways of looking at it. There were people that wanted him to be a certain way and people that accepted him for how he is. I chose to just accept him for who he is, and know that some days he's going to look right through me like he doesn't know who I am, and some days he's going to talk to me and never shut up. And I'm okay with that, because he's just a regular guy. He's not a regular baseball player. But he's just a regular guy that could play baseball really well. There's probably a lot of guys that wished they had that kind of stature, to be honest with you. I wish I did. But I was fine. I thought I was good for the role I had. I was a good player. But I was no Barry Bonds, and nobody else has been, either. They would just hold him to a different standard sometimes, and a lot of times that was unfair. That's just the way that I saw it. I would've liked to have seen him be a little more engaged and open up a little bit more. But that's not how he was. So, big deal."

Mohr adds that superstar athletes in other sports aren't that different from Bonds, bringing up a golf legend as an example. "It's kinda like Tiger Woods, right? They said that about Tiger Woods forever. Now that he's gotten older—golf's a little different; you can play as long as you're physically able to, into your 60s—he's opened up a little bit more. I think that those two are probably similar. Because I think people that didn't like Tiger, they didn't like him because he didn't open up to them and they wanted him to be something [else] rather than accepting him for who he is. So, I just think that's where you get the two different views about what they thought about Barry."

The bottom line, as far as Jim Leyland is concerned? "Barry was a team player, I don't care what anybody says. This guy, he could rub people wrong and everything, but I love him," Leyland, who managed Bonds for seven years in Pittsburgh, said in 2020. "I don't give a shit what they say. We had our moments, but I respected him [and] I really like him. We've very close to this day. All I know is he's one of the greatest players to ever play the game. People can make their own judgments, but he's one of the best players to ever play."

Barry and His Milestones: Who Says Nobody Cares?

My personal opinion is, until there's some sort of concrete evidence, until there's some substantial evidence that goes one way or another, you celebrate the record. He's a tremendous hitter. He's one of the best hitters of all time. He's one of the best players of all time. I enjoy watching him. It's special for me, someday, to tell my grandchildren that I got a chance to play against Barry Bonds. I'm going to congratulate him. It is an unbelievable accomplishment for his career. You think about it, that many homers, that's something special. Being a player, playing this game, you understand how hard it is and what he has to go through. So I'll congratulate him.

—David Wright, New York Mets third baseman,
as told to the *New York Daily News'* Adam Rubin (2006)

FOX announcer Thom Brennaman asked rhetorically, "Who says Barry Bonds doesn't care?" upon seeing Barry celebrate with Giants fans in the crowd following San Francisco's division-clinching victory over San Diego in 1997.

A better question is "Who says nobody cares about Bonds' career milestones?"

Many fans and media members across America have expressed that they didn't care when Bonds approached Hank Aaron's career home-run record in 2007. They didn't watch—or bother to wake their kids up to watch—Barry's 756th home run, the one that made him Major League Baseball's home-run king. They simply didn't care, they say. While they're entitled to feel that way, it doesn't mean everybody shares that viewpoint.

Take former Kansas City Royals star Mike Sweeney, for instance. Sweeney never played with Bonds in the big leagues, but the five-time All-Star first baseman/designated hitter did spend time with Barry in

Japan as teammates on the U.S. All-Star team which played an eight-game exhibition series over 10 days in Tokyo, Fukuoka, Osaka and Nagoya in November 2000. In May 2007, three months before Bonds broke Aaron's all-time home-run record, Sweeney, who was in the Bay Area with his Royals as Kansas City was taking on the Oakland A's, was being interviewed by *San Jose Mercury News* writer Daniel Brown about a completely different topic. At the end of the interview—it was about whether hitters look at stadium radar guns—Brown was about to close his notebook. Sweeney, though, said something, unprompted, which caught him completely off guard. "Wait, one more thing," Sweeney said. "Go, Barry."

Sweeney proceeded to tell Brown about how Bonds was "a great teammate" who "played the game hard and he played it the right way," adding that he was "rooting for" Barry to break Aaron's home-run record. For many observers, the fact that Sweeney—the quintessential gentleman off the field (he was ranked the third friendliest player of baseball in a *Sports Illustrated* player poll in 2007 and was twice selected as a "Good Guy in Sports" in 2003 and 2004 by *The Sporting News*)—got along with one of the most polarizing athletes in American sports history came as somewhat of a shock. But as far as the Royals first baseman/designated hitter was concerned, his first-hand experience convinced him that Bonds' negative reputation was undeserved. "I was expecting something different, but he was nothing but a class act," Sweeney told Brown, reflecting back to their time as teammates on the Japan tour. "I know some people might not feel the same way, but I'm rooting for the guy—11 more [homers to surpass Aaron], right?"

As for the idea that nobody cared about Bonds' records, Sweeney completely disagreed. "If I was the commissioner," he continued, "I'd be there for that 756th home run… if I were [Bud Selig,] I'd be there just as a fan. How many people today would have loved to have been at the game when Hank Aaron hit the home run out in the bullpen that Tom House caught [the one which broke Babe Ruth's old record of 714]? You don't have to be a fan of Hank Aaron to be a fan of the game. It's history." Just as how you didn't have to be a fan of Barry Bonds to be a fan of the game, and of that historic moment.

Giants play-by-play announcer Jon Miller perhaps said it best about the misconception about the idea that no baseball fans in

America cared about Bonds' home-run chase. Or that nobody wanted to see him break the record. Or that everybody felt that perhaps he should have walked away from the game rather than play long enough to approach that record. In every major-league city the Giants visited as Bonds neared baseball's career home-run record, Miller recalled in Ken Burns' documentary *Baseball: The Tenth Inning*, that stadium was packed. "And as he approached Aaron's record, every game was sold out," said the veteran broadcaster. "Not just in San Francisco, but Chicago and L.A. [and] every city the Giants went into, [you] couldn't get a ticket for those games. So, those fans, I don't think, were hoping he was going to retire before he got to their city, because they had already bought the tickets to see him play, and I think they were hoping to see him hit one." Games at Pittsburgh's PNC Park, meanwhile, weren't sold out when the Giants came to town, but when Bonds, who'd been booed by Pirates fans in every visit since his departure as a free agent after the 1992 season, had a two-homer game the year he broke Aaron's record (smacking Nos. 736 and 737), fans stood and cheered him following the second round-tripper.

And it wasn't just 2007 when fans showed up to watch him. The numbers show that Bonds turned the Giants into one of the game's top draws as he was hitting home run after home run during the 2000s, with spectators flocking to the ballpark when his team came to town. From 2001 to 2004, the Giants ranked second in the National League in road attendance every year. The average crowd for a Giants road game in 2004, when Bonds batted .362 with 45 homers, was more than 36,000. The following year, when Bonds missed all but 14 games because of three surgeries on his right knee, the average dipped to 31,740, abruptly dropping San Francisco to 10th in the NL. The Giants jumped back to fifth in 2006, with Bonds in the lineup again. And the fans were back again the year he was chasing the all-time home-run record.

The year Bonds hit his 700th homer in 2004, Hall of Famer and Giants legend Orlando Cepeda echoed the sentiments of Sweeney and Miller. "He amazes me the way he plays the game of baseball," Cepeda said of Bonds, adding that he'd said even a decade earlier that he'd never seen someone swing a bat as well as Barry. "In all his years, I've seen him look bad at the plate two times. Guys look bad at the plate five times a day... People should come to the ballpark just to say, 'I saw Barry Bonds.' I played with Hank Aaron, Willie Mays and Frank Robinson. There's nobody better than Barry Bonds, and he's nearly 40 years old... To me, he's one in a million. You won't see anything like that again. The things he's doing are unreal. He thrills me every day. I'm praying I can be like him in my next life."

Miller added in a separate interview with *TV Guide* in 2007 that, as a Giants broadcaster, Bonds' 500th homer in 2001 stood out for him "because it was a Giants-Dodgers game, which on the West Coast has the same feeling as Yankees-Red Sox." As a baseball fan, how could one not care when Bonds came up in a key moment of a San Francisco-Los Angeles game? "The Giants were down 1-0 in the bottom of the eighth inning [actually, San Francisco was trailing 2-1] and Rich Aurilia led off with a triple," explained Miller, "so at that point the whole park wasn't even thinking home run. Everybody had been thinking home run the whole night, but now the game was on the line and Barry needed to get a base hit or a fly ball to get that run in from third. And then all of a sudden he launches one into the night. It was breathtaking."

The point was that you didn't need to be a fan of Barry Bonds to be in awe of what he could accomplish at the plate with the game on the line. Even for baseball fans who didn't like the Giants slugger, seeing Barry come up to bat was must-see TV. After all, "if he hits one [out of the ballpark]," Miller believed, "the people will be glad they were watching—even if they say something like, 'The cheater hit one.'" Added Jeff Borris, a one-time agent of Bonds': "Whether you love Barry Bonds or hate Barry Bonds, you still watch Barry Bonds."

At least you'd be watching. Barry himself has said as much. "Whether you hated me or liked me, you were there. And I only wanted you there. I just wanted you to see the show. That was it," Bonds was quoted as saying in the *New York Daily News* in 2012. "All I ever wanted was for people to have a good time and enjoy it. It was fun to come out and people would boo or yay or whatever. They all showed up to see whatever would happen next and it motivated me to play hard."

* * *

When Bonds hit his 500th career home run, a two-run shot off Dodgers reliever Terry Adams in front of a Pac Bell Park record crowd of 41,059 on April 17, 2001, none of his teammates or coaches rushed out of the dugout to greet him.

The non-reaction by those in the Giants' dugout was made a big deal by some in the press because Mark McGwire's Cardinals teammates all greeted "Big Mac" at home plate when he hit his 500th homer for St. Louis in August of 1999. "When Bonds hit his 500th home run, only one person came out of the dugout to greet him at the plate: the Giants' batgirl. Sitting in the stands, you could've caught a cold from the freeze he got. Teammates 24, Bonds 1," *Sports Illustrated*'s Rick Reilly wrote in a column stating that Barry didn't have any friends on the team. "Bonds isn't beloved by his teammates. He's not even beliked." (To be fair, Reilly has also been critical of six-time NBA champion Michael Jordan in his columns over the years, one of the rare sportswriters who has criticized the Basketball Hall of Fame legend. Barry didn't respond publicly to the story, but former Warriors forward Rick Barry said, "What Reilly wrote was such bull. As long as Barry shows up ready to play, what difference does it make?") At least one Giants player, though, has said the non-reaction in the aftermath of No. 500 wasn't pre-planned and certainly wasn't sinister. "There was nothing malicious about it," first baseman J. T. Snow told sportswriter Jeff Pearlman years later. "He hit it, we were watching it, and by the time he rounded the bases it was too late. It happened too fast. It was only after the fact that guys were like, 'Wow, nobody went out there.'"

The truth was, Bonds got to celebrate the moment with those closest to him, and with the crowd of 41,059 adoring fans cheering him on. After he circled the bases, he was greeted at the plate first by batgirl Alexis Busch and then by a smiling Rich Aurilia, who'd scored on the homer, and the Giants shortstop hugged and congratulated him. More importantly, Bonds was then greeted on the field, in foul territory behind home plate, by his father, mother, wife and brother. Moments later, Hall of Famers Willie Mays and Willie McCovey met Barry on the field as part of an eight-minute ceremony. Following the hugs on the field, Bonds posed for a picture with Mays, McCovey and his father, and then he took a microphone to address the crowd. After thanking his parents, Mays and McCovey over the stadium public address system, Bonds thanked the fans. "... [And] most of all, thanks to all of you. I love you," he told the crowd, which was cheering their hero throughout. "I'm proud to be a San Francisco Giant. All of the people in San Francisco are part of this. Even though I hit it, it felt like the whole town did this."

Critics have pointed to that incident in which all of the Giants stayed in the dugout and suggest that none—or very few—of Bonds' teammates cared about him and his milestones. But journalist Joan Walsh, who was in attendance the night of the 500th home run, refuted that notion in a column for *Salon* in August 2001, noting that, later in the dugout, "teammates hugged and high-fived him in the celebratory chaos that followed." Dustan Mohr, who played for one season in San Francisco in 2004, also vehemently disagrees with the idea that teammates didn't care. The reserve outfielder wasn't with the team when Bonds slugged No. 600 off Pittsburgh's Kip Wells in August 2002, when Giants players reversed course and slowly filed off the bench and met him in front of the dugout for congratulatory high-fives and hugs.

Mohr was with the Giants, though, when Bonds hit his 700th round-tripper in September 2004, which saw the team react in the same fashion as when Barry hit No. 500—the players stayed in the dugout, although they were also waiting there to high-five Bonds when he returned. But Mohr, who waited at the top step of the dugout, explains he was told by certain members of the team to not be out there at home plate to greet Barry. "Yeah, I was pissed off about that whole scenario, and I'll be honest with you," Mohr says now when reminded that he was the first to greet Bonds at the top step of the dugout following home run No. 700. "I wanted to go to home plate. I certainly don't want to say anything controversial—and I'm not going to mention any names—but I was ready to go. It's his 700th home run. It's a big deal, obviously. Only two other guys had done that. So, this guy has hit his 700th home run, and we're not going to greet him at home plate? It was my first year there. I was told, 'You'd better not go out there.' But yeah, I was happy as hell for him because, regardless of whether you liked him or not, there was a lot of work that went into accomplishing something like that.

"And it wasn't just big for him. It was big for the Giants. It was big for the city of San Francisco, because baseball is such a numbers oriented game, especially when it comes to career records. [If you look at] other sports, I don't know that anybody knows how many yards Jerry Rice had. I don't know if they could cite it right off the top of their heads. But there was a time when everybody knew [that] Hank Aaron [hit 755 home runs] or [that] Babe Ruth [hit 714]. But I remember that moment, and I was upset about that. I was upset that we stayed in the dugout. I wasn't upset that he hit it."

When asked to clarify if other Giants players felt the same way as he did, Mohr emphatically says yes: There were other teammates who wanted to be out at home plate to congratulate Bonds, too. "I would say that quite a few did. I think that one of the reasons that Barry and I got along so well is that I respected Barry and I recognized how great of a player that he was. But outside of that, we were both just baseball players, men, husbands, dads and things like that. Our dialogue, our banter, was even better; it was just that of two buddies in high school. I think so many people just see him as on a pedestal, and rightly so, but I think just having somebody to talk to— and there were others; it wasn't just me—and just sort of treating him like he was one of the guys, I think he respected. And I think he liked that. Although I'm sure you'll find some guys that would say that's a crazy statement. But I just talked to him like I would anybody else. I was never afraid to speak up. If I had an opinion, I would say it."

Mohr points to an incident in which he spoke up early in the season—despite the fact he was only in his first month on the team— after San Francisco was swept at home by lowly Pittsburgh. "For instance, I can recall we got swept at home by the Pirates that year. We ended up losing the division by one game. That last game against the Pirates when we got swept, with all due respect to the Pirates because they're big-leaguers too, but this is our house, and we just got swept by a team we're supposed to beat, and [I basically said that] that's going to come back and hurt us. That can't happen. Some people didn't like that, but that was the truth of the matter. But my point is I wasn't afraid to say whatever was on my mind." Because he wasn't afraid to speak up, as Mohr recalls, Barry respected him for that.

"I think there were quite a few guys—I think it was more than half—that wanted to go out there," Mohr continues. "But there were certain few—who were probably veterans on the team, I'd say—that felt differently. And that's fine. Everybody's entitled to their opinion. But I just felt like, not only did he deserve that, but us not doing that hurt us as a team, collectively, because whether you like him or not, or whether you like anybody or not on your team, you're still a team trying to accomplish one goal. That kind of thing, I think, can hurt a team in terms of its chemistry. That's what upset me about it, really."

The 700th homer, a third-inning solo shot off Jake Peavy which gave the Giants a 4-0 lead against San Diego in a game they'd win 4-1, was perhaps anticlimactic. But No. 500 was an eighth-inning, two-run blast which turned a deficit into a one-run lead against the hated Dodgers. One could argue that Mohr's assessment—that a non-reaction by teammates could hurt the Giants as a team in terms of chemistry—was valid in that instance, particularly when No. 500 was such a meaningful homer that particular night against Los Angeles, and the team's goal was, after all, to win. "Not only that," Mohr continues, "but Barry didn't deserve for us to stay in the dugout like that. I didn't think it was right. But hey, I was one guy. I was a new guy. So, that's just the way it went down. But I made damn sure I was on that top step when he got there."

As for Bonds' 756th home run—the one which broke Hank Aaron's career record on August 7, 2007, against the Washington Nationals at AT&T Park—Mohr also refutes the idea that nobody cared. "I was watching it. I played with Mike Bacsik, who gave up the homer. I played with Mike in the minor leagues with the Indians [in Class A in 1998 and Double-A in 1999]. But I was watching it."

Mohr goes back to 2004 because that was the only season he played with Bonds. "I didn't agree with the media all the time. But I also had knowledge that they didn't. I mean, they're going by what they see. I'm in the locker room. I know what's really going on," he says, referring to the fact that what is reported by the media isn't always a true reflection of what actually happens. "But [the teammates who wanted to celebrate Bonds' 700th homer but were told not to] should've been mad about it. If you don't care about one guy on the team, no matter who it is, then your team is weaker for it. That, I thought, was unfortunate. I'm not going to go as far as to say that's why we lost Game No. 161 that cost us the division. [San Francisco was eliminated from postseason contention that afternoon in L.A., with the Giants bullpen giving up seven runs in the ninth inning of the 7-3 heart-breaker.] But I just think that's part of it. Those little things like that. If you're not pulling for one another, regardless of whether you like a guy personally or not, that's not relevant. It's not in anybody's contract that you have to like all of your teammates, but you have to play with all of them and do your job alongside all of those guys. As soon as that infiltrates your clubhouse, where there's a guy on the team that's not liked, then…"

Then, unfortunately, it becomes a situation like in Barry's Pittsburgh days when an anonymous Pirate was quoted as saying, "I'd rather lose without Barry Bonds than win with him," even though the objective in professional sports is to win. Professional baseball players are paid, after all, to win games. That anonymous Pittsburgh player, of course, got his wish when the Pirates trudged through a two-decade run of irrelevance after Bonds' departure. Mohr brings up a more recent example in baseball. "I can't speak to how the Nationals felt about Bryce Harper. But I do have a pretty good idea. And then he's gone [after the 2018 season, signing a free-agent deal with Philadelphia in March 2019], and who wins the World Series?" Mohr asks rhetorically. The Nationals, after having never even won any of their four postseason series in Harper's seven seasons in Washington (they lost in the division round in 2012, 2014, 2016 and 2017), finally captured the World Series in 2019. The Phillies, meanwhile, finished fourth in the NL East at 81-81. "And Bryce Harper is probably looked at, in some people's eyes, a little similar to Barry—where he seems a little bit selfish, a little bit about himself. And you get guys in the locker room that are constantly annoyed by it, and it just permeates through the locker room. It may not seem like a big deal. But it is, in my mind. It just can't happen.

"You touched a nerve when you brought that up—because I still haven't forgotten that. I was mad. In fact, I told Barry after the game. I apologized to him. I said, 'I'm sorry that we weren't at home plate there for you.' He didn't really respond. He just gave me a little dab, a handshake. I think it was kind of understood. But he didn't really say any words. That was, besides losing Game No. 161 to the Dodgers, the only negative about that year that I had. I loved being out there."

And some Giants teammates have gone on the record to say they loved being there to watch Bonds rewrite the history books. When Barry hit No. 714 at Oakland's McAfee Coliseum to tie Babe Ruth for second on the all-time homer list in 2006—Bonds had played in only 14 games in 2005 after undergoing three operations on his right knee—Giants shortstop Omar Vizquel was quoted in *The [Santa Rosa, CA] Press Democrat* as saying he was "glad to see it," adding, "Tying Babe Ruth is an incredible feat… That's one of the reasons I came to San

Francisco. I wanted to see the best home run hitter in the game hit those balls." First baseman/outfielder Mark Sweeney called the moment "pretty awesome" saying, "It was special to be a part of that."

As for home run No. 715 eight days later at home against Colorado, the one that moved Bonds into sole possession of second place on the all-time list, his Giants teammates toasted him with champagne in the clubhouse following the game. "Everybody was waiting for a moment like this," Vizquel told the Associated Press. And, for the record, after both of those homers, his Giants teammates filed off the bench and met him in front of the dugout, exchanging hugs and handshakes.

As for the reaction around baseball among the players after Bonds moved past Ruth? Padres pitcher Jake Peavy, who'd surrendered No. 700 to Bonds in 2004, told the Associated Press, "I'm happy for Barry and his family. I'm sure it takes a lot of pressure off him. Maybe he can relax and play his game now. That's an unbelievable accomplishment and Barry's one of the best that's ever played the game." Some players felt that fans outside of San Francisco should perhaps have embraced Bonds' achievements. "I think it's sad to hear fans boo him," Baltimore Orioles second baseman Brian Roberts told the Associated Press. "I think they should appreciate what they're witnessing. I can't imagine what he goes through on a daily basis." Padres catcher Mike Piazza, who played for the hated Dodgers between 1992 and 1998, said, "The bottom line is, you're witnessing history. I think that's what people really kind of need to appreciate a little bit. It's not every day you see a guy hit 700 home runs, it's not every day you see a guy become the second all-time home run hitter. It's something special."

"To pass Babe Ruth doesn't even seem normal," said Mets left fielder Cliff Floyd. "You tell your kids you played with this guy and they're going to think, 'Yeah right.' Well, I've got proof." Mets third baseman David Wright shared Floyd's sentiments. "It's special for me, someday, to tell my grandchildren that I got a chance to play against Barry Bonds," Wright offered. "… It is an unbelievable accomplishment for his career. You think about it, that many homers, that's something special. Being a player, playing this game, you understand how hard it is and what he has to go through. So I'll congratulate him."

Giants pitcher Jason Schmidt, who would hit seven big-league home runs, said he had a hard time putting the accomplishment into perspective. "You sit there and think about [all those] home runs. As a pitcher, I'm not much of a hitter, but you get up there and face these pitchers and look at what they throw, for someone to accomplish that, it's incredible."

* * *

Another good question is "Who says nobody cares about Barry Bonds?" because it's not exactly true, either.

Certainly, outside of San Francisco he's not a beloved figure, but to suggest that his former fans in Pittsburgh—or even his former Pirates teammates—loathe him would simply be an exaggeration. He may not even be the biggest villain in recent Pittsburgh baseball history when it comes to former Pirates superstars who bolted town via free agency— but he has often been portrayed as such in the press. There have been stories written, for instance, about how none of the Pirates cared when Bonds, who signed as a free agent with the Giants in December 1992, returned to Pittsburgh's Three Rivers Stadium for the first time as a visiting player on Friday, April 9, 1993. "Prior to the game, he entered the Pirates clubhouse to greet his former teammates," Jeff Pearlman wrote in the 2006 book *Love Me, Hate Me*. "Instead, not one player or coach so much as glanced in his direction."

But not quite, per newspaper reports from that night. Bonds was seen, wrote a San Francisco newspaper scribe in a story published the following day, shaking hands with former teammates Lloyd McClendon, Bob Walk, Randy Tomlin (that night's starting pitcher) and Tim Wakefield, along with former coach Bill Virdon. Bonds "hugged Randy Tomlin, joked with Andy Van Slyke and wrestled with Lloyd McClendon," added *The Baltimore Sun*. The *San Jose Mercury News*, meanwhile, confirmed the fact that Bonds "chatted briefly with" both McClendon and Van Slyke. Another newspaper account noted that "Bonds got a chilly reception in the Pirates' clubhouse, but found a few friends." Despite having a swarm of media members following him and recording his every move, Barry was then able to make his way to the manager's office, where he and Jim Leyland, according to the *San Francisco Chronicle*'s Bruce Jenkins, "exchanged a very warm and genuine embrace" and Leyland "looked downright happy to see him." While they didn't talk then—not with all of the media members following Barry around—the two did get a chance prior to the game;

during batting practice, the *San Jose Mercury News* and *Pittsburgh Post-Gazette* both reported, Bonds, with his right arm around Leyland's shoulder, had a private chat with his former Pirates manager for 10 minutes.

As for the fans? Yes, he was booed, consistently, noted the *Chronicle*'s Jenkins, "but the treatment wasn't nearly as savage as when Bobby Bonilla received [in his return to Pittsburgh the previous season]" after the former Pirates third baseman/right fielder had signed a five-year, $29-million contract with the New York Mets. "Overall, you'd have to call it a triumph for Barry," added Jenkins. Another newspaper account of the day had Bonds given a standing ovation from a number of fans in the stands along the left-field line when he ran to his position in left field in the bottom of the first inning. "Throughout the stands," noted sportswriter Bill Modoono, "the boos and cheers were about equal. When he came to bat in the second, the boos increased, but cheers still could be heard clearly." (Bonds, by the way, went 2-for-4 with a double, triple, RBI and three runs scored—including a two-out, run-scoring two-bagger off tough lefty John Candelaria in the eighth which started a three-run rally—but the Giants still lost 6-5 after Pirates rookie Kevin Young delivered a two-run homer in the bottom of the eighth off stopper Rod Beck. In his first at-bat, Bonds reached on an error by pitcher Randy Tomlin, was balked to second and scored the game's first run on Robby Thompson's single.)

Certainly, not every former Pirates teammate greeted Barry in the Pittsburgh clubhouse that afternoon in 1993. Not every fan welcomed him back in his return to town. Was he loathed by many ex-teammates and Pirates fans? Yes. But to suggest, years later, that not one player or coach so much as glanced in his direction—or that he was, in the fans' eyes, the biggest villain to ever return as a former Pirate—would be a gross exaggeration. Pittsburgh, said one writer, was a place where Bonds "is loved and hated, to say nothing of admired and reviled... Even in Pittsburgh, a tough-talking town where the boundaries of good and evil are well established, Bonds has a very mixed identity."

And, as time went by, it appeared the old wounds surrounding Bonds' departure had started to heal, even for the haters. In Bonds' final series with the Giants in Pittsburgh—in August 2007—he received a warm ovation from the crowd at PNC Park. Fans might have booed him and showered him with fake money for years since 1993 when he left Pittsburgh to sign with San Francisco—although it should be pointed out that anybody who played for the Pirates and left often got booed when they returned as visiting players—but the fans mostly cheered Bonds this time when he jogged to left field in the first inning. Bonds responded by waving his hat to acknowledge them, and made a curtain call and bowed to the crowd after the Pirates saluted him with a video tribute. When Barry returned to PNC Park seven years later to present Pirates center fielder Andrew McCutchen with the 2013 National League MVP Award during the 2014 Opening Day ceremonies, he drew many more cheers than boos from the sellout crowd—roughly 70% cheers to 30% boos, according to accounts by multiple media sources.

Bob Walk, a former Bonds teammate and a broadcaster with the Pirates since 1994, was in the booth the night Barry homered twice at PNC Park in April 2007. Although Bonds was booed when he hit the first round-tripper, the reaction was different when he connected for his second. "By the time he got the second home run, half the people in the stadium were standing up clapping and cheering," Walk recalled later that season. "I think they are starting to give in to: 'Hey, this guy is something special. And he's not the only guy to have left here. Everybody has left. Nobody has stayed around.'" Another point that can't be overlooked is the fact the Pirates, following the departure of Bonds in the winter of 1992, developed a reputation of not re-signing their quality players, one of the reasons Pittsburgh didn't have a winning season for 20 consecutive campaigns between 1993 and 2012.

In an interview with the author today, Walk puts it this way: "He was one of the greatest players in Pirate history, no doubt about it. I think the fans need to give him that. And they also have to understand [the fact] that [organization never really tried to sign him to a long-term deal]. And I don't know this for an absolute fact because I'm not in the general manager's office. So, I don't know. But from what I understand, he was never made an offer of a long-term contract. They never really tried to sign him. And I think he didn't like that. They took him to arbitration every single year. Some other guys got long-term contracts, and he wasn't offered one. And I think that that is another one of the reasons why he decided, 'Hey, after six years, I'm out of here.'"

To understand the situation from Barry's point of view, it was certainly disappointing that Bonds was never truly supported by Pirates management. He took the Pirates to salary arbitration in 1989, the first in what turned out to be a series of bitter wrangles over money that would turn the Pirates fans against him. Although Bonds eventually developed into the best player in the game in the early 1990s—he became the only player in club history to capture two National League MVP awards—the fans came to regard him as a greedy and surly athlete. And a choke artist. But, in fact, it was the Pirates' front office which had, beginning in 1989, promoted the view of Barry as a failure in the clutch in order to defeat him in arbitration. "The club commissioned an Elias Sports Bureau study," noted the 2006 book *Game of Shadows*, "showing that 'in late inning pressure situations' Bonds batted only .103, perhaps the worst clutch performance by a star player in the history of the game. Because of his complaints about money and his demands to be traded, the Pittsburgh writers awarded Bonds their 'MDP' award, for 'Most Despised Pirate.'"

In the arbitration hearings in the spring of 1990, the club also argued that Bonds did not drive in enough runs (58 in 1989) compared to other young stars like Mark McGwire (95), Eric Davis (101), Will Clark (111) and Kevin Mitchell (125)—despite the fact Barry was used as a leadoff hitter the majority of the 1989 season. (Although the Pirates dismissed Bonds' numbers, he scored 96-plus runs for the third straight season, and he averaged 23 homers and 27 stolen bases a year from 1987 to 1989 as a leadoff hitter. The sabermetric stat "Wins Above Replacement," or WAR, hadn't been invented yet, but his 8.0 WAR in 1989 was higher than that of Mitchell, the National League MVP.) Team management used a similar tactic in the club's arbitration hearing with Bobby Bonilla, attacking his shoddy infield defense even though the Pirates were the ones who'd asked him to switch from the outfield, his natural position, to third base.

For Barry, whose father Bobby Bonds had been treated unfairly by his ballclubs and by the media in his playing days, the Pirates' tactics in arbitration hearings, naturally, only made him mad. It didn't help that among Pittsburgh's eight arbitration-eligible players that spring, the three who lost were Bonds, Bonilla and R. J. Reynolds, all of whom were black. Three of the five victors, meanwhile, were white. When one looks at how Bonds couldn't help but reflect on the way his father had been poorly treated throughout his own major-league career, it's not hard to see why Barry felt racism existed even in sports and, specifically, on the Pirates. "My dad always told me that if I wanted to do the same thing for the white man for less pay, then go right ahead," Barry said in 1991. "But that means you got to do double-time for the same pay. Because we're already two steps behind. Now, I've made the two steps to be on that same line." Yet why were he, Bonilla and Reynolds the arbitration losers? Why was the team's most cherished player Andy Van Slyke, a white player? "Barry and Bobby both lost arbitration cases," pitcher John Smiley once recalled. "Doug Drabek and myself both won, [and] they were trying to say it was a black thing. I don't think his agent was too prepared. How can you put up numbers like that and lose an arbitration case?"

For Barry, it was the organization's way of saying they didn't care about their best players. "We're going to win a championship here, and it will be about the same time everybody becomes eligible for free agency," Bonds said in 1990. "And we're going to say, 'You didn't care about us when we were second- and third-year players. You didn't care about us when we went to arbitration.'" And as promised, Bonds and Bonilla led the Pirates to a pair of division titles in 1990 and 1991, before Bonilla left via free agency. Bonds then helped the Bucs to a third straight division championship in 1992, cementing his legacy as one of the best players in club history. He'd, in fact, taken the Bucs to new heights; with 95, 98 and 96 victories between 1990 and 1992, it marked the first time in Pirates franchise history that the club, which had begun play in 1882 as the Pittsburgh Alleghenys, had won 95-plus games in three consecutive seasons. Certainly, in a town such as Pittsburgh—one that prided itself on a hard-working, hard-nosed, blue-collar steel mill image—Bonds' unhappiness with his contract situation didn't go well with Pirates fans. Bonds' perspective, though, was that he should have been judged by his performance on the field, not the off-the-field stuff. "Reporters don't give people exciting things to talk about," Barry said before the 1992 season. "When they talk [negatively] about players, they're depriving the fans. They're making people come out here and boo you and scream at you, but this is America's pastime and everybody should be able to enjoy it."

Did Bonds have a legitimate reason to be unhappy with his contract situation? Consider this: After Barry was named the National League's MVP following the 1990 season, he felt he belonged in the $3-million club. But the Pirates balked, holding to an offer of $2.3 million in arbitration and winning. Yet, in April 1991, Pittsburgh signed Van Slyke, who was in the final year of a three-year deal, to a three-year contract extension worth $12.6 million—which, at the time, made the center fielder the Pirates' highest-paid player—a significant raise from his three-year, $5.5 million contract. Although Bonds (.301, 33 homers, 114 RBIs and 52 stolen bases in 1990) had outperformed Van Slyke (.284, 17 homers, 77 RBIs and 14 stolen bases) and everybody else in the league, Pittsburgh management refused to extend Barry's contact. "We wanted to sign Andy all along," general manager Larry Doughty said then. Team president Carl Barger called Van Slyke "the cornerstone upon which [the organization] could build." And just how much did the organization respect Bonds? Consider this: After Bonds left as a free agent, the Pirates immediately gave his old uniform number, 24, to an obscure rookie left-handed reliever named Dennis Moeller, who'd just been acquired from Kansas City. (Pittsburgh acquired Moeller, along with righty Joel Johnston, in November 1992 in exchange for second baseman Jose Lind. The left-hander, who'd never pitch again in the big leagues after May 21, 1993, would win only one game in the majors.) As of this writing, the Pirates have given Bonds' old number to 11 players since 1993.

Don Slaught, a catcher who played on those three division championship teams with Bonds on the Pirates, says that Barry simply wanted to be recognized as the best. "He should have won three MVPs in a row," Slaught tells the author when the subject of Bonds comes up. "Best player I've ever seen. Best left fielder I've ever seen. We got along great. Just because if you understand Barry, he just wanted you to believe he was a great player. He didn't care whether you liked him or not. He just wanted the respect of being the best player. Barry and I got along great."

And when Bonds felt that the Pirates weren't willing to reward him for being the game's best player—in the organization's viewpoint, the small-market club wasn't going to be able to afford to keep him— he, like Bonilla, left town for greener pastures. In December 1992, he signed a $43.75 million, six-year deal with San Francisco, making him the highest-paid baseball player of all-time. In regard to his salary, Bonds, who considered baseball pure and simple entertainment and deemed himself entitled to compensation equal to that of any star entertainer (an idea few elite athletes would disagree with), said, "I'm worth it." Few Giants fans would argue. Bonds' arrival immediately sparked the revitalization of the Giants franchise; he helped turn a 90-loss team into a 103-win ballclub, as he batted .336 with 46 home runs and 123 RBIs to earn the first of five NL MVP awards in San Francisco. The Pirates, meanwhile, were never the same; Pittsburgh suffered through 20 consecutive losing seasons before winning 94 games in 2013. As of this writing, the Bucs—who reached postseason play for three consecutive years beginning in 2013 but were eliminated in the Division Series in 2013 and lost the wild-card game in 2014 and 2015—still haven't returned to the NL Championship Series.

Barry: Not Going Backward

To me, it's very difficult to compare greatness—but Barry's got to be near or at the top. I remember when they had that argument about who's the greatest heavyweight, and they made up those computerized fights between Muhammad Ali and Joe Louis. I'll just say that Barry's the greatest of his era, and that Hank, Willie Mays and those guys were the greatest of that era.

—Dusty Baker, as told to the Associated Press (2007)

Barry Bonds, according to father Bobby, always wanted to improve as a player every year in the major leagues. "I've never heard Barry say, 'I had a great year. Dad, I'm happy with that year,'" Bobby told *The San Francisco Chronicle* in 2001. "The only thing I've heard him say in his 16 years in the big leagues was, 'I know I can do better.'"

Jim Leyland, who managed Bonds for seven years in Pittsburgh, knew all about Barry's commitment to the game. Barry was relentless about getting better, striving to be better at every aspect of the game. "A lot of people don't know how much Barry Bonds worked his whole career," Leyland once said in 2015. "He worked hard. His off-season regimen was unbelievable. He's really familiar with hard work. That guy trains as hard as anyone." Jim Warren, one of Bonds' personal trainers in his early years with the Giants, had worked with countless professional athletes and once called Bonds "the hardest-working guy I've ever trained, by far. I've never had anybody work harder than Barry." In a separate interview in the mid-2000s with writer Jeff Pearlman, Warren also said, "I've trained a couple of hundred NFL players and probably 50 Major League Baseball players and a ton of world-class sprinters and triathletes, but in 25 years I've never found anyone who took training as seriously with as much passion and commitment as Barry. I've never had anyone show up

93

early, work hard, stay on task, do the shit nobody wants to do and stick with it every single day."

Royce Clayton saw Barry's regimen first-hand in San Francisco. Speaking in a phone interview a day after a public memorial service was held for L.A. Lakers legend Kobe Bryant and daughter Gianna at Staples Center (Bryant and his 13-year-old daughter had been killed, along with seven others, in the 2020 Calabasas helicopter crash on January 26, 2020), Clayton recounted, "It's crazy, because there's a lot of stories I could say about Barry. But I understood Barry. We just lost Kobe Bryant, and they talk about how hard he worked. But Barry worked equally as hard, as the best player in the game, but didn't want anybody to know it. There were a lot of things behind the scenes that Barry did that he didn't want people to know. He just did it on his own time. He took me to the ballpark every day, and he talked to me about looking for certain things, and pitchers tipping pitches. But he grew up around the game—and around so many great players growing up. He had such an advantage, with Willie Mays, and his father was Bobby Bonds, for crying out loud. He grew up around the game. He saw things that, man, [for me, it was] probably not until the latter stages of my career [that] I was slightly able to pick up. That's one of the nuances [of the game that he knew, and showed what type of] a student of the game that he was.

"He studied the game. He worked hard. He knew his body. [He] took care of himself. The list goes on and on about how this guy became the best player in the game. It wasn't by happenstance. None of it was by happenstance because there's intellect there, there's definitely God-given ability and there's undeniable work ethic to be the best. I remember him talking about, like, 'Why is everybody making a big deal about Michael Jordan?' when he was winning MVPs back-to-back, like nobody else in professional sports. And there's MVPs they didn't give him, just because they felt like they didn't want to give it to him."

Clayton isn't exaggerating. Let's consider Bonds' seven National League MVP awards, when no other player in baseball has won a league MVP award more than three times. Out of the four major North American professional sports, only Wayne Gretzky, a nine-time winner of the Hart Trophy in hockey, won more MVP awards than Bonds. Gordie Howe (six in hockey), Kareem Abdul-Jabbar (six in basketball), Peyton Manning (five in football), Bill Russell (five in basketball) and Michael Jordan (five in basketball) are the only men to have won as many as five league MVPs in their respective sports. Of course, it's tricky to compare other sports—in which only one MVP a year is awarded—to baseball, which hands out two awards a year, one in each league. Still, Bonds could easily have had as many Most Valuable Player awards as Gretzky. "Don't forget Bonds also should have won the MVP in 1991, when his numbers [.292, 25 homers, 116 RBIs, 107 walks and 43 stolen bases] were clearly better than Terry Pendleton's [.319, 22, 86, 43 and 10 in the same categories]," *The [Santa Rosa, CA] Press Democrat*'s Jeff Fletcher once noted, echoing the sentiments of Clayton and Bonds' many other peers. "Bonds [.306, 49 homers, 106 RBIs and 117 walks] also had a reasonable claim to the 2000 award, over teammate Jeff Kent [.334, 33, 125 and 90 in the same categories]." In both seasons, Bonds finished with the better WAR (or wins above replacement, a statistic which measures a player's total contributions to his team), although that sabermetric statistic didn't exist in those days. "I mean, that just tells you how great this guy was as a baseball player," Clayton continues, "where he could've gotten [additional] MVPs that they didn't give to him because they just felt like, 'Oh, let's give it to somebody else.'"

In the 1991 case, Pendleton, whose experience, maturity and defense helped the Braves go from the NL's worst record in 1990 to pennant winners just one year later, might have appealed to many voters because of the improbability of the 31-year-old free-agent signee hitting 52 points above his career average—and 89 points higher than the .230 he'd batted the year before with the Cardinals—to capture the batting crown by one point over the Reds' Hal Morris. But pundits speculated even then that Pendleton's personality—along with Bonds' sometimes uncooperative relationship with reporters—might have played a role in Barry losing the MVP award to the Atlanta third baseman. For Bonds, not winning the MVP meant he was going to work even harder in the off-season. "I don't know what I didn't do," he said then when asked to comment on his second-place finish. "I stole bases. I drove in 100 runs. I hit homers. I don't know what else a complete athlete can do. Maybe this will be the little button that will spark me again next year. Maybe this is a message from God: I didn't work hard enough this year. I just don't understand it."

And Clayton, along with others including Leyland and Warren, knows how much Bonds worked to become the best player in the game for the rest of the decade—and certainly of his own era.

* * *

To reach the major leagues and stay there, baseball players not only have to have talent, they also have to possess a huge amount of confidence in themselves and their abilities. Barry Bonds certainly had all of those qualities and, for him, it was also a matter of striving for consistency. "I don't want to go backward," he said following the 2002 season. "Eventually I'm going to go backward. I really take pride in staying consistent throughout my career. If I do something, I have to do it again." After signing a six-year contract with the Giants in December 1992 which made him, at the time, the highest-paid player in baseball history—and coming off an MVP season—Bonds continued to deliver every single year for the rest of his career. Even in his final seasons in 2006-07, he strived to put up his usual numbers so that fans who paid to watch him didn't get cheated. Part of his success included, for instance, making sure he was walking to the plate with the right style of bats. When Barry, known to be consumed by every detail about his bats (they had to have the right weight and proper wood quality), discovered that his bat supplier, the Original Maple Bat Corporation, was for sale on eBay in 2006 for $3.5 million, he asked company founder Sam Holman how much it would cost to guarantee he'd get his full supply of 34-inch, 31.6-ounce maple bats. As Holman later recalled, "Barry just said, 'I want to ensure that I get my bats.' He said, 'I don't care if I pay for everyone else's bats. I want to make sure that I get mine.'" It can be debated whether Bonds was motivated solely by helping himself or by helping Holman's cause or by both—but the check for $40,000 that Barry handed Holman helped stabilize the Ottawa-based bat company. Bonds "saved us," Holman said—the money allowed Original Maple Bat Corporation to purchase more wood at a crucial time and also helped the corporation become better suited to selling its products to consumers—and the company was no longer for sale. "We're here because of his graciousness," Holman added. To understand the proper context of that $40,000 check, *The New York Times* wrote, the payment covered 80 bats, meaning each bat that Bonds used in 2007 cost him $500. For comparison's sake, according to the *Times*, other major-leaguers, from Albert Pujols to Alfonso Soriano, paid about $75 for their bats from the same company. "With all of the controversy and everything else that goes on with him, his peers look up to him,"

Holman responded when the *Times* asked for his thoughts on Bonds' name being linked to PEDs. "They tell me, 'He still puts wood on the ball like nobody else.' He's the king of what he's doing."

Indeed. With the right bat, Bonds could put wood on the baseball like no one else. But the story doesn't end there, as he needed the right feel of the bat to be able to properly do his job—and Holman always made sure to listen and create the bats that were exactly what Barry needed and wanted. Bonds, who'd first learned about Holman's company in 1998 from outfielder Joe Carter, used the Ottawa-based corporation's bats throughout the 2001 season, when he broke baseball's single-season home-run record. A couple of hundred round-trippers later, Bonds in 2007 used those bats to pass Hank Aaron's all-time record. Along the way, Bonds told Holman what type of bats he needed, and Holman always delivered. When Bonds, for instance, told him that his hand would cramp when he palmed one of the bats, Holman designed a new model with an extra-large knob, which was based on the diameter of a baseball which Barry could hold comfortably. And late in his career, Bonds, thanks in part to those bats, was still hitting balls out of the ballpark.

But very few players are able to, year in and year out, actually produce at the levels that are expected of them—and those who don't, end up being labeled "busts" or "underachievers" by the press and the fans. Ruben Sierra, for instance, was a young superstar ticketed for the Hall of Fame early in his big-league career with the Texas Rangers in the late 1980s. The switch-hitting slugger had a cannon for an arm, power from both sides of the plate and hit for a high average—and, according to multiple newspaper accounts of the day, he believed he was going to be as big as or bigger than Ken Griffey, Jr.

Sierra, however, wound up wearing out his welcome in Texas, Oakland, New York, Detroit, Cincinnati, Toronto and Chicago—and was then briefly out of the majors—before reinventing himself as a bench player in the latter part of his career. But while with the A's in 1993, when he was in what should have been the prime of his career, Sierra batted only .233. He suggested that the low average was a result of pitchers working around him because A's slugger Mark McGwire had often been out of the lineup because of injuries. "I don't have anybody like Rafael Palmeiro or Julio Franco like I had in Texas," Sierra said. When A's management countered that pitchers didn't throw strikes to him because he wasn't selective enough at the plate, the switch-hitting slugger scoffed. "You can't change people. Am I going to tell [Twins superstar outfielder] Kirby Puckett, 'Go to home plate and take a walk'? That's crazy stuff. Why [is] he going to take a walk when he know[s] how to hit?" Sierra told a reporter in 1995. When other critics pointed out he was swinging at bad pitches, he fired back. "I'm not going to make a mark taking a walk. [I've] never been like that in my life. I'm an RBI man." He added that not everybody understood the difficulty of having to stand at the plate for 162 games and consistently have balls thrown at his head and the next one down in the dirt.

Including this example is not a knock on Ruben Sierra, who did make an excellent point. He is mentioned here to illustrate just how difficult it is for a hitter, especially one who didn't have enough talent surrounding him, to live up to massive expectations—and to put up good numbers when opposing pitchers are consistently pitching around him, not giving him pitches in the strike zone. Other sluggers, unlike Sierra, might show more patience at the plate, yet not as much as Bonds, who did it for the long haul. Jose Canseco, for instance, became the fourth player in major-league history to draw seven consecutive walks in 1992—this happened over a two-game stretch that August with Oakland—but missed a chance to break the record when, perhaps anxious to swing the bat after receiving all those bases on balls, he swung at a 3-and-2 pitch that was almost in the dirt. Barry Bonds? He'd have gladly taken the walks. And, for the most part, he'd only swing when he saw a hittable pitch. "He was as close to Ted Williams as anybody I ever saw, and I saw Ted Williams as a kid," said veteran sports columnist Bob Hertzel, who covered Bonds as a beat writer for *The Pittsburgh Press*. "I'm old. Ted Williams wouldn't flinch until he swung at a ball. Barry was the same way. I don't ever remember Barry taking a half swing." Over a two-game stretch in 2004, Bonds saw 29 pitches and only five strikes. He swung once, connecting for his ninth home run—and 19th hit—in 38 at-bats. Only 36% of the pitches he saw in 2003 were strikes, yet Bonds wasn't fazed—he cracked 45 home runs and walked 148 times in 130 games.

And while Bonds might have been arrogant, he more than lived up to expectations and produced year after year after year for the Pirates and Giants, even when pitchers were unwilling to pitch to him. "He is someone who does not have to worry about stats because he is going to get them anyway," Duane Kuiper, a member of the Giants' broadcast team, opined in 1997. "With Matt [Williams] injured the last couple of years [in 1995 and 1996], he showed he was able to put up the numbers without a whole lot of protection… If the Giants had been competitive last year [in 1996], he would have had 50 home runs and 140 RBI."

In an interview with the author today, former big-league third baseman Steve Buechele, who played in parts of the 1991 and 1992 seasons in Pittsburgh, marvels at the fact that Bonds always drove in runs despite pitchers' unwillingness to challenge him as Barry didn't always have decent protection in the lineup. "I got to hit behind him the first year I got traded there, so it made life a bit easier for me, hitting-wise, and probably a little bit tougher for him," Buechele says now. "He was obviously a super talent."

And he didn't just talk. He produced. When pitchers threw him a high-and-tight fastball—a location pitch thrown above the strike zone and close to the batter—Barry routinely had a response. He knew pitchers would throw him inside but he was going to take them deep on the next pitch. "All you do is wake up the lion when you throw at my head," Bonds told reporters after a 2000 game in which he homered into the upper deck after Oakland's Tim Hudson threw high-and-tight at him. Pitcher Jeff Juden recalled a spring-training intrasquad game from 1996 in an interview with writer Jeff Pearlman a decade later, remembering Bonds telling him as Barry prepared to walk to the on-deck circle. "This guy's gonna start me with a little doo-doo fastball inside to try and back me off the plate. Then he's gonna throw a little changeup down and away. I'm gonna sit on both those pitches and then he's gonna try and sneak a fastball by me. I'll take him out on that pitch to left field." To Juden's amazement, pitcher Steve Mintz did throw an inside fastball on the first pitch and a changeup away on the second, before Bonds sent the third offering 400 feet away for a home run to left. "One of the most amazing things I'd ever seen," added Juden.

* * *

When it comes to Barry Bonds, the all-time home-run king has always been held to a different set of standards. Bonds wasn't the only player linked to performance-enhancing drugs. Among hitters, he just happens to be the most scrutinized.

Long-time Red Sox designated hitter David Ortiz was one of 104 players who reportedly tested positive for performance-enhancing drugs when Major League Baseball surveyed all of baseball in 2003—results that were supposed to have been anonymous. But the Red Sox slugger, a fan favorite and World Series hero, has said he never knowingly took steroids. In 2016, MLB Commissioner Rob Manfred revealed that there were at least 10 false positives among the 2003 survey tests, adding it would be "unfair" for Ortiz, who passed 12 years' worth of drug tests after MLB implemented its drug-testing policy, to be tarnished by his positive test in this survey and that it's unknown whether the Red Sox star actually used a performance-enhancing drug.

Ortiz, whose name will appear on the Hall of Fame ballot for the first time in 2022, has been said to have mostly gotten a pass by the media in spite of his name being linked to PEDs. Perhaps the biggest question about his Hall of Fame chances centers around the fact that Ortiz had a whopping 88% of his career plate appearances as a DH, as there has been a stigma among pundits that designated hitters, because they don't take the field to play defense, aren't complete players. But some have suggested that Ortiz's Hall of Fame candidacy received a major boost in 2019 when Edgar Martinez, the long-time Mariners star who was essentially a full-time designated hitter for his final 10 seasons (and had 72% of his career plate appearances as DH), was elected to the Hall, perhaps paving the way for Ortiz's eventual election.

There is little question that Ivan Rodriguez is one of the best all-around catchers in baseball history, and no hard evidence has linked "I-Rod" to performance-enhancing drugs. But former Rangers teammate Jose Canseco, who according to many observers has proved to be reliable in matters relating to steroids, stated in his 2005 tell-all book *Juiced* that he personally injected Rodriguez. That allegation, however, wasn't a factor for the Hall of Fame voters in the catcher's first year of eligibility; I-Rod was named on 76% of the ballots cast by veteran members of the Baseball Writers' Association of America, more than the required 75% for election.

Looking at the sport through the eyes of the players, ballplayers do indeed take various supplements just so they could take the field because Major League Baseball has one of the toughest schedules in pro sports. With the grueling schedule of 162 games over the course of six months, cross-country flights, extra-inning contests and back-to-back games night after night—not to mention day games after night games—it's not really all that shocking that players use supplements to fight fatigue and stay "up." Ortiz, for instance, has said that he wound up on the list of 104 players who allegedly tested positive during MLB's 2003 survey of steroid use because he used nutritional supplements and was careless about their contents. "Most guys were taking over-the-counter supplements then. Most guys are still taking over-the-counter supplements. If it's legal, ballplayers take it. Why? Because if you make it to the World Series, you play 180 games. Really think about that for a second," Ortiz wrote in 2015 on *The Players' Tribune*, a website founded by Derek Jeter which gives professional athletes a platform. "[You play] 180 games. Your kids could be sick, your wife could be yelling at you, your dad could be dying—nobody cares. Nobody cares if you have a bone bruise in your wrist or if you have a pulled groin. You're an entertainer. The people want to see you hit a 95-mile-an-hour fastball over a damn 37-foot wall."

If one understands what Ortiz was talking about in terms of the pressure for players to continue performing at a high level over the course of a lengthy Major League Baseball season, one can certainly see why ballplayers do choose to take various supplements.

Perhaps more players take supplements and other medication simply to endure the daily grind of playing 162 games a year—and even to live up to massive expectations and not let their teammates or the fans down—than the media reports or the fans know or care. Roy Halladay, widely considered one of the best pitchers of his era, was elected to the Hall of Fame in 2019 in his first year of eligibility, 14 months after he was killed at the age of 40 when his plane crashed into the Gulf of Mexico off the coast of Florida. But Halladay had demons that few knew, as his family admitted later that the star pitcher for the Blue Jays and Phillies was an "addict." During his career, he was taking painkillers to pitch through his severe back and shoulder pain, sleeping pills to help him rest through the night before each start, and anti-anxiety medicine to try and prevent him from vomiting each time he took the mound. Halladay, according to the autopsy report, had opioids, amphetamines, anti-depressants and anxiety medications in his body the morning his plane crashed. "This," wrote Bob Nightengale in the *USA Today* of the pitcher's drug addiction, "is the complicated legacy of Halladay." But Roy Halladay, as far as the baseball world is concerned, is still a revered Hall of Famer.

Bringing Halladay's name up is to demonstrate that we don't know what athletes do behind the scenes. Barry Bonds is a private person. Many professional athletes are. Roy Halladay, for the most part, was a private man, according to his wife, Brandy Halladay, when she delivered the Hall of Fame speech during the star right-hander's Cooperstown induction. His addiction, which was not known until after his death, was explored in the 2020 documentary *Imperfect: The Roy Halladay Story*. "He would get nauseous and throw up before every game," Brandy Halladay revealed early in the documentary. "He would take sleeping pills the nights before he pitched because he couldn't sleep, the anxiety of pitching the next day was so overwhelming to him." In that same documentary, Halladay was revealed to have purchased opioids to deal with pain in 2012 as he searched a solution to get back on the field and compete.

To summarize the situation succinctly, what goes on inside the bubble that is professional sports is not something the average fan understands. Fans saw how Halladay dominated on the mound throughout his career, but did they ever really know who he was as a person? One could say that Halladay had taken all of those painkillers—which were not provided by a team doctor but, rather, purchased from a doctor for cash—and sleeping pills in his determination to take the mound every fifth day for his ballclub. Even if Barry Bonds had indeed taken anything, one could reasonably make the argument that the purpose was for him to stay in the lineup and help his team. To borrow a line from David Ortiz, fans want you to entertain them by hitting 95-mph fastballs over the wall. They don't care about your personal life. They simply want to see you hit baseballs over a damn wall. You're an entertainer. Wouldn't you be cheating the fans if you weren't doing everything you could to get on the field and perform in front of them?

* * *

In January 2010, Mark McGwire acknowledged using steroids in 1998 when he smacked 70 homers and shattered Roger Maris' single-season home-run record of 61. Sammy Sosa, who blasted 66 homers in 1998 to also surpass Maris' single-season total, has never admitted using performance-enhancing drugs, but his name has been linked to PEDs.

When McGwire's acknowledgment came out, ESPN.com reached out to Ralph Houk, Maris' manager with the 1961 Yankees, to seek his opinion on the legitimacy of the former Cardinals slugger's home-run totals. "I think [McGwire] broke [Maris'] record fairly," Houk said then, just months before his passing at the age of 90 in July 2010, adding that he thought the effects of PEDs—whether amphetamines taken in the 1960s or steroids in later years—were questionable. "I wouldn't be concerned about it. [McGwire] was a good hitter that deserves everything he's got."

Regarding that last statement, Houk wasn't the only one who thought so. In 2020, ESPN.com did a story about the 1998 McGwire-Sosa home-run chase, speaking to five of the 17 pitchers who allowed homers to both sluggers that season. One of the five who shared their thoughts in the story was Diamondbacks right-hander Andy Benes, who opined that both McGwire and Sosa "are bonafide Hall of Famers" while admitting he'd go out for batting practice just to watch McGwire. "There are guys who have done PEDs who are in the Hall of Fame," added Benes. "... I could go back in the last 20 years, in the era that I played in, and say, 'That guy did something, that guy, that guy,' and some of them actually got in trouble for it—and they're still voted in. ... Those guys are Hall of Famers, some of the best to ever play the game... Some guys who did it [use PEDs] flew under the radar. They aren't looked at as cheaters, while other guys paid the price. I just look at those guys [McGwire and Sosa] as they made mistakes."

White Sox left-hander Jim Parque, another pitcher who gave up homers to both McGwire and Sosa in 1998, told ESPN.com that at the end of the day, a hitter still had to step up to the plate to hit the ball, whether they took PEDs or not. "No amount of banned or unbanned substance is really going to help you with that. It might speed up your bat, give you a little extra, but that doesn't really matter, because you still have to square up the ball, in a two-inch-by-two-inch area, on a ball that potentially [makes] you seasick because of how much the ball moves. Have you ever stepped into a box? You need Dramamine [an over-the-counter drug used to treat motion sickness] because the ball moves so much," said Parque, who added he felt "blessed" that he was able to face McGwire and Sosa—and an "honor" to be a part of history. (In a *Chicago Sun-Times* interview in July 2009, Parque admitted using human growth hormone six times during his stint with Tampa Bay in 2003, explaining that with his career in jeopardy, he "turned to performance-enhancing drugs, like some other players did." He'd never needed HGH before, he added, "but with a shoulder that wouldn't heal, it was realistically the only thing I could turn to.") Of the other three pitchers who spoke to ESPN.com—Mets right-hander Rick Reed, White Sox/Reds righty Jason Bere and Diamondbacks/Mets righty Willie Blair—all acknowledged they either were blessed or didn't feel cheated, and that the 1998 home-run chase helped bring fans back to the ballparks after the 1994-95 strike that included the cancellation of the 1994 World Series and drove many baseball fans away.

Of course, there will be pitchers and other players who feel differently about those linked to PEDs—and those five who did speak to ESPN.com certainly don't speak for everybody else—but if some of the pitchers who actually served up home runs to McGwire and Sosa believe the two sluggers should be in the Hall of Fame, then doesn't that suggest Barry Bonds, a far better player than either one of them, should be in?

Former big-league pitcher Tom Candiotti, who gave up two home runs to Bonds in his career, believes so. "To me, he is someone who was going to beat you any way he could. His hands were so quick that he turned on an inside fastball better than anyone I ever pitched to. Without a doubt [he was the best player I've ever seen]. Especially the guys that played against Barry, [they'll say the same]. Everyone knew how talented he was. If you just talked to any general manager from that day—let's say, Jim Bowden, for instance, who's on MLB [Network]—and asked him, 'Who's the best player you ever saw?' I guarantee you he would say Barry Bonds. I guarantee you. That's how good that guy was. He was amazing. You look at some of the numbers, especially with the new-fangled stats, with OPS and all that other stuff. My goodness, I mean, it's a whole nother category for that guy.

"And that's why I feel he's [deserving to be] in the Hall of Fame. He should [already] have been [inducted into] the Hall of Fame and I don't agree with all the stuff that he did, with the PEDs and all that stuff.

But, you know, he didn't even need them. But he was driven to be not only the best, he wanted to be the best anyway, whatever it took. And then you see like a whole generation of players doing it—Barry's not the first guy to do it—and he saw all these other guys doing it, so he goes, 'Well, I'm not gonna get left behind.' So, he started doing it too, and I think that's the same with a lot of guys. Once they started seeing guys like Canseco and these other guys do it, then all of a sudden, that next generation goes, 'Yeah, we've got to do this!' So, it was then [that] they end up getting caught and then the whole thing starts."

Barry and Race

I think one obvious fact is that the glaring focus on Bonds was unfair, given what we now know (and baseball insiders have long known) about the prevalence of steroids in the game. And though it was not mainly motivated by racism, I still believe race played a role. When I wrote my first piece about Bonds and race [in 2001], "If Jeff Kent Were Black," I got private e-mails from several well-known African-American sportswriters and sportscasters, thanking me for pointing out the double standard in white writers savaging Bonds and lionizing Kent, though they are both, on balance, talented, churlish jerks a lot of the time—one key difference being that Kent always cultivated the media.

—Journalist John Walsh, *Salon* (2007)

* * *

Critics of Barry Bonds will, as columnist Rick Reilly did in *Sports Illustrated* in 2001, point to the teammates whom Barry alienated and throw out comments such as "Teammates 24, Bonds 1," referring to the idea that in the Giants clubhouse it was 24 guys who subscribed to the team concept versus one standoffish loner unwilling to conform to team rules. In the eyes of the critics, it was 24 team guys versus one who was moody, self-centered and difficult.

Still, one could look in that same Giants locker room between 1997 and 2002, and see another player similar to Bonds: second baseman Jeff Kent, a superstar who, as SB Nation's *Beef History* once noted, could be just as grouchy and difficult as Barry. Yet Kent, it can be argued, was treated to a double standard by the media. David Grann of *The New York Times Magazine* once made a reference to this particular point in a September 2002 story, recounting an occasion in which Kent made some vile homophobic and sexist remarks in front of sportswriters—and nobody reported it.

"One day when I was in the locker room," Grann wrote, "not long after Kent and Bonds came to blows in the dugout... Kent, about to take off his towel, asked a pack of reporters if there were any 'queers' or 'women' among them—a remark that, especially in San Francisco, would have created a certain stir. Although he was surrounded by at least a dozen reporters who half have seized upon any number of Bonds' remarks, none, as far [as] I know, reported this. 'Is there a double standard because Kent talks to us?' one sports radio announcer told me. 'Definitely.'"

Another example of a double standard? In March 2002, the Giants were dealt a major blow with the news that Kent had broken a bone in his left wrist—with the second baseman claiming he'd slipped and fallen while washing his pickup truck, a freak accident— and would miss the remainder of spring training and likely part of the regular season. However, it was later revealed that Kent, in reality, was attempting to do stunts on his motorcycle on a highway—which was in direct violation of his contract—only to crash and injure himself. Although he was exposed for not being truthful, he still had one of the best seasons of his career, batting .313 with 37 home runs and 42 doubles, and the Giants won their first pennant in 13 years.

It wasn't the first time in sports history that an athlete had suffered an injury while engaging in risky behavior expressly forbidden by his contract, and in Kent's case the injury was laughed at more than criticized. Kent's injury, Chris Jaffe noted in *The Hardball Times* a decade later, "inspired a round or two of jokes made at the expense of" the Giants second baseman and that "comedians could start revving up their jokes at Kent's expense." But what if the player who'd violated his contract and suffered that injury was Barry Bonds instead? SB Nation's *Beef History* put it this way: "[The] famously no-nonsense Kent came through with some big-time nonsense... Kent got some minor scolding from the media, but that's one of those things that, like, man, imagine if it had been Bonds who got hurt dicking around on his motorcycle, then tried to lie about it. It would have been huge."

SB Nation's *Beef History* brings up other examples of the way Bonds and Kent, despite sharing similar qualities, being portrayed differently. Although Kent also rubbed people the wrong way, noted SB Nation, he was often portrayed in the press as a player who took the traditions of baseball extremely seriously, praised as a "blue collar," hard-nosed, gritty player; "in other words, white." When the star second baseman—who mostly ignored reporters before games— once kept the media waiting in Cincinnati, he wasn't a prima donna; he was just, in his own words, "busy lifting weights." Journalist Joan Walsh—a Giants fan who, by the way, is white and also a Jeff Kent fan—once noted that Kent was moody and sometimes cruel to teammates, "and much like Bonds, has few close friends among the Giants." Walsh brought up the 2001 Rick Reilly column in *Sports Illustrated* in which Bonds was heavily criticized, the one in which Kent offered several of those criticisms of Barry. "Few sportswriters," Walsh observed in a column of her own in August 2001 in *Salon*, "blasted Kent for breaching his own supposed 'team-first' ethics by attacking a teammate, in the heat of a pennant race no less," and she opined that a double standard did exist in respect to Bonds and Kent. The lack of criticisms toward Kent for his unflattering comments about Bonds in the Reilly article "showed the amazing extent to which reporters' own experience of a sports star— the petty slights or the charm and flattery—can control the way they cover him, and how the star is in turn perceived by fans." Translation? "Kent was more accommodating with reporters, and notably, had the same skin color as most reporters," concluded SB Nation. "Even though he could be just as grouchy and difficult as his black superstar teammate, Kent fit all the hardworking, blue-collar stereotypes of a white player, so he was treated to a double standard."

Walsh, meanwhile, wasn't finished. In her same column, she observed that Bonds and Kent were in many ways the same ballplayer: "proud, hardworking, self-critical loners, family men with few friends on the team." Both players "have been known to stare through fans like they didn't exist" and ignore kids requests for autographs. While Bonds was blasted for skipping the Giants' team photo, Kent missed the 2000 photo shoot, too, but wasn't criticized and the incident was hardly even mentioned by reporters. In short, in some ways "both guys are cocky assholes, but one is white and dutifully answers reporters' questions, while the other is black and does not. Guess which one's the media darling?" Furthermore, Kent's negative comments about Bonds to Reilly "were a breach of the team ethic Kent claims to revere, and hurt the Giants far more than Bonds' surliness with reporters."

Although Bonds was often criticized for being a diva, Kent—portrayed in the press as a hero for standing up to baseball's home-run king when they were teammates—did not receive as much of that type of criticism despite exhibiting many of those qualities. Batting behind Bonds, for instance, Kent made it known that he hated Barry stealing bases while he was at the plate—because it distracted him. According to Walsh, she'd been to five years of spring training and nearly 200 Giants games between 1997 and 2001, and she had never once seen him sign an autograph, toss a ball to a fan or chat up a kid in the stands—although she had seen Bonds do those things. Sports journalist Joan Ryan, meanwhile, once noted that when Kent hit a grand slam to reach 100 RBIs in four straight seasons in 2000, Giants fans shook the ballpark with a thundering ovation, demanding a curtain call. The problem? "Kent didn't budge from the bench," Ryan recalled in her 2020 book *Intangibles*. "The cheering hung in the air like an unreciprocated handshake until the crowd sank back into their seats. It was bizarre. All he had to do was step out of the dugout and doff his cap." When the aloof second baseman and another Giants teammate picked up their children at the same preschool, Ryan added, Kent didn't say hello or even make eye contact with the teammate—even if they were waiting right next to each other.

Kent, during his San Francisco years, was mostly given a free pass by the media, though; in stark contrast, Bonds, unfortunately, was always labeled more negatively. "It's worth mentioning that while Bonds was getting roasted in the middle of a historic achievement [in his single-season home-run chase in 2001], no one seemed too bothered by Kent's behavior," added SB Nation. It was, if one were to look at the situation objectively (the way Joan Walsh did), a matter of double standards.

* * *

As far as news and sports reporter Dennis Freeman is concerned, race is a factor when it comes to the hatred shown by the press to Barry Bonds. "For all the hell and scrutiny that Bonds has had to go through the past few years about his alleged knowledge of using performance enhancing drugs," Freeman wrote in 2011, "his white and non-Black peers, for the most part, have been basically given a salute for admitting they have used the substance. When major league baseball headliners like Alex Rodriguez, Andy Pettitte and Jason Giambi were found to have used steroids, all they had to do to gain sympathy from the media and the public was to shed a few fake tears, pretend to have a contrite heart, say all the right things and all would be forgiven."

As for Bonds, wrote Freeman, it was a different story because of race. "He's a man playing in a different bracket. That bracket Bonds belongs to is being black, supremely confident, the owner of numerous MLB records and unapologetic to his critics." Freeman, who has written about social justice and civil rights in addition to sports, opined that Bonds has, over the years, "been unjustly condemned" in the court of public opinion. "While white and non-Black [players] have been subjected to some criticism," the scribe continued, "Bonds [has] been outright vilified. The hating on Bonds has had a much sinister tone to it than regular criticism. And in my opinion, it has been driven and fueled by race. Except for O. J. Simpson, I've never seen such vile hatred distributed by the media and the public towards another prominent Black athlete."

A piece of tidbit that has perhaps been forgotten by many baseball fans is that the pitcher who gave up Bonds' record-tying 755th home run—San Diego Padres pitcher Clay Hensley—had once been suspended for testing positive for steroids while pitching in the minor leagues. Or, in the words of Freeman, Hensley "is a drug cheat, having been suspended for his use of steroids. But that conversation, of course, barely caused a ripple on the media's radar screen. This is not [a] sports thing. It's a black thing. The double standard of life is in black and white." The double standard, Freeman noted, meant that for white ballplayers, the standard of accountability is often lowered and memories become short as far as their wrongdoings are concerned. For Bonds, meanwhile, there has always been talk about having his accomplishments marked as tainted or have an asterisk put by them.

Those who believe that double standards exist in the case of Barry Bonds will point to the Jeff Kent situation in San Francisco. Others will point to the way Yankees left-hander Andy Pettitte has been forgiven for his use of PEDs. In the words of Freeman, Pettitte is "a cheater and a proven" who "was exposed as a fraud when he denied using steroids or HGH, according to a 2006 *Los Angeles Times* article." With Bonds, who didn't play again following the 2007 season despite being a productive player in that final year, he "lost at least two years of playing because of the allegations levied against him," believed Freeman. "Meanwhile, Pettitte pitched again with no repercussions. You can see the difference in favoritism in reporting by mainstream media when it comes to [any white ballplayers] or any other athlete not named Bonds."

Former Giants teammate Royce Clayton, for one, believes that race is indeed a factor in baseball. "That's just one of the things that [maybe I didn't understand then], but there's a lot that I understand now as a 50-year-old father and man, [about] what life is about," Clayton begins. "People beat down people for various reasons, and baseball mirrors society. I've always understood that. Baseball in America and racism run hand in hand. A lot of things that are said about Barry is because they didn't like him, his bravado, the way he went about it. But there were white dudes that did the same thing that were looked at as heroes, but they villainized Barry because he's Black, plain and simple. They didn't understand him. But they can say whatever they want to say about him, but I know I played with the best player who ever played the game. Hands down.

"I'll never forget how Barry took me under his wing when he came to the Giants in 1993, and I listen to things that people say about what he did or what he didn't do. But, I mean, I played with McGwire. [Clayton, who joined the Cardinals prior to the 1996 season, was traded by St. Louis, along with Todd Stottlemyre, to Texas for Darren Oliver and Fernando Tatis on July 31, 1998, a month before McGwire broke Maris' single-season home-run record.] Things that went on during that point in time, I didn't like it. Because you're glorifying people who weren't even close to this man's stature, who weren't even close to this man's ability."

Critics have ripped Bonds for being "jealous" of McGwire and the attention paid to the slugger known as "Big Mac" during the 1998 season when the Cardinals first baseman and Chicago Cubs outfielder Sammy Sosa both surpassed Roger Maris' single-season home-run record. (The story that emerged in 2006 from reporters Mark Fainaru-Wada and Lance Williams in their book *Game of Shadows* is that the attention accorded to those two sluggers motivated Barry to take PEDs to keep up.)

But if one took the time to understand Bonds, one would understand all Barry wanted was to be recognized as the best player in the game. And Bonds, with his combination of power and speed, was certainly baseball's best all-around player, with already three National League MVP awards under his belt by 1993. In the strike-abbreviated 1995 season, he enjoyed his third 30-homer, 30-stolen base season over the last six years. The following year, he had a 40-40 season. In 1997, it was 40 homers and 37 stolen bases as San Francisco won the NL West crown.

Then came 1998, when Bonds won his eighth Gold Glove and led the NL in Wins Above Replacement among position players (or WAR—a statistic which measures a player's total contributions to his team—although that sabermetric stat hadn't been invented yet) for the seventh time. Clearly the best player in the game, Bonds hit .303 with 44 doubles, 37 home runs, 120 runs scored, 122 RBIs and 28 stolen bases in 1998. He played all out, even when the games didn't count. Case in point: In a spring training game that year, when Osvaldo Fernandez had a no-hitter going in the fourth, Bonds made a terrific sliding catch on the rain-slicked field on a short pop fly to left. That same season saw him achieve the unprecedented 400-home run, 400-stolen base milestone when he connected for his 400th career round-tripper off Marlins pitcher Kirt Ojala in Florida.

Unfortunately, little attention was given to Bonds' outstanding year and his contributions were virtually ignored, thanks to all the hoopla surrounding the McGwire-Sosa home-run chase. That home-run derby, which ultimately saw McGwire finish with a major-league record 70 homers, is widely credited by sports analysts as having restored Major League Baseball among its fan base in the preceding years, as many fans had lost interest and felt betrayed by the 1994 strike. "Even batting practice has become a huge event in each city McGwire visits, drawing thousands of spectators who crowd in the stands behind home plate or sit in the left field stands, where the right-handed batter's lofty homers often land," observed *The Washington Post* in the middle of the 1998 season. Countless sports industry figures suggested then that all the home runs were helping the sport massively. "There's no question Mark's streak has had an impact on baseball this season," said a spokesman for a leading maker of batting gloves. "He's elevated the game's image. Now four years out of the strike, this is what we needed as an industry… someone to take over after Cal Ripken's 2,131-game streak broke Lou Gehrig's record [in 1995 for consecutive games played]." A spokesman for J.C. Penney Co. said nationwide sales of baseball merchandise was up 30% over the previous year, with a direct correlation between sales and more home runs.

The biggest impact McGwire had was on attendance and concession sales when his Cardinals visited other stadiums. When the Cardinals played the expansion Arizona Diamondbacks in mid-June at Bank One Ballpark—where nearly every game was a sellout—the big difference between that and other series was the 15,000 people who arrived two hours early for batting practice. Concession and merchandise sales shot up 10%, and sales at the Diamondbacks Team Shop were the best since Bank One Ballpark's inaugural week in April. "They came, they ate, they drank and they partied," said a spokesperson for the stadium's concessionaire. Noted *The Washington Post* in a July 1998 piece titled "McGwire's Heroics Driving up Profits": In the Cardinals' late-June series in Houston, "the team's average attendance jumped from 24,498 to 38,591 per game for a three-day homestand, which brought in an extra $167,424 in revenue based on the $11.88 average ticket cost at the Astrodome." In Minnesota in July, "attendance for the three games against the Cardinals averaged 31,067 compared with 13,870 the rest of the season. Based on Minnesota's average ticket price of $8.22, those 17,197 extra people per game brought in $141,359 extra over three days. When McGwire's home run sailed over the left-field wall, sports columnists said they could have sworn it was the loudest ovation they have heard this year."

Looking at the situation from the perspective of Bonds—an ultra-competitive athlete and the best player in the game—one could make a reasonable argument that Barry likely felt betrayed, too. Many players were using steroids, but there was hardly any outcry in baseball then. In fact, it was quite the opposite. "Nike reminded everybody that chicks dig the long ball!" sportswriter Joe Posnanski reminded readers in 2020. "MLB even put out a comic book of baseball players with enormous muscles. Muscles were in!" What everybody—Bonds included—saw was that home runs were king. Baseball, thanks to the home-run chase, was front-page news for the first time since the strike. Players were juicing and bashing baseballs out of ballparks at rates never seen before, and those players were being celebrated. Worse, PEDs were not being tested for, nor were they against the rules.

Baseball, in fact, seemed to love the idea of hitters getting stronger through chemistry. The perfect example was seen in August 1998, when Steve Wilstein, an Associated Press writer, saw a bottle of androstenedione—at the time banned in the NFL and the Olympics, but not in baseball—in McGwire's locker and wrote about it. In his story, Wilstein made it clear McGwire hadn't broken the rules of the game, but also wrote that androstenedione's ability to raise testosterone levels "is seen outside baseball as cheating and potentially dangerous." Furthermore, if McGwire was taking androstenedione, known in baseball clubhouses as "andro," what else was he taking? Yet nobody cared or wanted to investigate the matter any further; Wilstein, meanwhile, was widely criticized for even writing the piece.

Wilstein was even seen as a villain and his story was crushed. "In baseball's magic summer," SI.com recalled in 2013, "Wilstein became public enemy number one in major-league clubhouses, the subject of a backlash not only from teams and players, but from his fellow writers, who worried that players would become more guarded with all reporters as a result of Wilstein's 'snooping.'" At the time, McGwire, who looked like a bodybuilder, was being celebrated, praised as the hero of the country. He was a legend, not a pharmaceutical creation. "I was marching in that parade in 1998, when Mark McGwire hit 70 homers and was the great American hero," Posnanski reflected years later. "Back then nobody wanted to hear about andro or steroids or any of that. Forget Hall of Fame, he could have been a senator."

Posnanski was hardly alone. Dan Shaughnessy of the *Boston Globe*, like many others in the press then, scoffed at the notion that McGwire was a cheater. While acknowledging andro was a steroid, Shaughnessy insisted it was an all-natural, over-the-counter substance used to help an athlete train harder and recover faster, and was not that different from aspirin, steak, prime rib and Wheaties. "Giving credit to the substance for McGwire's success makes it sound as if the substance is adding 40 feet to McGwire's long fly balls. This is ridiculous," added the *Globe* columnist. "… [It] is misleading to write that he's using a 'performance-enhancing drug.' He's a baseball player, not an Olympic sprinter. There's nothing sold at drugstores that would help any of us hit a home run in the big leagues (unless the store has a book on hitting written by Ted Williams)." McGwire was, according to Shaughnessy, the "feel-good story of the baseball summer" and a victim of a "tabloid-driven controversy." McGwire and Sosa were, according to others, making baseball "fun" again with their home-run derby. Fans also seemed unconcerned about andro, as attendance records were smashed.

Other players seemed unconcerned, too. Hall-of-Famer-to-be Pedro Martinez, then with the Red Sox, admitted years later that he wanted to see McGwire break Maris' record because McGwire was "such a nice gentleman." Even commissioner Bud Selig appeared to suggest McGwire had done nothing improper when Wilstein's story came out, saying, "I think what Mark McGwire has accomplished is so remarkable, and he has handled it all so beautifully, we want to do everything we can to enjoy a great moment in baseball history."

And if the fans and the media—and even players around the big leagues, many of whom dropped whatever they were doing to watch McGwire hit during batting practice—wanted home runs, well, Bonds certainly showed the baseball world he could hit them. And if one took the time to really reflect back on the whole home-run chase in those days, one could reasonably argue that race might have played a role in McGwire's national hero status and in Bonds' unpopularity. As a proud, outspoken African-American athlete who knew he was the far better player, Bonds certainly would have been upset to see McGwire being glorified as a savior in the game. In Pittsburgh years earlier, he'd seen a similar script when the Pirates didn't want to reward him for being their best player, yet the organization, in his eyes, treated a less-talented Andy Van Slyke much better. Now in San Francisco, Bonds was still the game's best player, yet the baseball world was giving all its attention to McGwire and his home runs. Was race a factor? Would it have been so unreasonable for him to feel that McGwire was being embraced as baseball's golden boy—and not crucified for his androstenedione transgressions—partly because he was white? Wouldn't it be understandable, too, if Barry watched the McGwire-Sosa home-run derby play out and felt like he wasn't on a level playing field?

And when fans decided they wanted to see home runs—"[the

1998] home-run spree," as ESPN.com has said, "revitalized baseball following the crippling strike that wiped out the 1994 World Series"—Bonds showed he could outslug everybody else in the game. The sport, after all, had changed following the 1998 home-run chase; the long ball, apparently, was the only thing that the baseball world cared about, and the very thing that brought fans back to the ballpark (and sent them home happy). And if fans wanted to see a great show with those long balls, Bonds, who'd always viewed being a baseball player as being an entertainer, was going to give them a great one. At one point in 2001, he hit 38 home runs during a 61-game stretch, a 101-homer pace if projected to 162 games. "And [Barry] proved everybody wrong, like, 'Okay. You guys want to see somebody hit home runs. Watch what I can do.' I think that's what Barry did, and he proved everybody wrong," continues Clayton. "I think it's his way of saying that the best player in the world would've hit 100 home runs if they'd pitched to him, that year that he had 73. He made a mockery of the game."

Regarding that last statement, perhaps that's another way to view the situation from Bonds' point of view: The best player thumbing his nose at those in charge, saying, "Look what I've done with your rules." Given how baseball celebrated McGwire—and Sosa—and all those long flies during the 1998 home-run derby, and ignored Bonds' all-around contributions to the game, one could certainly argue that Barry, being the competitive athlete that he was, had every reason to be upset and, thus, be driven to show the baseball world he could hit more home runs than anybody else in the game. Baseball is supposed to be entertainment—to most people, sports are a welcome distraction from real-world problems—and Bonds was, indeed, entertaining and giving fans what they wanted to see.

* * *

Whenever Bonds mentioned race in his comments, those remarks were dismissed in the press. For Barry, the issue was real. For those who have looked at the issue in an objective manner—journalist Joan Walsh, for one—they wanted to understand Bonds instead of dismissing him. "Life is harder for Black superstars," Walsh opined in 2006 when reviewing the book *Game of Shadows*, "from Jackie Robinson to Willie Mays to

Curt Flood to, yes, Barry Bonds in 2006." Of course, that statement, regarding life being more difficult for African-Americans compared to non-Black people, is still true as of this writing. And, as sportswriter William C. Rhoden once quoted a defense attorney saying, "Black faces in high places get serious scrutiny."

Documentaries and columns have linked Bonds' personality to his fairly unhappy childhood as the son of Bobby Bonds, the star outfielder who was supposed to be the new Willie Mays but turned to alcohol and anger when he couldn't live up to the unrealistic expectations. Bobby, as we are told, could be an abusive father and husband. Barry, we are told, grew up in an affluent white suburb in the Bay Area with all sorts of advantages. Yet we aren't told to stop and thoroughly consider that sad possibility Barry Bonds, growing up sort of fatherless as a Black youth, did indeed feel racism being the lone Black kid in a wealthy white suburb. We are told in the documentary *Baseball* that when Willie Mays was described as an "instinctive" and "natural" ballplayer early in his career, there was a touch of racism in those comments. Yet we are expected to believe racism doesn't exist when it comes to the treatment of Barry Bonds decades later.

When he signed with San Francisco in 1993 to be the team's new left fielder, and his father was brought on to be hitting coach and Dusty Baker was named manager (giving the Giants three African-Americans in high-profile roles), Barry said, "I thought we were going to get lynched. I knew what I was up against." That's what he believed, and could anyone blame him? As the son of a 14-year major-league player, he grew up in the baseball clubhouse and around the sport's culture. He saw how poorly his father was treated. He knew that as a Black athlete, there was already one strike against him. And even if race wasn't truly a factor, Barry knew from experience he'd be criticized no matter what. He'd heard those types of criticism ever since he was a teen. Nothing he did was ever enough.

Kevin Donahue, Barry's basketball coach at Serra High School, once recalled Bonds getting criticized more so than other teammates. "Barry spent a lot of time in my office talking about problems... He was under a microscope because of who his dad was. People always expected him to perform well. When he made a mistake, people tended to be more critical of him." And, of course, everything Barry was facing—the unfair expectations and the criticisms—all goes back to his father and how he was treated. Even early in his major-league career, Barry had already heard all the criticisms directed toward him. Although he deserved the 1991 National League MVP, admitted many in the press, another lesser candidate (Atlanta's Terry Pendleton) received more votes as a way to punish Barry. Although he revived the Giants franchise upon his arrival in 1993, he was still criticized in the press, the same treatment he'd received in Pittsburgh.

Fitting in as an African-American in a baseball clubhouse isn't as easy as one thinks, confirms former Giants teammate Royce Clayton, who played for 11 clubs in the big leagues from 1991 to 2007. For Clayton, although the San Francisco clubhouse already had a number of veterans when he debuted in September 1991, it was a difficult culture to fit into, even for a first-round pick (15th overall in 1988) who grew up in Burbank, California. "For me, being drafted by the Giants and then breaking in with them was an honor. It was a good thing surrounded by a bunch of veteran players," Clayton reflects. "Will Clark. Robby Thompson. Matt Williams. Kirt Manwaring. They were the pillars of the ballclub. I broke in as a young shortstop, just trying to find my way. But it was tough. I couldn't really identify with [the guys, who were wearing] cowboy boots with bucket hats, [while] I was wearing Cross Colours to the ballpark. So, it was a big transition."

Clayton isn't the only one who had that experience. Utility second baseman John Patterson, who played for parts of four seasons with the Giants from 1992 to 1995, recalls the days before and after Bonds arrived. The clubhouse went from playing country music pre-Bonds, as Patterson recalls, to playing hip-hop when Bonds joined the team in 1993. "It's a different locker room," he says now.

"It was tough," Clayton continues, referring to his transitioning into the San Francisco clubhouse as a rookie. "[The team slogan and rallying cry] 'Humm Baby' was something that [then-Giants manager] Roger Craig and those guys came up with, but I just did the best that I could, do things the best of my ability and break into the league, be a good teammate and learn the right way. Those guys taught me a lot. But again, it was tough for myself to express myself as a player or an individual, just because of the surroundings that were put around the organization. For myself and Darren Lewis—he was our center fielder—we were the two young kids on the block. It was a tough atmosphere, especially being two young African-American kids. Me being from Inglewood, Darren being from the Bay Area. It was just a real tough atmosphere to penetrate and break in with. We had Dusty as the hitting coach, which was helpful. He helped us along the way. But then when we acquired Barry in '93, I can't tell you just how much it just changed everything. It changed myself as a player, as an individual. It changed, obviously, the city of San Francisco. It changed our ballclub immediately, as soon as we got Barry on that club.

"Speaking more of my experience personally, as soon as Barry came into the fold, on the first day of spring training, he came with high-top shoes on, earrings in [and] hat on backwards, and it just changed everything. It gave us a swag, it gave us a personality, and it really gave me and Darren, as two young players on that club, the opportunity to just be loose and go out and express ourselves and play the game that we were capable of playing."

Indeed. That "swag" was something which led to a change in the culture and the fortunes of the Giants. Suddenly, it was cool to be a Giant. "Immediately, Barry took me under his wing. I'd known Barry from my brother [Royal Clayton], who actually played at ASU with Barry. So I knew him. He'd come to the house a number of times, and I'd watched Barry play in college. So, I'd already had that relationship with him."

Clayton credits Bonds for changing the culture in the Giants clubhouse and made it smoother for him and other younger players such as Lewis and Patterson to fit in. But for African-Americans in baseball, nothing came easy. Although African-Americans are embraced in other American sports, it wasn't the same in baseball, as far as Clayton is concerned, during his time in the big leagues. "There's a lot that you have to deal with when it comes to this game, when it comes to certain situations," he explains. "Football is a game where you can be African-American and be memorialized and glorified. Basketball is the same type of game where you can be memorialized and glorified. But the reality is that baseball is not that game. Baseball is a game where Hank Aaron had been the home-run king, walking on this planet, since I was a kid. He'd held that title since I was a kid. And [yet] we talked about the second-best as if he was the best: Babe Ruth, who was not the home-run king. Henry Aaron was the home-run king, and because he's African-American, they didn't talk about him. They didn't glorify him. If he's walking on this planet, we should be showing Henry Aaron all the love, the due diligence and the respect in the world. And when Barry was chasing that record, all they were worried about was him breaking Babe Ruth's record. And he was like, 'Screw Babe Ruth! Hank Aaron is the home-run king! Hank Aaron is the number!'

"And it almost seemed like it was more of a big deal when Barry passed Babe Ruth, than when it was when he passed Hank Aaron. And I was just so happy in my heart to see that Hank Aaron stepped up and was happy to see Barry break that record, and I don't care what people say as far as 'asterisk' or whatever they want to do, or say this or that. I'm just proud that in history, whether you say Hank Aaron or Barry Bonds, whatever you want to argue about, an African-American is the home-run king. Period. And that record will never be broken."

As an aside, long-time Giants skipper Dusty Baker, who managed both Clayton and Bonds in San Francisco, certainly saw first-hand how African-Americans and minorities were unfairly treated during his own playing career, which spanned from 1968 to 1986. According to Jason Turbow's 2019 book *They Bled Blue*, the Dodgers parted ways with Baker, a left fielder, and pitchers Dave Stewart and Bobby Castillo during the 1980s, with each under suspicion of being a negative influence on left-handed reliever Steve Howe, whose career would be derailed by problems with alcohol and cocaine abuse. "Any time you see a correlation where there's one white dude and three minorities," Baker reflected later, "automatically we've got to be a bad influence." Then-Dodgers general manager Al Campanis, according to Turbow, supposedly asked Howe, "Why do you hang around the Blacks and Hispanics so much? Why don't you hang around with Rick Monday or Ron Cey, guys like that?"

Clayton certainly knows what he's talking about. The day Bonds hit his 60th home run of the 2001 season, a reporter asked Barry if he could remember the first time he understood Ruth's significance. "Naw," Bonds said truthfully, "but I'll tell you about Hank Aaron. Aaron was my guy." But, according to writer David E. Early in the *San Jose Mercury News*, not one reporter asked to hear what Barry had to say about Aaron. Bonds offered anyway, saying, "In the true history of baseball, Hank Aaron is the home-run king. Babe Ruth is not the home-run king, and I wasn't going to slight Hank by talking about Ruth when I don't know that much about Ruth."

Certainly, Bonds has a deep respect for the game, particularly for African-Americans in the game, yet critics will have you believe he has no respect for the sport. "I'm African-American, and our achievement is part of what I stand for in this game," he once said when the topic of Ruth came up again, several years before he broke Aaron's career home-run mark. "My heritage is what I need to know and need to talk about. How Jackie [Robinson] paved the way [by breaking baseball's color barrier in 1947]. About the Negro Leagues, from 'Cool Papa' Bell to Josh Gibson and Satchel Paige. Those are my people, the ones who opened the doors to give me the opportunity to play this game. Everyone already knows the American history of baseball. But in the African-American history, and in the American history of baseball, Hank Aaron is the home-run king, and that is that."

Barry and Other Double Standards

Barry Bonds of the San Francisco Giants, most everyone seems to believe, is a cheater and a creep who is rightly being pursued by U.S. federal prosecutors, a guy whose records ought to be expunged from the books. Shawne Merriman of the San Diego Chargers [who was caught using steroids and suspended for four games] will simply pay the modest price the National Football League demands for his sins, as have many of his contemporaries... Meanwhile, there is no media backlash, no preaching from on high, no congressional committee convened and no suggestion that he ought to give back the award he won last year as the league's outstanding defensive rookie.
—Journalist Stephen Brunt, The Globe and Mail (2006)

Looking at other sports, one also sees a double standard when it came to Bonds.

Consider the case of basketball superstar Michael Jordan, known for his intense work ethic and generosity, especially how he looked out for the younger players. A story surfaced in May 2020, however, about the way the NBA legend treated Horace Grant, his Chicago Bulls teammate between 1987 and 1994, which multiple players knew about but went unreported by the media until more than two decades later.

The story came out in 2020 when Sam Smith, a sportswriter who'd covered the Bulls during the team's heyday and the best-selling author of the 1992 book *The Jordan Rules: The Inside Story of a Turbulent Season with Michael Jordan and the Chicago Bulls*, appeared on a KNBR podcast and stated that Jordan once asked the staff not to feed Grant if the latter did not play well. "Players would come to me over the years," Smith offered, "and say, 'You know what he did? He took Horace [Grant's] food away on the plane because Horace had a bad game.'

[Michael] told the stewardesses, 'Don't feed him; he doesn't deserve to eat.'"

According to Smith on the same podcast, the players who told him about Jordan's treatment toward Grant would then ask, "Why don't you write this?" Smith's response? "And I would say, 'Well, I can't write it unless you said it.' I don't do 'league sources.' You can't do that kind of stuff on these kinds of things. 'If you want to be quoted, I've got no problem with that.'" Those players' reaction, Smith continued, would be something like, "No, no, no. We can't say that about Michael Jordan."

In his Hall of Fame induction speech in 2009, Jordan dredged up old grudges, railing on those who ever undervalued or overlooked him. He disparaged people who had little to do with his career, including former New York Knicks head coach Jeff Van Gundy and former Utah Jazz small forward Bryon Russell—for crossing him with taunts more than a dozen years earlier. Jordan even flew out his old high school teammate, Leroy Smith, to Springfield, Massachusetts, for the induction. Smith, of course, was the upperclassman his coach, Clifton "Pop" Herring, kept on varsity over him as a high school sophomore. Jordan waggled to the old coach, "I wanted to make sure you understood: You made a mistake, dude." Although he was widely criticized then for being arrogant and petty, he didn't hurt his image with the NBA community, a high-ranking team executive told *Yahoo! News* then. "That's who Michael is. It wasn't like he was out of character. There's no one else who could've gotten away with what he did [with that speech]. But it was Michael, and everyone just goes along." Despite giving that speech, Jordan is still revered today, with his supporters believing that his speech revealed the side of his competitive nature that made him the sport's best player of all-time.

Rick Reilly, for one, isn't one of those supporters. According to the long-time sportswriter, Jordan's Bulls assistant coach, Johnny Bach, told him early in Michael's career, "This guy is a killer. He's a cold-blooded assassin. It's not enough for him to beat you. He wants you dead." Reilly, in a 2009 ESPN.com column, proceeded to list a few examples, including an incident in which he witnessed Jordan "race his car up the shoulder of Chicago interstates just because he didn't have the patience to wait in traffic." He added that for Jordan, "it was never enough to win. He had to have scalps."

Even today, Michael Jordan is still relevant in the sporting world.

In 2020, ESPN Films and Netflix co-produced *The Last Dance*, a vastly popular documentary miniseries focusing on Jordan's last season with the Chicago Bulls in 1998. Although some, including filmmaker Ken Burns, criticized Jordan's involvement in the production of the series (which meant certain aspects that Jordan didn't want in weren't going to be in it), *The Last Dance* drew mostly positive reactions from the NBA community and positive reviews from those outside of the basketball community. Today, Jordan is still revered by sports fans, universally acknowledged to be not only the greatest basketball player of all-time, but the most popular, too. Barry Bonds, whose own 2006 reality TV series *Bonds on Bonds* on ESPN generated poor ratings and was widely criticized before the series was canceled after 10 episodes, unfortunately, is a different story.

There have been some who have tried to explain what made Bonds tick. "I think that he was absolutely brought up in the jock culture values of the clubhouse," journalist and author Robert Lipsyte once said of Barry in an ESPN2 documentary about the home-run king. "You intimidate, you bully and it's not enough to win. You must also dominate. And leave your enemy in the dust." But how is that different from Jordan?

* * *

When it comes to the Barry Bonds-Michael Jordan comparison, it's an unfair one simply because the two sports are completely different. In basketball, the game's best player can dominate a game and carry a team on his back. He could, literally, have the ball in his hands with the game on the line. In other team sports, in fact, you could always pass the ball (or the puck) to your best players. In baseball? In what's perhaps the ultimate team sport, the pitcher is the one who has a monopoly of the baseball itself, and each hitter occupies only one of nine spots in the batting order. In baseball, your best player still bats only once every nine times, and if opposing teams don't want his bat to beat them, they don't need to pitch to him.

That last point, as far as former Giants shortstop Royce Clayton is concerned, is all the proof he needs that Bonds is the greatest ever. You see, Bonds is the only athlete, says Clayton, whom opponents feared. And, as Clayton says, it isn't even close.

There was the game on May 28, 1998, when Arizona Diamondbacks manager Buck Showalter had Bonds intentionally walked with the bases loaded with two outs in the ninth inning—the first time in major-league history that a hitter was, officially, intentionally walked with the bases full. The strategy ultimately worked out in the Diamondbacks' favor as stopper Gregg Olson then retired Brent Mayne on a lineout to right, ending the game in an 8-7 Arizona victory. (Intentional walks have only been an officially tracked statistic since 1955. Before then, at least five other players are believed to have been intentionally walked with the bases full—all having occurred before 1945—but these are unofficial cases based on newspaper accounts of games. Bonds became, at the very least, the first hitter intentionally walked with the bases loaded since the end of World War II.) "You try to give your club the best opportunity to win a game," Showalter said that night, adding that walking Bonds "was better than the option we had."

There were all the other times when opposing managers ordered Bonds to be intentionally walked, not wanting to pitch to him. Advance scouts, whose job description includes providing scouting reports on how their teams could get opposing hitters out, had no answer for how to pitch to Bonds when Barry was slamming home runs in the 2000s. "If it's a game situation where he could drive in the lead run, even if the lead run is himself—don't pitch to him," an advance scout told ESPN.com in 2002. "No one on, tie game—you walk him." In 2003, when he walked 148 times in 130 games, only 36% of the pitches Barry saw were strikes, the lowest frequency in the majors.

"No doubt in my mind he belongs in the Hall of Fame," former Pirates teammate Bobby Bonilla told *The Athletic* in 2020. "I won't sugarcoat it or anything. All I know is I was part of meetings on other teams where they were told not to give B.B. a pitch to hit—period. None. Don't even go near the guy. And he still managed to hit 73 home runs [in 2001]. That's crazy. You can't sell B.B. short at all. He's one of the greatest players of all time. Of all time."

Former Pirates manager Jim Leyland told an AP reporter in 2007 that he didn't want to get into a debate about who was the greatest and who was better. "But I do know this: There's no player in the history of the game," said Leyland, "that's had the impact on the opposing managers that Barry Bonds has had in the last several years, as far as do you walk him? Do you not walk him? Do you pitch to him? Do you not pitch to him? I mean nobody." Added former Giants shortstop Neifi Perez in 2004: "They have to get him in another league. He's not for this league. They need to make another big league for him. It's unbelievable."

Perhaps the game was played and managed differently decades earlier, but even Babe Ruth wasn't feared to the extent that Bonds was in the 2000s. "Why shouldn't we pitch to Ruth?" New York Giants manager John McGraw famously said with bravado during the 1923 World Series, despite the fact that "The Babe" had averaged a major league-leading 47 home runs, with a batting average of .368, between 1920 and 1923. "I've said before, and I'll say it again, we pitch to better hitters than Ruth in the National League."

As far as Royce Clayton is concerned, no team in any other sport feared another athlete the way baseball managers and pitchers feared Barry Bonds in the 1990s and 2000s. "People can say what they want to say. And pile on Barry. Don't put him in the Hall of Fame," Clayton begins. "But here's the deal. I played—and everybody who puts on the uniform plays—for the respect of their peers. And everybody, when I came up as a kid as a 23-year-old shortstop, would ask me about how it is playing with the best player in the game, whether it was Tony Gwynn, Eric Davis, Darryl Strawberry, [Craig] Biggio [and Jeff] Bagwell… Every player in the world wanted to know how it was playing with this dude because he was that much better than everybody else."

Clayton points to all of the walks Bonds received. As of this writing, only 60 players in modern baseball history (since 1900), according to Baseball-Reference.com, have even walked 120 times in a season, period. But in 2004, Barry was intentionally walked a whopping 120 times; pitchers walked him in situations they'd never walked anybody before, and managers had given up on the idea of pitching to him—even when the game wasn't on the line. The last-place Diamondbacks, for instance, once intentionally walked him in a September game with San Francisco already ahead by six runs. Another time, they intentionally walked Bonds in the first inning. "We have about two guys on this staff who can throw to Bonds and throw that perfect pitch," Diamondbacks manager Al Pedrique (a former Bonds teammate in Pittsburgh) later said, adding that the two

pitchers instructed to put Bonds on, rookies Brian Bruney and Edgar
Gonzalez, simply weren't ready to face him. (When Pedrique ordered
the Diamondbacks pitching staff to intentionally walk Bonds again
throughout an entire three-game set against the Giants the following
week, *Sports Illustrated*'s Tom Verducci called the move one of
"professional cowardice.")

To put that number of 120 in perspective, the player who was
second in intentional base on balls that year, Jim Thome, received only
26 intentional walks. And before Bonds broke the record for intentional
walks in a season two years earlier with 68, the major-league mark had
been 45, set by Willie McCovey in 1969. Bonds, who walked 232 times
in total in 2004, was simply playing at his own level, one that no one—
not even Babe Ruth—can match. "You won't see another player [like
Barry]," Clayton continues. "We're playing with and against the best
players in the game, the best players in the world. And he instilled fear in
pitchers I had never seen before in my life. They were scared of him.
They were scared to throw that man a strike. And there's no other player
that you can ever say that I've seen, from Albert Pujols to Mike Trout to
anybody you want to say. They're not scared of any of these guys today.
They pitch to them. They did not pitch to Barry. Scared to death. There's
very few pitchers that would admit it. But everybody knew it." (On that,
not everybody agrees. Former Giants reliever Dustin Hermanson, for
instance, once said late in September 2004, "I don't think a lot of those
pitchers want to walk Barry. They want to go after him, but when your
manager puts up four fingers, what are you supposed to do?")

Clayton pauses for a moment and issues the author a challenge.
"Name me another athlete in any sport [who instilled] that type of fear
in [the opposition], where they were scared to compete against him. Just
answer that." When the author cannot do so—as there simply isn't
anything, in any sport, to compare with Bonds' 2001 to 2004 seasons,
when managers refused to pitch to Barry and intentionally walked him
an average of 71 times per year—the former Giants shortstop laughs.
(Some might argue, though, that NFL linebacker Lawrence Taylor of
the New York Giants, in his prime, was another player head and
shoulders above his peers, one who created fear and was a particular
emphasis of offensive schemes when his opponents played against
him.) "That's something that everybody knew," continues Clayton.
"And that's respect. Fear is respect. If I fear you, I respect you. Name

me another player in any sport that ever commanded that much respect, to where they were scared of him, scared to compete against him. Name me one. I could end the argument about anything that anybody wants to bring up, is to ask them, 'Well, you show me another athlete on this planet that the best in the world were scared to compete against him. Scared.' There's no other way to put it. [You can't even say that about] Kobe [Bryant or] Shaq [O'Neal in basketball]; there was nobody scared to play against them.

"[But] these pitchers were literally scared to compete against Barry Bonds. Scared. The opposing managers were scared. I played against Barry, and our managers were scared to let him beat you. 'Don't let him beat you, because he will.' And he played mind games and tried to embarrass [Cardinals manager] Tony La Russa, into pitching to him. He did, and Barry hit a home run. It's legendary. Like I said, I had the honor and privilege to play with, to me, the best player, the most dominant player in all of professional sports, if you really want to look at it for what it is. That's what Barry Bonds is."

Former Pirates outfielder John Cangelosi, who played in the majors from 1986 to 1999, wouldn't go so far as to say that managers or pitchers were "scared" of Bonds, but he does acknowledge that, since he was already out of the game after the 1999 season, he wasn't sitting in on major-league clubhouse meetings when Bonds was breaking those home-run records. "That one year when he had 73 home runs and all those walks—almost 200 of them—those numbers are sick, man!" Cangelosi—who played against Bonds in the National League while with the Mets, Astros and Marlins—says now. "You look at his on-base percentage. Every [6.5 at-bats] was a home run. He had only 400-and-something at-bats because of all those walks and 73 of them were home runs. That was incredible. [But as far as managers and pitchers are concerned,] they weren't 'afraid' of him. You go into a [team] meeting and [it might be something along the lines of], 'Okay, this situation comes up, we can't let Barry beat us.' Every hitter and pitcher has his own strengths and weaknesses. We're not 'afraid' of Barry, but it's just that if there's a situation in the game where you're going to let Barry Bonds or someone else, you let the other person beat you."

Whether or not anybody was scared to compete against Barry Bonds, both Clayton and Cangelosi have a point. Believe whatever you want about whether Barry took this or took that, the fact that he smacked 73 homers in 2001 is still an incredible feat. He had only 476 official at-bats in 153 games that season, largely because terrified opposing teams walked him a record-setting 177 times (he broke Babe Ruth's single-season record of 170, set in 1923). Long-time skipper Bruce Bochy, who had the unique perspective of managing Bonds and against him during his managerial career, once said, "You're thinking the whole time about having a pitcher ready just for Bonds. If it's the eighth inning and there's a guy on, or two, you're thinking, 'I've got to have somebody ready for Bonds.' He's the focal point. He's that good."

Regarding that last statement, everybody in baseball knew it. The following year, pitchers worked around him at an even more alarming rate, as he shattered the walks record with 198, including 68 intentional. He still managed to hit .370, making him the oldest first-time batting champion, with 46 homers and 110 RBIs in only 403 official at-bats. Then, in 2003, when he walked a major league-leading 148 times in 130 games, only 36% of the pitches he saw were strikes, the lowest frequency in the majors. He still batted .341 with 45 home runs in 390 at-bats. In 2004, he was walked an astonishing 232 times—again shattering his own mark for bases on balls in a single season—yet he homered 45 times in 373 official at-bats in 147 games while batting .362 to capture his second batting title in three years.

With his 45 homers in 2004 while playing home games at SBC Park, one of baseball's worst hitting ballparks, Bonds, who turned 40 on July 24 of that year, broke the single-season record for round-trippers by a 40-year-old, set by Detroit's Darrell Evans, who slammed 34 in 1987 while playing at Tiger Stadium, one of baseball's best hitting parks. (The Giants' home ballpark, whose original name from 2000 and 2003 was Pac Bell Park, was known as SBC Park during the 2004 and 2005 seasons. It was renamed AT&T Park in 2006, and as of 2019 has been known as Oracle Park.) That same year, Bonds, at 40 years and 71 days old, also became the oldest batting champion in big-league history, breaking the original mark set by Ted Williams, who captured his sixth and final batting crown at 40 years and 29 days with a .328 average in 1958. A point worth noting is that Williams had batted .388 in 420 at-bats the year before—"The Splendid Splinter" was still hitting .393 in mid-August in his bid to finish .400 for a season for the second time in his career—and won the 1957 batting title at age 39. "No one that old has ever hit anything close to that number," noted author Kerry Banks in the 2010 book *Baseball's Top 100*, "and no one has ever accused Williams of taking steroids."

Not many will argue that Bonds wasn't the most dominant player of his era. For writer J. P. Hoornstra, covering Bonds late in his career was a unique experience. He'd never seen anyone who had such an aura and a presence about him, an athlete who'd thoroughly mastered his craft and commanded so much attention. "Toward the end of his career, my first job after college was a newspaper in the Bay Area in 2003. I was probably as close as you can be to being in the media. Even though I didn't cover Barry every day, even on the days that I wasn't covering the games he was playing in, I had to edit a newspaper that went out to lots of Giants fans in the Bay Area. I was making news judgments about Barry Bonds' performance on the field in 2003, 2004, 2005 and part of 2006. So, I'd like to think that that qualifies me in the way that it would any BBWAA voter. On a couple of occasions I did interview Barry Bonds in scrums. I was in the same locker room with him. I saw how he interacted with his teammates. I asked Felipe Alou about Barry Bonds many times. I didn't speak to him individually, ever, and I wasn't around him every day. But to the extent that I was around him, it was different. I don't know what it's like to be covering LeBron James on any of the teams that he's played for, but I imagine it's quite similar in that he was so much better than any of his teammates—certainly by the end of his time with the Giants.

"He [garnered such a huge amount of] attention compared to any other player on that team. It's weird to have this guy with 700 home runs and nobody on the team is anywhere in his orbit, even when Jeff Kent won the MVP Award in the National League. Sure, you could make a reasonable case that Kent was as valuable to that team as Bonds was, if not more so, because Kent spent more time on the field, but Bonds was so much more talented that it was surreal to watch somebody who'd mastered the game so thoroughly in comparison to anybody else on his team and, to a degree, in comparison to anybody else on the field playing the game at the time.

"I'd never seen anything like that at the time and I've never seen anything like it since. I mean, Trout is the closest. And I've interacted quite a bit with Trout, and that isn't the same because Trout has had teammates—whether it's Albert Pujols or Shohei Ohtani—who either currently or previously, in Pujols' case, were capable of dominating the game in a way that Trout is. Or at least close to it. In terms of raw hitting ability, the closest thing I can tell you [is that] covering Barry Bonds is like covering Mike Trout. You almost have to see him for a different set of standards, whereby if Trout goes 2-for-4 with two swinging bunt singles, you as a writer could honestly look at that at the end of the day and say, 'Mike Trout did not have a good game.' Let's say he had the only two hits of the game and none of his teammates got a hit. But that doesn't mean I can, with intellectual honesty, go down to Mike Trout after the game and say, 'Mike, you had a good day at the plate. Tell me about that.' No. No, he didn't because, by Mike Trout standards, that's not a good game. He's just that much better than anybody else. The only other time I can really think of having such a completely different set of standards for a player, as a writer and a journalist, is probably Bonds from 2003 to 2006."

And that's part of the problem. Barry Bonds has always been held to a different set of standards.

* * *

It's worth noting that other sports treat alleged "cheaters" differently. Take football, for instance, where, according to former NFL executive Jeff Diamond, "PEDs are perceived by media and fans to be a much bigger no-no than deflated footballs or secretly videotaping opposing [coaches'] signals." The comments of Diamond, former president of the Tennessee Titans and former vice-president/general manager of the Minnesota Vikings, were in reference to the New England Patriots' duo of quarterback Tom Brady and coach Bill Belichick. Brady, a six-time Super Bowl champion with New England, was suspended for four games at the start of the 2016 NFL season for allegedly being part of a scheme to deflate footballs at the 2014 AFC Championship Game against Indianapolis. Belichick, meanwhile, was fined by the league for his role in Spygate, a videotaping scandal in which the Patriots were disciplined for taping New York Jets' defensive coaches' signals during the 2007 season.

Andrew Fillipponi, a Pittsburgh-based sportscaster, brought up this point on Twitter in January 2020: "What's the difference between Bill

Belichick and Barry Bonds? No one says Belichick isn't a Hall of Famer. Belichick was the mastermind behind a massive cheating scheme. And no one doubts his HOF credentials. At all." Pittsburgh radio host Colin Dunlap, meanwhile, tweeted in December 2017 that Brady "is a cheater. A proven one. Such a stain should never go away." He tweeted that "the fact that some don't see Tom Brady in the same light as Bonds" and other alleged "cheaters" was "mind-blowing" to him, adding on 93.7 The Fan, Pittsburgh's CBS affiliate, "I think there's a huge question with Tom Brady. I can't quantify it—and this is just opinion—that he was able to benefit and was able to complete five more passes in his career, 75 [more passes,] if he was able to complete 150 more passes in his career because of both Spygate and Deflategate. Again, the NFL came down on [them]. I didn't make these things up. That's why I have a hard time understanding where to put him among the greats, and not calling him a cheater."

The Spygate and Deflategate scandals have been well-documented. For instance, a *Business Insider* story in 2019 detailed the "cheating scandals" and accusations involving the Patriots during the Belichick-Brady era, suggesting that suspicions about the organization's brush-up against the NFL rule book went as far back as 2001 and citing an ESPN story which stated "league-wide 'paranoia' about how the Patriots would cheat" resulted in the NFL competition committee spending much of 2001-06 discussing theories of how New England might have pulled those tactics off. Many pundits say that those "cheating" controversies, however, are viewed differently from the steroid controversy in baseball.

"It's fascinating to see how alleged 'cheaters' are viewed by fans and media covering various sports and especially the Hall of Fame voters in football and baseball," Diamond opined in a piece written for *The Sporting News* prior to the 2016 NFL season. Although the long-time NFL executive noted he believed Brady and Belichick wouldn't have to wait long to be enshrined in the Pro Football Hall of Fame once they become eligible, he also asked rhetorically: "Why should Brady's fate, linked to fair play rather than PEDs, be different than the baseball outcasts?" One reason, he opined in answering his own question, is the fact that "the baseball voters obviously view alleged cheaters with disdain and clearly do not accept the 'everyone in that era was doing it' argument or the fact that baseball's drug program was essentially nonexistent during the steroid era." Because of that, it's virtually assured that Brady, a four-time Super Bowl MVP known as an athlete with a good image overall and one who's always been cooperative with the media, will receive better treatment when it comes to his own sport's Hall of Fame than Bonds, who was never suspended for PEDs, and other baseball stars linked to steroids.

Although one player alone cannot carry his team to a championship in baseball—and although other sports greats including Patrick Ewing, Charles Barkley, Karl Malone, Barry Sanders and Dan Marino never won championship rings—critics have knocked Bonds for the fact he never led his Pirates or Giants to a World Series title. Critics will say that Bonds wasn't able to lift the level of play of others, whereas an all-time great like Tom Brady, widely considered to be the greatest quarterback of all-time, or Joe Montana, the owner of four Super Bowl rings, could.

Or the way Michael Jordan could, which the five-time NBA Most Valuable Player and six-time NBA Finals MVP proved time after time after time with his six championship rings, including a pair of three-peats (1991-93 and 1996-98).

To Dustan Mohr, that's an unfair comparison. "I never played with Michael Jordan, obviously," Mohr says when asked specifically to discuss the criticism Bonds faced about not being able to lift his teams to championships the way Jordan did in the NBA. "I've seen a lot of things and watched a lot of things. I think he was very vocal to his teammates. It wasn't just him going out there and being Michael Jordan. He knew how to do that. Barry didn't say a lot during games. He didn't really get excited a whole lot. He stayed kind of even keel, one level. I think that could be where that came from. He wasn't sort of a cheerleader, and he rarely said very much. He was always watching the game, the pitcher, to see what's going on. That's just how he went about it. I think that that's what [Bonds' critics] would be referring to. He just wasn't that way. He was different from Michael Jordan in the sense that he didn't talk a lot. He just did his thing and played. Maybe they—those who said that—would've wanted him to be a little more engaged in terms of rooting for his teammates. I'm not saying he wasn't rooting us on; I'm just saying that he just didn't talk a whole lot. He was just focused, and making sure that he took care of his job. That's the way I viewed it."

Royce Clayton, meanwhile, refutes the myth that Bonds didn't lift the level of play of his teammates in San Francisco. From Day One of spring training in 1993, says the former Giants shortstop, Bonds, in his first year with the Giants, gave the rest of the team a swagger they hadn't seen before on that ballclub. "Man, Barry brought that swag to the team, and it didn't just affect me," Clayton says. "It affected everybody that was a part of it. Some players, I'm sure, didn't particularly care for it. But when all was said and done, man, that team was together and bonded. Everybody carried that same personality, that same swag that Barry brought to us."

Even during spring training, John Patterson says, Bonds wasn't about to let the opposition bully the Giants. Patterson, a utility second baseman with the Giants from 1992 to 1995, recalls an incident at Scottsdale Stadium when the Padres' Phil Plantier was hogging the batting cage and wouldn't leave—even after Bonds politely told him time was up. "It was funny. I was heading down to the cage when all of that took place," Patterson says now. "As the story goes, Plantier was down there hitting. It's timed, where you take 10 swings or whatever. Plantier was taking swings. Barry goes, 'Hey, your time is up.' I don't think Plantier realized who was telling him that. So, Plantier kept swinging, and Barry then just went in and interrupted his B.P. It was pretty obvious that Barry came out on top of all that."

What Patterson recounts is the clean version, but as the story goes, Plantier told Bonds to "fuck off," only to have Barry respond by saying, "You don't say shit like that in my house!" and swatting the Padres outfielder across the face with the back of his hand. The incident was the talk of the Giants clubhouse for the rest of spring training, because Bonds' attitude was new and fresh for the team. "Nobody else on our team would have had the balls to do that, but Barry did," confirms Patterson. And when the team took the field throughout that season, Bonds' presence simply lifted the confidence of every Giants player. "You knew you had the best player and he was hitting third [in the lineup]," says Patterson. "He was durable and he could put his team on his back for a month if he was hot. You always had a chance to win. He could do it basically with all five tools: He was a Gold Glover [and] he could steal bases, hit bombs [and] take a walk if he had to. He was just a stud."

When asked about that Plantier incident, Clayton puts it this way: "As far as how we went about it, [the attitude became] 'This is our situation. This is our team. We're gonna win this whole situation in the NL West or whatever comes before us.' And, like I said, Barry brought that swag to the team and it affected everybody." That was certainly true, as the Giants were transformed into a team which every National League club feared in 1993, going from a mediocre 72-90 fifth-place outfit in 1992 to a 103-win powerhouse, which in any other year would have been good enough for a division title or, at the very least, a postseason berth under today's wild-card format. "That '93 team was a special team," reflects Clayton. "We won 103 games [but] came up one game short. And this was before the [era of the wild card and expanded] playoffs. Man, I don't think there was any team in Major League Baseball that wanted to play us."

Thus, to suggest that Bonds, whose teams finished either first or second in their division 14 times in his 22 big-league seasons, never lifted the level of play of his teammates the way that a Michael Jordan could would be hogwash. His presence in the Giants' batting lineup boosted the performance of virtually every player who hit in front of or behind him. Bonds was such a dangerous hitter that he was walked more than anyone else in baseball, whether it was 1993 or 2003—Barry, the all-time leader in that category with 2,558 walks, led the league in walks 12 times while finishing second four other times—meaning pitchers had to throw strikes to the hitters in front of and behind Barry to avoid walking multiple batters in a row. Thus, other Giants saw more pitches over the plate, boosting their chances of getting a hit.

As for the oft-reported stories of Bonds not stretching on the field with the rest of the Giants players before batting practice? Not something that his teammates cared about. Besides, Bonds had played for Jim Leyland in Pittsburgh, where the Pirates skipper never cared if players stretched before the game. "Just prepare yourself," Bonds, who by then was already used to his own pre-game preparation, recalled years later of Leyland's message in Pittsburgh. "That was the best team I ever played on," third baseman Matt Williams, a member of the Giants' 1989 World   Series team who later reached the Series with Cleveland in 1997 and won a ring with the 2001 Diamondbacks, said years later, referring to the 1993 club. "We all benefited from Barry showing up. He was the best left fielder I've ever seen. The best hitter I've ever seen. So what if he wasn't out there to stretch with us? I didn't care."

* * *

In December 2007, former Senator George J. Mitchell released a 409-page report—informally known as the Mitchell Report—that tied 89 Major League Baseball players to the use of illegal, performance-enhancing drugs. The report, which was completed following a 20-month investigation into the use of anabolic steroids and human growth hormone in Major League Baseball, used informant testimony and supporting documents to provide a portrait of what Mitchell described as "baseball's steroids era," with players from all 30 teams being named—including more than a dozen who'd had significant roles with the Yankees and 11 players from the 2000 Los Angeles Dodgers. Although more than 700 people, including 60 former players and two active players, were interviewed during the investigation, Mitchell acknowledged that his report was inhibited by limited cooperation and the absence of subpoena power, and that there was still much about drug use in baseball that he didn't know.

The Mitchell Report was critical of the commissioner's office and the players' union for knowingly tolerating performance-enhancing drugs, citing numerous instances where club officials knew about particular steroid use among players and did not report it. Mitchell himself stated, "There was a collective failure to recognize the problem as it emerged and to deal with it early on," adding that "baseball's steroids era" started roughly in 1988 but it took 15 more years for baseball to start random testing. Larry Starr, a trainer for 30 years with the Reds and Marlins between 1972 and 2002, was interviewed by Mitchell's investigators several times, but his information was entirely omitted from the final report. Starr, however, has spoken freely about the subject with the press, once telling a reporter, "I have notes from the Winter Meetings where the owners group and the players' association sat in meetings with the team physicians and team trainers. I was there. And team physicians stood up and said, 'Look, we need to do something about this. We've got a problem here if we don't do something about it.' That was in 1988."

As for Commissioner Bud Selig's claim that he didn't know about the steroid issue in baseball until 1998, Starr was unconvinced. In a 2009 interview with a Chicago writer, Starr suggested that if the commissioner's office hadn't turned a blind eye to the use of performance-enhancing drugs that started in the 1980s, the so-called Steroid Era might have been avoided. "Someone ought to ask Mr. Selig whether he had any suspicion at all. Was there any one time from 1990 to 2003 that you had any suspicion that people were doing something wrong or cheating? If he says no to that question, he must not have watched many games."

He wasn't calling Selig a liar, but he offered the following story when he suggested the commissioner must not have been paying attention when the commissioner claimed he didn't know baseball had a steroid problem. "I used to have a neighbor across the street, a 45-year-old lady who is a big baseball fan," Starr said. "Every time I took the garbage out, she would corner me and talk baseball. She would inevitably ask me what's wrong with these players because they look like giants and are hitting balls one-handed out of the ballpark. If she's seeing it and is only watching 20 to 30 games a year, [you would think] someone who has spent a lifetime in the game would notice something."

Others have questioned Selig's leadership—or lack thereof—during the Steroid Era, criticizing the commissioner for not taking an active enough role to stem the tide of steroid use in baseball until it had blossomed into a debilitating problem for the industry. The actions of Selig, who initially served as the acting commissioner in 1992 before being named the official commissioner in 1998, were "either dishonest or incompetent—or both," opined David Locke in a 2005 piece titled "Steroid Scandal Means It's Time for Selig to Say Goodbye" in the *Seattle Post-Intelligencer*. Critics are quick to point out that we knew about steroids all along, yet baseball didn't have an official steroid policy until 2002 and MLB didn't begin widespread testing for performance-enhancing drugs until 2003. The Mitchell Report, for instance, lists 85 newspaper and magazine articles between 1987 and 1998 that discussed suspicions of increasing steroid use in baseball, right up until an Associated Press reporter noticed a bottle of androstenedione—a testosterone-producing supplement—in Mark McGwire's locker and MLB was forced to address the issue. In 1995, Padres general manager Randy Smith was widely quoted as estimating steroid use among 10 to 20% of major-league players. But nobody cared; fans got the home runs they wanted, as baseballs were flying over fences and into the stands at an unprecedented rate, with a single-season record of 4,962 homers being hit during the 1996 season. The *New York*

Daily News reported in February 2005 that Major League Baseball security ignored an FBI agent who warned about the game's growing steroid problem 10 years earlier, when special agent Greg Stejskal, who'd gathered enough evidence during a steroid investigation he conducted, told an official in the MLB security office in 1995 or 1996 that Jose Canseco and many other players were using illegal anabolic steroids. Baseball, said the agent, did not act on the information.

"The sad thing is all these GMs, they all knew it," former knuckleball pitcher Tom Candiotti laments now, referring to the sport's growing steroid problem. "Everyone in baseball knew it." Then, there was the time when McGwire was caught with androstenedione in 1998 and said, "Everybody else is using the same thing I am," but Selig didn't launch a study into andro until 1999. "The study revealed what the Olympics and the NFL knew: It is a steroid," Locke remarked. "Shockingly, it still took Selig until 2002 to ban andro. He ignored the escalating calamity for three more years before constructing a policy."

Critics have opined that Selig turned a blind eye to the use of PEDs because the long ball was what brought fans to the ballpark; baseball was still recovering from the 1994 players' strike and the game needed offense, so the commissioner made the decision that the steroid issue wasn't worth fighting. "Selig's version of leadership includes gag orders on anyone in baseball," added Locke. "When Padres general manager Kevin Towers admitted in spring training he was aware of the steroid issue, he was summoned back to San Diego where he was scolded and told to pipe down."

Nonetheless, Bud Selig is in the Hall of Fame, elected by the Veterans Committee and inducted as part of the 2017 class. If the commissioner who oversaw the sport during the Steroid Era is in the Hall of Fame, Bonds' supporters have asked, what is the logic for keeping Barry Bonds out? (Selig, meanwhile, has reminded his critics that he began negotiating in 2002 with the Players Association to implement steroid testing. "Let me say this, I fought long and hard for the [drug-testing] program," Selig said in 2017, "and we put in the toughest program in North American sports. It's ridiculous to think anything else.")

Not only is Selig in the Hall of Fame, but championship teams with players linked to PEDs are still being celebrated. Despite the fact the

Mitchell Report listed key members of the Yankees' World Series teams in the Joe Torre era, for instance, there was no national outcry for those championship teams to have an asterisk added to their accomplishments in the record books. According to a 2008 piece on ESPN.com, Torre managed 20 of the 86 players named in the Mitchell report, more than any other big-league skipper (although many of those players played only briefly for Torre and did all or most of their alleged doping while with other clubs). But as ESPN.com's contributors spoke to Torre and Tony La Russa, both Hall of Fame managers, along with current and former players, trainers, front office officials and owners, a picture emerged of a culture in which loyalty and secrecy trumped integrity— and winning trumped everything. "Baseball," noted ESPN.com, "was practically an incubator for performance-enhancing drugs because almost everyone in a position to speak up chose not to."

When asked his thoughts about PEDs in the game, Torre acknowledged he was torn by his desire to see the game remain clean while needing to support his players. "You've got to manage these players and you want to earn their trust, so you've got to allow them responsibility to take care of themselves," he explained. "I'm not saying you don't talk about it. You're always cautioning them that you don't want to be embarrassed by this or that. [But] you don't follow players around or peek around the corner or whatever." As La Russa put it, "This is America, you know. It's not a police state."

Hall of Fame pitcher Tom Glavine added that any major-leaguer or coach who might have suspected steroid abuse was unlikely to speak up, simply because of the game's culture: What goes on in the clubhouse—whether it's team fights or arguments or other scandals— stays in the clubhouse. "All that stuff is supposed to remain in-house," Glavine explained in 2008. "That's the culture of the game and it doesn't matter if a guy has a drinking problem, or a guy is doing drugs or a guy is doing things in their marriages they shouldn't be doing. You just don't discuss that." All that has ever mattered, Glavine added, is performance. And, of course, the use of PEDs by teammates often helped the ballclub. "And therein lies the problem," continued Glavine, who explained that in his case he didn't want to believe that players would be taking PEDs. "If they are going out there on the field and performing, then there is reason for everybody in the whole chain of command to not worry so much about what is going on. The end result is the guy is performing; and when guys are performing, everybody wants to leave him alone and let him do [his] thing."

Former pitcher Tom Candiotti says everybody in baseball knew about the growing steroid problem—well before the late 1990s. "It's funny because everyone's talking about all the PEDs [more than a generation later], after the testing with A-Rod [Alex Rodriguez] and all these guys in the early 2000s," says Candiotti now, "and I'm going, 'Whoa, wait a minute.' All this stuff was happening way back in the 1990s and even the 1980s, but they just happen to call that the 'Steroid Era' or whatever because he was doing it and he flunked a test or whatever, but there's plenty of guys that were doing it back then." But, as many former players, including Candiotti, acknowledge, when players were performing, everybody just left them alone and let them continue producing.

* * *

One could make the argument that fans seem conflicted about performance-enhancing drugs. On social media today they call out players whom they perceive to be cheaters, and yet, despite the BALCO steroids scandal, they showed up at major-league ballparks in record numbers in 2005 (with attendance figures at an all-time high of 74,915,268). They continued to show up despite the fact that the Congressional hearing in March of 2005—in which several prominent major-leaguers, along with commissioner Bud Selig and MLB Players Association executive director Donald Fehr, were summoned to testify in front of Congress—made the sport look bad. Attendance figures increased yet again in each of the next two seasons (76,043,902 and 79,484,718)—and did not decrease significantly in 2008 (78,624,315) even after the Mitchell Report—the result of Senator George J. Mitchell's 20-month investigation into the use of anabolic steroids and human growth hormone in MLB—was released following the 2007 season.

Fans want to see home runs and boo when there's a drop-off in production of their favorite players (the mentality of sports fans, after all, is "What have you done for me lately?" and "It's all about what you do next"), yet when players do use performance-enhancers to achieve the gaudy numbers that are expected and demanded, fans are turned off. For a prime example of the fans' being conflicted, look at Yankees

141

slugger Jason Giambi, who admitted during his 2003 testimony to a federal grand jury in the BALCO case that he'd taken steroids. Details of his grand jury testimony were leaked to the press in December of 2004, and when Giambi slumped at the beginning of the 2005 season, Yankees fans booed and heckled him for his admitted drug use. Yet when Giambi finished the year with a .271 average, 32 home runs and 87 RBIs—a dramatic improvement over his 2004 showing of .208, 12 homers and 40 RBIs in 80 games—those same fans voted him "Major League Baseball Comeback Player of the Year" (fans voted for the winner in 2005, the first year MLB established the award, which is different from the award given out by *The Sporting News*)—in spite of the fact he might only have been coming back from self-inflicted problems related to his use of illegal drugs.

Ironically, during commercials while watching a game on television, fans are routinely bombarded with images of products promising magical pain relief, better sexual performance, more hair and other miracle cures. Somewhere, there was always a pill that could make every problem disappear, including erectile dysfunction. Besides, was it really important if baseball was phony, that the game was played by chemically-enhanced ballplayers? Wasn't baseball— like other sports—just a great escape from the stress of everyday life, a form of entertainment to distract fans for a few hours every night? And if fans wanted home runs—and many fans do enjoy the home runs and strikeout pitchers—weren't they getting what they wanted from players who were using enhancers to attain them?

Tom Trebelhorn, who managed the Cubs in 1994 when Sammy Sosa was in his third season with the North Siders, once praised the Chicago slugger's work ethic in a 2012 interview with the author— saying that Sosa's drive and determination were a big part of the success in his career—before adding, unprompted, that critics were unfair and being too judgmental with their constant "Did he take it? Did he not take it?" questions about which ballplayers were taking performance-enhancing drugs. "In fact, every generation's got some kind of substances that supposedly helped them," added Trebelhorn in the same interview. "In the old days, [it was] amphetamines. In Babe Ruth's era, you could get cocaine at the drugstore... There's all kinds of different stuff going on. So, I think it's unfair, really, to get excited the way we are [when it's reported in the news that certain players took these] supposedly performance-enhancing drugs—because who doesn't take them? I mean, you talk about Viagra and Cialis… What's more performance-enhancing than that? Those same guys [baseball fans] who are taking that are going, 'Oh, those records shouldn't count because of this and that.' Well, then your record shouldn't count [either]!"

Trebelhorn's counterargument was valid: What, after all, is cheating? That's the exact question Barry Bonds asked while speaking to the press in the spring of 2005, when he didn't admit to steroid use but rationalized it. "You're talking about something that wasn't even illegal [in the game] at the time," Bonds said. "All this stuff about supplements, protein shakes, whatever. Man, it's not like this is the Olympics. We don't train four years for, like, a 10-second [event]. We go 162 games. You've got to come back day after day after day. We're entertainers. If I can't go out there and somebody pays $60 for a ticket, and I'm not in the lineup, who's getting cheated? Not me. There are far worse things like cocaine, heroin and those types of things. So we all make mistakes. We all do things. We need to turn the page. We need to forget about the past and let us play the game. We're entertainers. Let us entertain." Bonds then asked, rhetorically, what the definition of cheating was, wondering if it was "cheating" to make a shirt in Korea for $1.50 and sell it for $500 in the United States. He added, "You can't see, things look fuzzy, so what do you do? You go get glasses. Is that cheating? You get glasses so you can see, so you can do your job. What's the difference?" On the other hand, Bonds also said, "I tell my boy [son Nikolai], 'If I see you doing steroids, I'll bust you up.'"

Those who believe that the Steroid Era was no surprise and that we should simply accept it, meanwhile, have also made some compelling arguments over the years. For starters, modern ballplayers were going to start breaking records because baseball was trending in that direction. Hall of Famer Mike Schmidt is one who subscribes to that theory. "One thing everyone can agree on is this: even if steroids had never been invented, it got easier to hit a home run after 1990," the former Phillies third baseman once wrote. "Harder balls, maple bats, small parks, small strike zones, fewer inside pitches, elbow pads and yes, bigger biceps (whether produced by hours of hard work in a gym or a series of injections in the butt), all combined to increase home-run totals."

Indeed. Modern baseball players, like in other sports, were getting bigger and stronger. By the 1990s, baseball players had realized that lifting weights—with or without steroids—made them stronger and it didn't ruin their swing. Other factors also contributed to the explosion of offense in baseball in the decade: Two rounds of expansion (in 1993 and 1998), along with injuries, diluted available pitching talent more than hitting talent. Furthermore, pundits opined, pitchers couldn't pitch inside—the tactic of throwing a pitch close to the batter to make it more difficult for him to swing the bat—without starting a brawl. "That's why stat guru Bill James has said steroids may have had minimal impact on home-run totals," attorney and baseball author David Ezra, citing several of the aforementioned factors, reminded readers on USNews.com in 2009.

Besides, Bonds was hardly the only one reaching career highs in home runs at an advanced age, Ezra added. "As soon as 37-year-old Carlton Fisk bought a Nautilus machine and changed his diet, then went out and hit 37 home runs in 1985 (11 more than he ever hit in his 'prime'), Maris' record was doomed," he noted, referring to the Hall of Fame catcher known for his Herculean exercise regimen. "Born bigger and faster, modern players were avoiding alcohol and tobacco, watching their diets and hiring strength coaches. Of course they were going to break records. Ted Williams, Hank Aaron, Jim Rice—they never lifted weights. Barry Bonds trained four hours a day in a sweaty weight room and we're shocked when he hits a lot of home runs. Please!" (That brings up the point where some refuse to point any accusatory fingers despite the *San Francisco Chronicle*'s reporting that Bonds admitted before a grand jury to inadvertently taking steroids. "Who's to say you can't get that big?" Mets outfielder Cliff Floyd told the *New York Daily News* in 2006. "Am I being naive? You might say so. I don't feel I am. I'm saying, if you worked out three times a day, your body will change. I don't care how old you are. I don't care how small you are. Your body will change.")

A second argument made for simply accepting the Steroid Era is that baseball has always found ways to do only some minor tinkering if its leadership wanted offense. "Look at 1930," Ezra continued. "With the stock market crash heralding the Great Depression, a shot in the arm might boost attendance. Presto! A tighter baseball with less prominent seams went farther when hit and was less apt to curve when pitched." That season, as the records show, the entire National

League batted .303 and the Cubs' Hack Wilson, who was only 5-foot-6, homered 56 times and drove in 191 runs. Ten major-leaguers batted .367 or higher, including Chuck Klein (.386, 40 home runs and 170 RBIs) and Al Simmons (.381, 36 and 165 in the same categories). When home runs dropped from 1,565 in 1930 to only 1,088 the following season, baseball fans accepted the decline as "there were no steroids to blame for 1930's excess; no steroid testing or perjury trials to blame for 1931's precipitous decline," Ezra noted. Of course, despite the absurdity of the numbers compiled by Wilson, Klein and Simmons in 1930—all of whom are Hall of Famers—we'd never suggest that their stats be wiped out of the record books.

How does 1930 relate to the Steroid Era? Well, following the 1994 strike, baseball wanted offense and fans got the home runs they wanted. The Steroid Era is part of the game's history, just as 1968, when the pitcher's mound was raised, is a part of baseball history. "Nobody thought about putting an asterisk next to Bob Gibson's numbers when he dominated after the pitcher's mound was raised,"

Steve Lyons, who played nine season in the big leagues from 1985 to 1993 before becoming a television sportscaster, once said. "They didn't alter the record books during the 'dead ball' era to account for the lack of home runs hit." Every generation in the sport's history has its faults, but nobody is calling for wholesale eradication of the multiple generations of players who used amphetamines. Nobody's trying to revoke Gaylord Perry's Hall of Fame pass because he threw a spit ball or Whitey Ford's Hall pass because he doctored baseballs, either. Nobody's trying to remove Ty Cobb from Cooperstown because he sharpened his spikes—just in case he had to come in cleats up to take out a shortstop on a double play. Nobody thinks Babe Ruth's statistics are tarnished or illegitimate because he never played in a racially integrated league. "You simply have to recognize the era for what it is," as Lyons once said, "and move on."

But when it became convenient for the media and fans to use Barry Bonds or other players they didn't like as scapegoats for home-run records being broken, they blamed steroids for everything. Case in point? Now, when a pitcher has a better year than he did the previous season, whispers about HGH use surface. (After Cubs ace Jake Arrieta, for instance, had a breakout season in 2015—and threw no-hitters in both 2015 and 2016—the following spring he had to endure unfounded accusations by the media that he was aided by the use of performance-enhancing drugs. And it wasn't just the press; even some of the best players in the game, Arrieta revealed, were spreading baseless rumors that he was using PEDs.) If an infielder hits 30 home runs now, people wonder if steroids are part of the reason. Blaming steroids for everything, though, is oversimplifying things. Steroids couldn't help players refine their batting eye or hit Randy Johnson's slider.

For every alleged steroid user who thrived, another was mediocre. Marvin Benard, for instance, admitted to the Associated Press in 2010 that he used steroids during the 2002 season to deal with a nagging knee injury, but he wasn't breaking home-run records. He batted .276 with one home run in 123 at-bats. Or take the Giambi brothers, both of whom were BALCO steroid/HGH users in 2003, as we're told. One hit 41 home runs; the other batted .197 with five homers and one strikeout every three at-bats. Or the Cansecos, with Jose hitting 462 career major-league homers and twin brother Ozzie going homerless. Perhaps, some have argued, that's why the Mitchell Report revealed that "a number of studies have shown that use of human growth hormone does not increase muscle strength in healthy subjects or well-trained athletes."

With respect to the Hall of Fame, some have argued that it didn't make any sense for some players to be suspected of possibly doing PEDs, and other players from the exact same era be assumed to be 100% clean, especially when performance-enhancing drugs didn't necessarily make baseball players look like NFL linebackers. Those who make this argument will point out that the entire era is tainted, and there's absolutely no way for anybody to know who was clean and who wasn't. A case in point is that the first major-league player suspended for using PEDs was outfielder Alex Sanchez, who stood at 5'10" and weighed 180 pounds—and had four career home runs in 1,351 at-bats at the time of his suspension. Several others who have been caught using PEDs and steroids included players who didn't exactly have bodybuilder-type bodies, either.

But, of course, some players who failed drug tests during their careers have been forgiven. Bonds, meanwhile, never failed a drug test, yet, as of his writing, still doesn't have a plaque in Cooperstown. "I know there's something in him that would like to be in the Hall of

Fame," Royce Clayton says. "But I'm sure there's another side of him that doesn't really care, because he understands what he did and he understands what he represented. This is the media's last control mechanism to have something over this man, and they're holding on to it, because they couldn't do anything to stop him from what he did on the field. And that's the power that he still has.

"[As for] some of these players [who'd failed drug tests] going out on these campaigns and to try and get people to forget—and trick people—I'll say it out loud. I think it's a travesty that A-Rod—who's tested positive twice—is being glorified [and] my kids have to watch this man on TV. Why is baseball allowing him to be on networks and TV and all these other things, knowing that he disgraced the game? Twice! And I'm very adamant about it because I didn't do it. I played 17 years without touching that stuff. But they pick and choose who they want to put on the forefront... [As far as PEDs being prevalent in the game] everybody knew it. I competed against them. I know. You pick and choose who you want to put in there, and turn a blind eye to what they did and yet you want to scrutinize Barry. But that's the just world we live in. But who cares? There's no stopping it. It's racist as hell, absolutely. That's what this country was built on. Let them have it. Who cares?

"But we know who was going out there and playing ball, and dominating the game the way that he did. There's nothing that's going to erase that. It's already done."

* * *

Barry Bonds was generally considered someone who was not going to be kind to an interview request, and not someone who was gracious or cooperative with his time in that regard. But... "Everybody was the same," Dustan Mohr says, saying that Barry wasn't the only player who didn't always feel like talking to the media—or to anybody else, for that matter. The press, however, picked on Barry just because he's Barry. He certainly wasn't the first high-profile professional athlete to be difficult with media members requesting an interview to do a story. He won't be the last. Yet other athletes, even among his contemporaries, aren't singled out or remembered for that.

One example is NBA superstar Clyde Drexler. In 2014, Richard

Hoffer, the same writer who penned "The Importance of Being Barry," recounted another *Sports Illustrated* assignment from 1993-94, when he traveled to Portland to do a story on the Trail Blazers' Drexler. The future Basketball Hall of Famer, however, kept Hoffer waiting for about two days, at which point the writer, not wanting to waste his time, decided to just scrap the story and return home. The Clyde Drexler story ended up not being written. Another example is Blue Jays left-hander David Wells, who during the first half of the 2000 MLB season registered an incredible 14-2 record and was going to be featured in a story in *Sports Illustrated*. However, the Toronto pitcher refused to be interviewed for the story, with the reason being that a few seasons earlier he'd posed for a picture as Santa Claus which was supposed to go on the *SI* cover but it didn't. After a similar incident happened again, Wells informed *SI* representatives that he wouldn't be talking to them anymore. The writer assigned to interview him for the 2000 piece, Jeff Pearlman, ended up writing the story using quotes from Wells from other sources.

Clyde Drexler and David Wells are just two examples of athletes on a long list of sportspeople who didn't cooperate with the press. Of course, today, the fact that they didn't speak with *SI* has likely been long forgotten. As for Bonds, who actually did speak to the writer in 1993? Hoffer, the writer who did the Bonds piece, was interviewed in a 2014 story for SI.com as part of the magazine's 60th anniversary, with "The Importance of Being Barry" being republished in full, bringing that story back to the forefront.

Royce Clayton brings up that *Sports Illustrated* story about Bonds and shares Barry's side of the story. "One of the things I did want to say that very few people know, is that during that '93 season, Barry lived right down the street from me, and he'd come over all the time. I'd go over to his house and eat with him. He would come over. This reporter, whom I didn't know at the time, started following Barry around. Everywhere we'd go, this guy was around and just kind of following Barry," Clayton says, referring to Hoffer. "I asked Barry, 'Who's this dude, man?' He's like, 'Oh, it's a writer from *Sports Illustrated*. I'm finally going to do an article…' Barry never let anybody into his life. He never talked to the media in that respect. So, I saw this go on for a couple of weeks. One day, I kinda forgot about it. Barry comes knocking on the door. He had a *Sports*

Illustrated article in his hand. He slapped it down on the coffee table. And he said, 'Man, this is why I don't talk to these people.' It really hurt him. I looked at the cover. It's a picture of him leaning on a bat and it says, 'I'm Barry Bonds, and You're Not.' To do that, and to portray him in the way that they did, after he opened up to this man, I felt was a slap in the face. It was disrespectful. And it was uncalled for. From that point on, Barry never dealt with the media. He just never did. I think it's something that drove him."

Bonds has certainly been sharing his perspective with those he trusts, including Clayton. Whenever he gave interviews, Barry would wonder how things were going to be edited, believing the media might twist the narrative to make him look bad because that's precisely what he'd experienced earlier in his career. "None of them know me anyway," Bonds once said during his Pittsburgh days, referring to his critics in the media who made it seem he couldn't do anything right. "They know me from the time they come into the locker room and want to do an interview. Most of the time, it's a bad time. A lot of them get upset if I want to sit in the training room and collect my thoughts and relax."

The focus, he believed, should be on his accomplishments on the field, not what he did off the diamond. "Reporters don't give people exciting things to talk about. When they talk [negatively] about players, they're depriving the fans. They're making people come out here and boo you and scream at you, but this is America's pastime and everybody should be able to enjoy it… When they make players look bad, all it does is take dreams and hopes away from little kids. I've never had any problems with the fans. The fans have only had problems with what they've read and believe. I'm not trying to give anybody a bad influence and I haven't done anything to hurt anyone. I'm trying to do the best that I can. But I can't satisfy everybody." As if that wasn't enough, there was also the fact that the press was often expecting him to do the impossible—simply because his father was Bobby Bonds. "Everybody thinks just because your dad was a major-league player, you had special privileges that made you a better player. If that was the case, everybody who's been in this game, all their kids would be playing. There's a lot of good ballplayers who didn't have fathers that played in the majors. Babe Ruth is one of them. Where's his son?"

What he didn't say publicly then was the fact that what was written about him hurt him a great deal—which Royce Clayton alludes to—but Bonds addressed that point years after his career ended. "You're human. We're human. And you get your feelings hurt. Mine got hurt a lot more," he acknowledged in a rare interview in 2019. "For somebody to come up to me—and I'm just a human, a person, I'm just a baseball player, just a person, and I'm trying to do the best I can out here that your money can buy, and it's not going to be perfect—and I have someone that says, 'I want to do this wonderful piece on you.' And next minute it's like, 'Bonds [blah blah blah with a negative spin].' And I'm like, 'Wait a minute. Didn't we just have an earlier conversation about how wonderful this was going to be?' And I got [Bonds blah blah blah]. I took it to heart. That physically and mentally hurt me. Then when I got to the point in my career where I could dictate it my own way, I was a brat. I got even. That's how I'd sum it up. I said, 'Okay. Now you need to talk to me, you ain't talking to me because you were the one who said you were gonna be nice to me, and then you weren't nice to me. So, now you're never going to talk to me.' And so I went to the extreme because of the OCD in my head. That introvert, loner person said, 'Go straight to hell.' And then I couldn't get out of it. Then I got caught in it. That's when I said, maybe if I can perform, I can ease it, because I'm never going to say the right thing…"

Clayton understands Bonds well because Barry shared his viewpoints with him when the pair were teammates. "There are things that he taught me and told me that I'll keep to myself, about certain things that kept his fire burning, because we all need something to drive us as athletes," Clayton continues, before implying that race played a part in the way Bonds was treated by the press. "But this is something that he carried for me, for all of us, for all African-Americans, but he took it out on that baseball. I'll tell you that much. But just the things that [relate to] people's perceptions and how they cast people. Look, people are different. I was fortunate enough to play for 11 different teams. There's all different types of personalities. Nobody's perfect. If you worked for Bank of America, there's introverted people. There's people who are more social. But they're just people, at the end of the day, that have feelings and they have kids. And to have somebody that disrespects you and write things about you that casts a light that you don't want shed, it doesn't encapsulate everything about that man, I felt was just wrong. And I don't think he'll ever get a fair shake as far as the media perspective. But at the end of the day, who gives a shit? That's the way I look at it. And that's another thing he told me. The media is as powerful as you let them be. I'll have to give you the power in order for you to have some type of power. But if I take that power away from you, you're powerless. And I think that's what Barry did. He just took the power away from the media. His embodiment of what he went out there and did on the field spoke volumes of what he was, which is the best player to ever play the game."

Clayton's comments about the power of the media are worth exploring. As can be seen with the 1998 McGwire-Sosa home-run chase, the media played a key role in squashing the androstenedione controversy when Associated Press writer Steve Wilstein's story about the bottle of androstenedione found in the locker of Mark McGwire came out. It was an example of how powerful the media could be; the press crushed the story instead of investigating further into it. Conversely, when the media wants readers to know something, it gets written about.

In the case of Bonds and Cooperstown, some pundits are of the opinion that Hall of Fame voters are punishing Barry for the way he treated the media during his playing career—by keeping him out of the Hall.

Hogwash, says former New York *Newsday* sports editor Adrian Brijbassi when asked his opinion on whether he believes the writers who have refused to vote for Bonds are doing so because of the way Barry dealt with the press. "If he was the only one of that group who's not in the Hall of Fame, you can make that case a little more strongly," says Brijbassi, who was at *Newsday* when the BALCO case broke. "But I think because some others of his peers who were also caught cheating [or suspected of cheating] haven't been elected, you can say that there's been equal treatment for people caught in the BALCO scandal [or linked to PEDs]. And also, Barry Bonds wasn't the only player who was tough on the press. The Hall of Fame has a number of them who have been elected, so I think it would be unfair to the writers to allege that they've been holding him to a higher standard than they have other players who have been elected before him, and that someone like Mark McGwire, considered very decent to the press, isn't in the Hall of Fame as well."

Sports columnist Dieter Kurtenbach, who has opined in the *San Jose Mercury News* that Bonds belongs in the Hall of Fame, shares a different view. He has suggested that the writers were the ones who were unfair, bringing up the fact that the baseball world didn't care about performance-enhancing drugs during the 1998 Mark McGwire-Sammy Sosa home-run chase. Nor did they care, Kurtenbach noted, when Baltimore's Brady Anderson smacked 50 homers in 1996—after the Orioles leadoff hitter had averaged 16 round-trippers in the previous four seasons. But the writers' attitudes toward PEDs only changed, he added, after Bonds started hitting home run after home run after home run. "[I believe] that it was his less-than-warm temperament, not his PED use, that's holding him back from [Hall of Fame] enshrinement," Kurtenbach wrote in 2018. "Remember, everyone loved the home run race of 1998, which helped make baseball the cash cow it is today. The sport had no problem turning a blind eye to PED usage then. (Remember Brady Anderson?) But once the less-than-gregarious Bonds hit 73 homers in a season, the blind eye towards PED use was pulled wide open. Perhaps that was a coincidence, but I doubt it."

Casey Olson, a Seattle-based sportswriter, has argued that steroids weren't a banned substance until the 2000s and PEDs were just part of baseball's culture in the late 1990s. "And that is why it is so hard for me to stomach a lot of the baseball writers singling out Bonds and Clemens when plenty of other players were doing the exact same thing." A big reason that Bonds and Clemens, Olson opined, were "getting a brunt of the ire from the writers and the general public is because they were always surly with the media and because they were, by most accounts, not very nice human beings."

Kurtenbach and Olson certainly weren't alone with the viewpoint that the writers who haven't voted for Bonds are simply punishing him for the way he'd dealt with the press. Over the years, in fact, writers have admitted to peers that they punished players by not voting them for the Hall for precisely that reason. Former White Sox and Mets beat writer T. J. Quinn wrote in 2012 that he enjoyed his role as a Hall of Fame voter, before adding, "But too often, I've seen writers use their votes as a way to punish or reward players, and I don't think journalists should be in that position." Although most of the writers he knew took their votes seriously, added Quinn, who gave up his Hall of Fame vote in 2010, he'd "heard other writers say they couldn't wait for certain players to make the ballot so they could leave their names unchecked." For instance? "Eddie Murray's name came up that way more than once," he noted. "I voted for Albert Belle because I thought he was one of the most dominant players of his era. He didn't get enough votes to stay on the ballot, in large part because of the way he treated reporters."

As long as voters hold grudges, sports columnist Cathal Kelly opined in *The Globe and Mail* in 2017, none of the "jerks" linked to PEDs will get a fair shake. "None of Clemens, Bonds or [Alex] Rodriguez is getting into the Hall," Kelly wrote in the *Globe*. "Their real sin wasn't taking drugs. It was being thought of as jerks. Steroids are the excuse that will allow the writer-voters to take their revenge."

* * *

Of course, not every writer wishes to take that so-called "revenge." To vote for the game's very best players, some Hall voters have reasoned, is the whole point of the exercise.

"To vote for Bonds and Clemens is not to condone the morality of their behavior," Tim Cowlishaw of *The Dallas Morning News* argued in 2012. "It's to recognize that their achievements put them among the greatest baseball players of all time." For Cowlishaw, the argument was simple. "I'm going to do something unimaginable to many. When I fill out my Hall of Fame ballot, I'm going to vote for the best baseball players… Roger Clemens and Barry Bonds are Hall of Fame players. I can't view them as anything else. If they did things to enhance their performance in the latter stages of their careers—the same thing countless others were doing—so be it. I'm voting them for the Hall of Fame, not the seventh level of heaven." After all, he noted, the sport wasn't even testing for PEDs at the time. "Major League Baseball was not testing Clemens or Bonds or McGwire during their time in the spotlight. MLB has not seen fit to take away any of their awards or remove their numbers from the record books. So why should it be left to the longstanding members of the Baseball Writers' Association of America to sit in judgment in these matters?"

Those who don't think Barry should be allowed in the Hall of Fame might argue that even Hall of Famers don't want to see known steroid users enshrined. Hall of Fame second baseman Joe Morgan famously sent an email to all Hall of Fame voters in 2017, urging them to keep "known steroid users" out of Cooperstown, because in his estimation, the Hall is a "place to look up to" where the "hallowed halls honor those who played the game hard and right." In reality, though, not all Hall of Famers share Morgan's view. Count Willie Mays, Bonds' godfather, among one of those who'd like to see Barry in. "Give somebody the honor who deserves to be in the Hall of Fame," Mays said in August 2018, on the night the Giants retired Bonds' number. "On behalf of all of the people in San Francisco and all over the country, vote him in."

Hall of Famer Mike Schmidt has said he'd have no issue with Bonds or Roger Clemens in the Hall. "I would not have a problem with Bonds or Clemens [being inducted]. Here we are convicting them of PED use and we don't know anything more than we read," the former Phillies third baseman told CSNPhilly.com in 2013. In the case of Bonds and Clemens, Schmidt added in that same interview, they never failed a drug test—"I'd need to see a legitimate test to know if what we're talking about was actual fact," he was quoted as saying—and he didn't like it when players are accused of using PEDs without evidence.

Although long-time Braves pitcher John Smoltz shares Morgan's view that anybody who used steroids should be kept out of Cooperstown, he has also acknowledged that proving who cheated would be difficult. "I'm trying to figure out what is actual and what isn't," Smoltz, who was inducted into the Hall of Fame in 2015, was quoted as saying in 2017. "To me, the one thing forgotten in this thing is the mission statement. Character is a big part of it. You have to not only have the numbers, but the character that matches it... If you have first-hand knowledge that a player used, or has publicly acknowledged it, I think it's an easy decision. When it is circumstance and evidence, and you don't know and just follow the rumor mill, that's difficult for the writer to be judge and jury." Regarding Bonds specifically, Smoltz added, "Barry Bonds is the greatest player I have ever played against. Barry Bonds could do things like no other player. I have tremendous respect for Barry Bonds." If he and Roger Clemens—and anyone else linked to steroids—were clean, Smoltz said, let them in. But... "I have no knowledge. None. I can just follow the speculation scale like everyone else," the Hall of Fame right-hander said.

Like Smoltz, Hall of Fame shortstop Barry Larkin has said he doesn't want to see cheaters in Cooperstown, although there has to be definitive proof that a player actually cheated. The former Reds star, inducted into the Hall in 2012, told the Associated Press in his induction year, "I think if you cheated, no, you don't deserve it because I know how difficult it was for me to get there and how difficult it was for me just to compete on an everyday basis. I think if you cheated, I think you made a decision and I don't think you belong." At the same time, he added, "There can't be hearsay. If you can prove it, then that's what it is. If you can't prove it, you're innocent until proven guilty."

Larkin wouldn't jump to conclusions about which players cheated, though. When the names Bonds, Clemens and Sammy Sosa came up, he told the Associated Press that "playing against some of these guys, they were the best, period." But as far as their induction? "I'll leave it to you guys [the BBWAA writers]." He does add that pitchers who took PEDs don't get talked about enough. "[When] we talk about steroids… most of the attention goes to the guys who got bigger and hit home runs. How about those guys that it wasn't so obvious, that were able to hang on to that slider just that much longer and make that ball break, so instead of hitting the ball off the sweet spot, you miss the sweet spot by that much. When I think about it, living through it… personally, [for me, it was about] my confrontation with the [pitcher]. If a guy hits a ball to shortstop, regardless of whether he was on [steroids] or not, he hit me a ball to shortstop. But that pitcher who threw that ball that moved up my barrel that much that I missed it, those were the guys I was concerned about."

Gaylord Perry, who admitted to doctoring baseballs during his Hall of Fame career (he was inducted in 1991), opined in 2017 that Bonds deserved to join him in Cooperstown, while adding that Pete Rose should never be enshrined in the Hall. "Pete did the worst thing possible, worse than steroids. He put money on games, win or lose. He's paying the price… [But] I think [Bonds will] get in eventually. If you have a player like that, pretty soon, you put him in." Chipper Jones, a member of the Hall of Fame Class of 2018, has also said that Bonds should have a plaque in Cooperstown. "I have no problem, whatsoever, saying that Barry Bonds is the best baseball player I've ever seen don a uniform. I have no problem with that. I think he's a

Hall of Famer whether there's a cloud of suspicion or not," Jones told ESPN radio host Dan Le Batard months before his own Hall induction in 2018.

For baseball writer J. P. Hoornstra—along with those who believe Barry Bonds belongs in Cooperstown—the Hall of Fame is a museum, not a shrine. "I don't think," begins Hoornstra, "you can tell the story of Major League Baseball without [Bonds]…"

Barry and the Hall

Bonds is not in Cooperstown because a sizable bloc of writers simply don't like him and the era that he represents—they hold their Hall of Fame vote (and the establishment itself) with an irrational reverence. To me, that's unacceptable, and it's counterintuitive to what I believe the true mission of the Baseball Hall of Fame is. The standard for enshrinement in Cooperstown should be simple: If you're telling the story of baseball, do you have to include this person? After all, that's all the Hall of Fame is—a museum of baseball. ... And if any baseball writer believes they can tell the story of baseball without including Barry Lamar Bonds, I'd recommend that they find a different line of work. Actually, they should present that story to their editor and see how well that goes over.

—Sports columnist Dieter Kurtenbach,
San Jose Mercury News, 2018.

Throughout the history of baseball, superstar players have done questionable things that raise eyebrows, some of which will be covered over the next few pages. Bringing up these examples isn't meant to diminish those stars' legacies. These examples are cited to show that even the elite players aren't perfect; nobody is. Their flaws are somehow less reported by baseball writers—perhaps even ignored by those covering the game—and, certainly, less remembered by baseball fans. Or perhaps not even known by baseball fans because the examples didn't make national headlines or dissected on sports talk shows. Or they have been forgotten because those players are considered legends and heroes. Barry Bonds' "flaws," however, are more prominently talked about and remembered.

Without getting into the home-run king's links to performance-enhancing drugs, there's the matter of the Giants' catering to Bonds' needs—which some will refer to as "demands"—during his time in San Francisco. "He was the most pampered athlete, ever. Ever. At any level. Anywhere. Any time. Any sport. It doesn't matter. He was sickeningly pampered. I believe he had four lockers when he was with the Giants. They kissed his ass the entire time. He had his own TV in front of his locker [and] a huge leather massage recliner chair—when everybody else was on a folding, metal piece-of-crap typical locker-room chair," says veteran sports radio personality Ted Sobel when the topic of Bonds comes up. "He acted—always—liked a pampered, spoiled child. Always. A couple of times in San Francisco I was there, and I saw his pampered routine in front of his locker. That was unbelievable to me."

It's important to note that the way the Giants "kissed Bonds' ass the entire time," as Sobel calls it, was nothing new to sports. Superstar athletes from every sport—not just baseball—and from every generation, have enjoyed a different set of rules than their less-talented counterparts. The practice of superstars calling their own shots and receiving special treatment dates at least to the days when the Bambino was still a pitcher in Boston. Unable to get Babe Ruth to abide by curfew, Red Sox manager Ed Barrow reached a compromise in 1919: The Babe could return to the team hotel whenever he pleased just as long as he left a note in Barrow's mailbox stating what time he came back. "I don't know whether he ever lied to me or not. I took his word," Barrow was once quoted as saying. "And besides, who could complain about a few wild nights when there were all those home runs in the afternoon?"

The Los Angeles Lakers, writer Daniel Brown opined in the *San Jose Mercury News* in 2005, certainly couldn't complain when Kobe Bryant was putting up points on a nightly basis for the NBA club. Bryant wielded "a staggering amount of power for a 26-year-old shooting guard," Brown wrote then, bringing up Kobe's highly-publicized 2003 sexual assault case (which was ultimately dropped) as an example: While he was on trial, "the team paid half the bill for a private jet to shuttle the player from games to his legal appearances in Colorado, an arrangement hard to imagine for a benchwarmer." Brown also noted that the Lakers even "let Bryant dictate some of their most important personnel moves—his clashes with Coach Phil Jackson and center Shaquille O'Neal resulted in the ouster of both." (The aforementioned criminal case was dropped after Bryant's accuser refused to testify. A separate civil suit was later filed against Bryant by the accuser, and that case was settled out of court and included Bryant publicly apologizing to the accuser, the public and his family, while denying the allegations.)

The reality in sports is that players who are superstars often feel they can do whatever they want. Sportswriter Casey Olson, who has argued that Bonds belongs in the Hall of Fame, once shared a story about the way Bonds treated a teammate—but is quick to add that this sort of behavior was not uncommon when it came to elite superstars. "My college roommate was drafted by the San Francisco Giants and spent a spring training with the big league club in the late '90s. He tells the story of sitting down on the team bus moments before Bonds got on. Wearing a full-length fur coat, Bonds got on the bus, looked right at my buddy and, with a few F-bombs mixed in, told him that he was in his seat and to get to the back of the bus. You can't get more entitled than that. But that's just the way the top alpha-males in professional sports act. It's the same way guys like Babe Ruth and Michael Jordan acted. Awful human beings? Obviously. But that shouldn't keep them out of the Hall of Fame. Bonds, along with [Roger] Clemens, are two of the best baseball players to ever lace up a pair of spikes."

When Cal Ripken, Jr., generally regarded as the man who saved baseball following the 1994 players' strike, was closing in on Lou Gehrig's major-league record for consecutive games played in 1995, the Baltimore Orioles Hall of Fame shortstop stayed in hotels separate from the team and dictated his own pregame work schedule. Ripken also had the equivalent of valet service at his home ballpark, Camden Yards. "The danger, though, is whether such treatment risks alienation of the rest of the clubhouse," wrote the *San Jose Mercury News* in 2005. "It rankled a few teammates in the Ripken case, especially after Brady Anderson, only briefly an elite player, started getting the same special hotel arrangements on the road. Some of the Orioles wondered if the courtesy extended only to white players."

But enjoying a different set of rules wasn't the only lesser-remembered story about baseball's all-time iron man. There was also the time when, because of an injury to Orioles starting third baseman B. J. Surhoff, manager Davey Johnson temporarily moved Ripken to third in 1996—a move that didn't affect Ripken's iron-man streak.

But Ripken's response, according to New York beat writers John Harper and Bob Klapisch in the book *Champions! The Saga of the 1996 New York Yankees*, was that "he stopped talking to Manny Alexander, the kid who would play short during the move." It became an uncomfortable situation for the "intimidated" second-year infielder, who played poorly during what turned out to be an eight-game stint at shortstop. "Of course, it couldn't have helped that Ripken," added Harper and Klapisch, "didn't so much as say hello to Alexander during that time"—not the type of behavior one might expect from a Hall of Famer when a common tradition in baseball is to support a teammate even if he was replacing you.

Harper and Klapisch recalled another incident involving Ripken in *Champions!* In a 1996 game against the Yankees with Baltimore down a run in the eighth inning, Davey Johnson pulled Ripken for a pinch-runner, sending Alexander, who had a much better chance of scoring from first on a double than Ripken did, to replace him. Never before had Ripken been replaced at such a meaningful moment of a ballgame ever since the iron-man streak had begun 13 years earlier, but the concern that night for Johnson, who was in his first season managing the Orioles, wasn't about hurting anybody's feelings—but trying to win a key game against the Yankees. Besides, pulling Ripken didn't affect his consecutive games played streak. But, as Harper and Klapisch noted, "Ripken hadn't even reached the dugout yet and Baltimore reporters were on the phone, calling their editors with news that would shake the city. The move created such a media frenzy that Johnson would say, 'It was like I was impeaching the president.'" Ripken could have made the decision a non-issue, Harper and Klapisch opined, by acknowledging Johnson's right to try to win the game. Instead, after sitting solemnly in the dugout through the final innings, he told reporters, "I don't wish to make a comment one way or the other. I'll just let that stand as my response." As far as Harper and Klapisch were concerned, Ripken's response was "transparent enough" and that the loose translation was that "Davey Johnson is a peabrain." The two New York beat writers added that "Ripken set the tone in the O's clubhouse, and his resentment toward Johnson became contagious. It would grow closer to mutiny in the coming weeks" as the season progressed. Although many fans were shocked that Ripken had such a "selfish" side—judging by reactions of callers to local sports talk radio shows the night he was pulled for a pinch-runner—the incident was quickly forgotten.

Today, Cal Ripken, Jr., because of his work ethic, is remembered as the man who saved baseball following the 1994 players' strike. He is remembered for his iron-man streak—his breaking of Lou Gehrig's record was a celebration of his work ethic, the antithesis of baseball's image in the wake of its labor war between millionaires—not for the special treatments he received with the Orioles or for the incidents with Davey Johnson and Manny Alexander.

Carlton Fisk, who in the 1975 World Series hit one of the most memorable home runs in baseball history, wasn't—and still isn't—known for being a "nice guy." Fisk "never won any nice guy awards," author Doug Wilson wrote in *Pudge: The Biography of Carlton Fisk*, adding the Hall of Fame catcher was a man of immense pride and principle who lived by a strict code. "He was who he was— a complicated man." In *Men's Journal* in 1993, writer Pat Jordan described Fisk as a man "angry at a lot of things." Examples included autograph seekers ("I *hate* that! Sometimes I just wanna scream, 'What the fuck do you want?'"), people who wanted to know more about his life ("Why the fuck should I tell them?"), and store clerks who couldn't make proper change ("And we wonder why the Japanese are killing us!"). And sportswriters who didn't use tape recorders ("They make you slow down, repeat yourself; you lose your train of thought") and players who were "stupid," like Nolan Ryan ("His priority was not to win but to strike out as many as he could, to make batters look foolish"). Jordan added many other examples of things that made Fisk angry—although it should also be noted the veteran sportswriter and author has said over the years that he admires the Hall of Fame catcher. Added James Warren in the *Chicago Tribune*, Fisk came across as a player who, although principled, was "at times dogmatic and often inhospitable" and "prides himself in not having friends in the sport and in chiding those he doesn't believe play the game the 'right' way."

And there was also the perceived lack of appreciation and respect he felt. "[No] matter how many games he caught, how many home runs he hit, it was never enough. He never felt appreciated enough, never respected enough," Brad Balukjian wrote in the 2020 book *The Wax Pack*, referring to the way the Red Sox and the White Sox handled

Fisk's contract negotiations throughout his career. In his final season in 1993, Chicago kept him on the team long enough to break Bob Boone's career record for most games caught, 2,225, and then released him a week later. Fisk was furious, oblivious to the fact that at age 45, he was hitting just .189 and had thrown out only one of 23 would-be base stealers. (He also hated the fact that his age was pointed out by the media—"I hate *that*, too! Being defined by my age, not my talent.")

For more than a decade after his release, Fisk still felt bitterness toward White Sox management—until the club announced in 2005 that he'd be honored with a statue to be placed on the left-field main concourse at U.S. Cellular Field. But even in retirement, the Hall of Fame catcher still spoke bluntly, sometimes when perhaps a platitude might have been preferred. At the 1999 All-Star Game, for instance, he ripped Juan Gonzalez after the Rangers slugger declined his invitation to the Midsummer Classic because he was tired and needed rest. "I think he's totally out of line. I know some players prefer three days off. Well, you can rest when you're dead, I think. This is a great honor," Fisk, the honorary captain for the AL All-Stars, told reporters. But that's the way Fisk was. "He could be blunt, brutally so, and if the truth hurt, then so be it," added author Doug Wilson.

Still, Carlton Fisk is a beloved figure in baseball. He's remembered for waving his 12th-inning home run inside the left-field foul pole at Fenway Park that gave Boston a 7-6 victory over Cincinnati in Game Six of the 1975 World Series—a series his Red Sox went on to lose—not for his pugnacious or irascible nature. He's remembered for playing the game the right way, not for his feud with White Sox management over his diminished playing time in his final season in 1993. Not for being a private person.

Nobody in his or her right mind would say Cal Ripken, Jr. and Carlton Fisk don't belong in the Hall of Fame. Discussing their stories here, in particular, isn't meant to knock either Hall of Famer. But the two examples serve as a comparison in terms of how differently ballplayers are perceived, how some superstars' faults are overlooked while those of others—such as, say, Barry Bonds—aren't. Bonds has always been called out for receiving special treatments on the Giants. For being surly. For wanting to keep his life private. For lashing out at others. For wanting the recognition he believed he deserved. Or for feuding with Giants management. And teammates.

Not that he took any of those criticisms personally. "You can't sit there and evaluate me when you don't know me," Bonds said early in his career when asked his thoughts about being disliked by many. "That's what writers and reporters and critics do. They evaluate someone you don't know. Unless you spend time at my house and know what I do, you don't know me. So I don't take any of this personally or anything."

* * *

To properly understand the mindset of Hall of Fame voters who have refused to check Bonds' name on the ballot—despite the fact Cooperstown already displays plaques of various former players who didn't necessarily check off all the boxes on the so-called "character clause"—the author seeks the opinions of journalist Adrian Brijbassi, who doesn't believe Barry belongs in Cooperstown. While he's not (and has never been) a Hall of Fame voter, Brijbassi, now a travel journalist, was a sports editor at New York *Newsday* when the BALCO case broke.

In terms of "bad characters" already in Cooperstown—for instance, Ty Cobb and Cap Anson, who were known for being racists—Brijbassi explains it was a different era in society, let alone sports. PEDs or steroids, meanwhile, are a different matter, says the former *Newsday* sports editor, who strongly believes that Hall of Fame voters are justified in not voting for players believed to have used PEDs or whose names have been liked to steroids. "I think [in terms of the] Hall of Fame vote... you have to look at players within their generation. Ty Cobb was not the only racist. He was just one of the more famous racists of that time. You could say that a large majority of white Americans of that time were racist, and Cobb was just reflective of them. But I think larger than that, you're looking at what the players do on the field; that's the number one criteria. And were they honestly working at their craft while they were putting up the statistics that they did? Those are what someone who's voting on the Hall of Fame would be thinking about—not 'Is he a good person or not?' That becomes far more subjective. And who is a baseball writer to judge someone's moral character? That's not what they're supposed to be doing. '[Is so-and-so] a good player?' That's what you're judging. And obviously Bonds was one of the best players in history, but you just can't also look at it [in terms of], 'How good would he have been without that level of PEDs?'

Brijbassi is right in suggesting that a large majority of white Americans of Cobb's time were racist. Yet it's also true that the transgressions or flaws of some of the game's superstars in the sport's history have been overlooked. Many of the faults that the media has found in Bonds were exhibited by other superstars throughout the history of baseball. Besides, before and during the Steroid Era, rampant use of greenies was well-known around baseball. How is it fair that Barry Bonds has been singled out? Some say that it's because he brought attention to himself, suggesting that one of the problems with being a great player in today's era of 24-hour sports channels and all-sports talk radio was that you were going to be singled out.

Of course, in the days of Babe Ruth and Joe DiMaggio, with sportswriting reduced to sonnets of heroism for a nation weary after two World Wars and the Great Depression, the flaws of ballplayers were essentially invisible to an adoring public. But in Bonds' days with the 24-hour sports coverage, Barry's flaws are regularly pointed out, his every strikeout met with cheers by writers who didn't like the Giants slugger. "The game has changed since the time I first knew it, when I was watching my dad [Bobby] and Willie [Mays] playing, and even later, when I saw Reggie [Jackson, a cousin]," Bonds told the *San Francisco Chronicle*'s Glenn Dickey in 1998. "It seems people used to love the game and love the players. Now, there just seems to be such a negative attitude. I think we've let people get too close to us, and everybody seems to focus on the flaws, the negativism, instead of just enjoying the game." In another interview, he shrugged off the fact that so much negativity had been written about him. "Those people don't pay my bills," he said, referring to those who took shots at him. "Those who judge people they don't know, they have to be in more pain than the people they're judging."

The way sportswriters glorify the superstars of the past and the way they rip into Bonds are certainly unfair, as all sports heroes are flawed and no era is perfect. Bonds was arrogant? Well, many superstars are like that. Case in point? Ted Williams, who, according to Ken Burns' 1994 documentary *Baseball*, once said, "No one could throw a fastball past me. God could come down from heaven and he couldn't throw it past me." Bonds wasn't well-liked in the clubhouse? He angered many by not stretching with teammates? He couldn't get along with people? Throughout the history of baseball, some of the greatest players in the game weren't well-liked by their teammates. There have been references, notably in Burns' *Baseball*, of Ty Cobb's teammates "despising" The Georgia Peach. Red Sox outfielders were said to have criticized Ted Williams for being uninterested in anything but hitting. Williams, it was said, was unmoved. "Tell them," The Splendid Splinter remarked, "I'm going to make more money in this game than all of them put together." Rogers Hornsby, according to numerous accounts, was not well-liked. Characterized once by Bill James as perhaps the biggest "horse's ass" in baseball history, Hornsby was another Hall of Famer whose play in the field was said to be indifferent. According to a teammate, Hornsby, then playing at third base, wouldn't think of working on his fielding and cared only about his batting average.

Of course, some of those traits—whether they are hostile attitudes or disagreeable personalities—have been said to have helped make great ballplayers as dominant on the field as they were. Cobb, who still holds the record for the highest career batting average at .366, was a prime example. "If I hadn't been determined to outdo the other fellow at all cost, I doubt I would have hit [even] .320," Cobb said in 1925. "In other words, my lifetime batting average has been increased at least 50 points by the qualities that I'd call purely mental." While every rookie got a little hazing and most just took it and laughed, Tigers outfielder Sam Crawford once recalled, Cobb rebelled when he was hazed. Cobb alienated his teammates and made them his enemies. "He came up with an antagonistic attitude, which in his mind turned any little razzing into a life-or-death struggle," Crawford once told writer Lawrence Ritter. "He came up from the South, you know, and he was still fighting the Civil War. As far as he was concerned, we were all damn Yankees before he even met us. Well, who knows, maybe if he hadn't had that persecution complex, he never would [have] been the great ballplayer he was. He was always trying to prove he was the best, on the field and off. And maybe he was, at that."

Bonds, say critics, wasn't pleasant with the media and fans. But in another era, neither was Williams. The Red Sox Hall of Famer feuded with the press, lined baseballs at fans who jeered him and was once fined for spitting at them. He was on uncomfortable terms with the Boston media throughout his player career, as he felt the newspapers liked to discuss his personal life as much as his baseball performance. Williams, for instance, once told Huck Finnegan of the Boston *American*, "Every time I go up to the plate in batting practice, some guy I never saw before comes up and says, 'I'm from such and such a paper, or news service. My managing editor sent me out to get a story on you and your girlfriend.' So I burn up and say, 'I'm not looking for any story about your managing editor and *his* girlfriend, so scram.' Then they all get on me, and I'm never the Most Valuable Player because I don't want writers butting into my personal affairs. Why can't they stick to baseball?" (Williams, who won MVP awards in 1946 and 1949, finished second in 1941, 1942, 1947 and 1957. He famously lost out to Joe DiMaggio in 1947, when he captured his second Triple Crown—leading the AL in batting average, home runs and RBIs—and had a statistically superior year to the Yankees superstar but lost the MVP by a point when a reporter left him off the ballot.) Unhappy about being booed by the Boston rooters in his first big-league season, he also refused to tip his cap to the fans for the remainder of his playing career, even after rounding the bases following a home run in his final career at-bat at Fenway Park. Long after his career, Williams acknowledged, in an interview on *Baseball*, he didn't handle the press or the fans well, but he also suggested the Red Sox didn't, either. "Sometimes, I wonder if it didn't have a good effect because I was mad at the world and mad at everybody, and I go to the plate more determined than ever," he reflected.

Bonds enjoyed his privacy. He preferred to let his on-field performance do the talking. But so did other superstars before him. So did the aforementioned Williams. "Joltin' Joe" DiMaggio, meanwhile, was known to be "distant, quiet, serious-minded, understandably wary of the press," noted the 1994 book *Baseball: An Illustrated History* (the companion book for the Ken Burns documentary, *Baseball*). He was so reticent, Hank Greenberg once said, that "if he said hello to you, that was a long conversation." DiMaggio was so protective of his privacy, a teammate once remembered, that he led the league in room service. "DiMaggio, as a ballplayer, was very difficult to know," legendary broadcaster Red Barber once said. "He was a loner. He said very, very little. You don't find many quotes in the papers of DiMaggio's playing days because he didn't say very much. He just performed." Like modern athletes, he held out for more money—including in 1938, a Depression year—and missed the beginnings of seasons. Yet Joltin' Joe, spoken of glowingly by members of the media to this day, isn't criticized for being quiet or aloof. Or for holding out or being greedy. He's still revered today as one of the greatest Yankees legends ever.

That's because DiMaggio, according to many in the press who covered him, was a great sportsman, an exemplary citizen and everything we wish our sports heroes to be. Yet the beloved "Joltin' Joe" isn't scrutinized about some of his off-the-field activities, which, the *New York Post* once penned, included having friends in the mob. Then, there was also his family life. "His first marriage—to Dorothy Arnold, a bit player in films—was a disaster," noted the *Post*. "She thought she was getting an icon of American decency. Instead, her new husband drank and chain-smoked and cheated constantly. They had a baby, Joe Jr., but DiMaggio barely paid attention to him and regarded him as an irritant." When the baby got sick, apparently, "Joltin' Joe" would check in to a hotel. "He was concerned with image, with how things looked," Joe Jr. was once quoted as saying of his father. "He wasn't concerned with me as a person." Arnold eventually filed for divorce, and a decade later DiMaggio married Marilyn Monroe, whom he brutally beat more than once. Joe Jr. once recalled being woken up one night by their fighting. "I was asleep downstairs," Joe Jr. was quoted as saying, "and I woke up to the sound of my father and Marilyn screaming... After a few minutes, I heard Marilyn race down the stairs and out the front door, and my father running after her. He caught up to her and grabbed her by the hair and sort of half-dragged her back to the house. She was trying to fight him off but couldn't."

Bonds, say critics, was a "mean-spirited" and "horrible person." Well, there are worse people in the Hall of Fame. Cap Anson played an important role in keeping Black players out of Major League Baseball. Ditto Kenesaw Mountain Landis. Ty Cobb was widely considered a racist and an all-around nasty man. Tris Speaker and Rogers Hornsby were rumored Ku Klux Klan members. If we're talking strictly about personality, well, when Red Sox owner Harry Frazee sold Babe Ruth to the Yankees, he defended the move by saying Ruth was "one of the most selfish and inconsiderate men ever to put on a baseball uniform."

Another story has Ruth calling everybody "Kid," not bothering to remember anybody's names—although his idiosyncrasies are thought of as endearing and rarely criticized. Bob Gibson, known for his fierce glare and menacing mound presence, refused to speak to opposing players even off the field and twice threw at hitters in Old-Timers Games—but the Cardinals legend is fondly remembered and those stories about him are generally regarded as funny.

Bonds didn't always sign autographs for fans? He's hardly the only athlete in the world to act unkindly to those seeking an autograph. And if the conversation is about rude interactions with fans, the incidents which happened at the turn of the 20th century are virtually unfathomable today and would make Bonds look like a saint. Although extremely rare in the 21st century, attacking fans was not an unusual occurrence in the early years of baseball, with even some of the game's biggest stars involved in such activities. Notable Hall of Famers who assaulted heckling fans, in fact, include Ty Cobb, Babe Ruth, Cy Young, Rube Waddell and Fred Clarke. Young, usually a mild-mannered man, for instance, once charged into the stands to challenge a fan who called him a quitter, noted author Charles Leerhsen in *Ty Cobb: A Terrible Beauty*. Clarke, a Hall of Fame left fielder and manager, meanwhile, was said to have once pushed a heckler down a flight of stairs during a game. True, those incidents occurred in a completely different era, but Google "Mike Milbury shoe incident" and "Ron Artest brawl," and you'll see more recent examples of professional athletes confronting spectators during a game. Bonds might not have wanted to sign items or acknowledge fans at times, but he certainly never fought with them. Not even the time when a fan at San Diego's Petco Park threw a syringe in his direction while he was standing on the field. Bonds, instead, picked up the syringe—about the size of a fat cigar—and carried it off the field so that no one would get hurt. "If that's what they [fans who throw objects onto the field] want to do, embarrass themselves, then that's on them. That has nothing to do with me at all," said Bonds, who, at the time, was under investigation by baseball for alleged steroid use.

If anybody wants to bring up that particular allegation, you could certainly argue that Barry Bonds, because he sought ways to remain a productive player throughout his entire career, always helped his team—not hurt it—in the process. A star athlete, after all, always faces the pressure of having to live up to his previous performance and his multimillion-dollar salary, and in Bonds' case he was consistently staying on the field and remaining productive for the Giants over the course of his 15 years in San Francisco. *USA Today*'s Bob Nightengale, who is among those who believe Bonds belongs in Cooperstown, is certainly one who subscribes to that theory. "No matter what you believe—whether he took steroids or didn't—it's like, if there's no speed limit, people aren't going to go 55 miles an hour. Everybody tries to get the top edge. And why are we penalizing Bonds and Roger Clemens, when there was no testing at the time? They never tested positive. The biggest thing is they were never suspended. So, the big difference between a Barry Bonds and an Alex Rodriguez, or a Manny Ramirez, is he only helped his team win. These other guys who got suspended, those teams [were hampered]; they hurt their teams because of their suspensions."

In regard to Rodriguez, Nightengale is referring to the Yankees third baseman's being suspended for 211 games in 2013 for his involvement in the Biogenesis PEDs scandal, a suspension which was later reduced to 162 games and kept him off the field for the entire 2014 season. In the case of Ramirez, the superstar outfielder was suspended 50 games while with the Dodgers in 2009 for violating baseball's drug policy by taking human chorionic gonadotropin, a women's fertility drug which is often taken after steroids. In the spring of 2011 while with Tampa Bay, Ramirez was informed by MLB of another violation of its drug policy; given a 100-game suspension, he chose to retire rather than be suspended. "So, to me," continues Nightengale, "it's a big, big difference. People can say what they want now, but teams wanted guys who were on performance-enhancing drugs, guys who were in the gym longer, ate better than everybody else, got their sleep and controlled their bodies better. So, it was actually encouraged, and not discouraged at the time."

Indeed. Everything that Bonds did was to help him remain on the field and stay productive. That Bonds tried to stay on the field benefited his teams. Not all superstars did. Even Babe Ruth, recognized as the game's greatest hero, couldn't always stay on the field, missing countless games due to suspensions. His career was shortened, it can be argued, because of poor decisions off the field with all of his eating and drinking. He could have done more, pundits have said, if he'd been able to keep it together. In a game in 1917, Ruth, then a pitcher with Boston, lasted only one batter before being ejected for punching home-plate umpire Brick Owens; he was ultimately fined and suspended for 10 days. The Babe's off-the-field antics during his Yankees years also got him suspended several times. In the fall of 1921, he was suspended until May 20, 1922, by Commissioner Kenesaw Mountain Landis for participating in a barnstorming tour following the World Series, which violated the rules of the time. In the first week of his return in 1922, Ruth was thrown out of a game for throwing dust in the face of an umpire, and then climbed into the stands to confront a heckler. For his actions, Ruth was suspended by league president Ban Johnson, who suspended him again in June and September for his poor conduct toward umpires. Although New York reached the World Series that year, the Yankees lost to the Giants, with Ruth hitting .118. Three years later in 1925, with the Yankees seeking their fourth pennant in five years, Ruth reported to camp overweight, feverish and often drunk. He needed abdominal surgery and missed the first seven weeks of the season. The press reported that he'd eaten too many hot dogs and drunk too many sodas; it was, one reporter wrote, "the bellyache heard round the world." (According to *The Baseball Hall of Shame's Warped Record Book* several decades later, the Bambino had fallen ill injecting himself with an extract from a sheep's testicles in an attempt to improve his power at the plate, and the Yankees covered the news up by telling the press that Ruth was sick with a bellyache.) When Ruth returned, Yankees manager Miller Huggins, tired of his slugger's constant drinking and carousing, fined him $5,000 and suspended him until he apologized. The suspension lasted nine days, and that season The Babe missed 56 games and the Yankees finished seventh.

And one can't argue that Bonds' 73 home runs in 2001 didn't help the Giants win. One could, however, argue that the various alcoholics in the Hall of Fame, from Grover Cleveland "Pete" Alexander to Rube Waddell, more often than not took the field in less-than-prime conditions for games. As for Mickey Mantle, a first-ballot Hall of Famer known for his carousing? One could argue that manager Casey Stengel, in not naming Mantle to his personal all-star team in his 1961 autobiography (The Ol' Perfessor listed six outfielders on his AL team), felt Mickey wasn't always giving his best effort. Three years earlier, when Stengel was asked by a sportswriter to name his all-time team, he included the name of Yankees right fielder Hank Bauer but not Mantle. Bauer was startled upon learning of the response and asked The Ol' Perfessor why he was named instead of Mantle, who'd finish his career with 536 home runs. The response: "You gave 110% every time you were in the lineup." Alexander, Waddell, Mantle and many others who deprived their teams of their best performances through some combination of substance abuse and not taking enough care of their bodies. Wasn't that cheating the fans and their own teams? Yet Hall of Fame voters and those in the anti-Bonds faction have issues with Bonds helping his team win ballgames.

Bonds, say critics, got into a shouting match with Pirates skipper Jim Leyland during a spring-training workout in 1991 that was caught on TV cameras, with the manager yelling, "I've kissed your ass for three years! I'm not going to do it anymore! I'm sick of people who don't want to be here! If you're not happy, go home!" Well, see the earlier entry on Babe Ruth, with Miller Huggins suspending The Babe in 1925. Yet in the case of Bonds vs. Leyland, both men have said the incident was over immediately—in fact, Barry, the runner-up for the National League MVP Award, would carry the manager on his shoulders off the field when the Pirates clinched the division title that season. And when critics kept rehashing the shouting incident, Bonds responded, "I'm sure these people [the media and fans] have problems at home. They yell and scream at each other. Everyone has problems with their friends and stuff. Mine just happened to be on TV." You certainly can't argue against that viewpoint. After Bonds left the Pirates, whenever Barry's Giants were playing Leyland's ballclub, he could be seen seeking Leyland out during batting practice, where he'd put his arm around his former manager. The two men are still, to this day, close friends.

The Hall of Fame is for the greatest players who ever lived. Barry Bonds was one of them. You can't tell the story of baseball in the 1990s without mentioning Bonds. You can't tell the story of the game in the 2000s without mentioning his name, either. Just because the era in which he played is unsavory doesn't mean we can pretend it didn't happen. There is no doubt, many have made the argument that he should be in the Hall of Fame.

* * *

When it comes to Bonds and the Hall of Fame, the so-called "character clause" has been brought up, namely his link to performance-enhancing drugs, along with his treatment of the media.

J. P. Hoornstra, a member of the Baseball Writers' Association of America, speaks candidly when asked about the Hall of Fame's character clause as it pertains to Bonds when it comes to stories about how Barry handled the media during his playing career. "As it relates to how I think of his Hall of Fame credentials, the veracity of any of that [how Bonds treated members of the media] wouldn't affect my thoughts about him as a Hall of Fame baseball player," Hoornstra begins. "But I will say this. There is a line when it comes to character that I would draw, separate from performance-enhancing drugs that speaks to how I evaluate how baseball players treat fellow human beings, whether that's reporters or teammates or everyday people outside the clubhouse. And I've heard stories about players who are in the Hall of Fame treating reporters—particularly women reporters— that are just abhorrent that I, frankly, consider even worse than using performance-enhancing drugs, a worse indictment of their character because at least in the case of performance-enhancing drugs, inherently, you're taking it because it makes you better as a baseball player."

Hoornstra doesn't name examples—and the author doesn't ask—but there have been enough stories in the papers over the years about male athletes who treated female reporters poorly that it's common enough knowledge. One such player in baseball was Hall of Fame pitcher Jack Morris, who in 1990 was quoted as saying, "I don't talk to people when I'm naked, especially women, unless they're on top of me or I'm on top of them" when *Detroit Free Press* sportswriter Jennifer Frey approached the then-Tigers pitcher (who wasn't naked at the time) in the Detroit clubhouse. (When Morris' comments made their way to then-team president Bo Schembechler, he stated that the newspaper had a "lack of common sense" for assigning a woman to a locker-room interview. Nobody from the Tigers, it was later reported, apologized for Morris' comment to Frey, which was heard by several reporters and a number of Detroit players.) The following year, when Morris was with the Twins, Frey was assigned to cover the American League Championship Series between Minnesota and Toronto. When she ran into Morris, the pitcher screamed, "You're a bitch!" and Twins center fielder Kirkby Puckett had to keep Morris from physically attacking her.

Over time, the pitcher's interactions with Frey have been largely forgotten. But not by everybody. In August 2018, when the Tigers asked fans to recall their favorite memories of Morris on Twitter, baseball analyst Keith Law felt he should bring attention to the way Morris conducted himself off the mound. Law tweeted in response: "[M]ine is when he sexually harassed a young woman reporter and then later had to be physically restrained from attacking her while he was screaming that she was a b—." Hall of Famers should conduct themselves at a higher standard than most, and Law was reminding the baseball world that Morris simply did not. Morris was eligible for the Hall of Fame from 2000 to 2014, but did not receive the required 75% of the vote in any of his eligible years. After falling off the regular ballot, Morris was elected to the Hall in December 2017 by the Modern Era portion of the Veterans Committee, who apparently decided to overlook the pitcher's treatment of Frey, who'd passed away in 2016.

Today, Jack Morris is remembered as being the Tigers' workhorse and one of the best pitchers in baseball in the 1980s, his incidents with female reporters forgiven by most. He's remembered for his 10 shutout innings in Game Seven of the 1991 World Series with the Twins, and as one of baseball's "big-game pitchers," praised for his—in the words of Toronto sportswriter Stephen Brunt— "genuine tenacity" and "character in the clubhouse." And for his competitiveness and desire to win. He's fondly regarded in Detroit, Minnesota and Toronto, cities in which he won World Series rings— and teams for which he has done broadcasting work following his playing career.

Any reasonable person will, like J. P. Hoornstra, conclude that treating fellow human beings in a disrespectful manner is a far worse indictment of a person's character than using performance-enhancing drugs. With respect to performance-enhancing drugs specifically, many observers believe that it's a temptation which is hard to resist. For those who slam Barry Bonds and other suspected PED users, comedian Chris Rock once suggested that they look into the mirror first. "Who in the whole country wouldn't take a pill to make more money at their job?" Rock asked rhetorically on Ken Burns' documentary *Baseball: The Tenth Inning* before providing his own answer. "You would… 'Hey, there's a pill and you're gonna get paid like Steven Spielberg.' You would take the pill. You just would." Steve Lyons, who played in the majors between 1985 and 1993, put it this way: "The will to win takes on strange bedfellows. And the pressure today's players place on themselves to win sometimes clouds their moral fortitude. Ask yourself if you would have the guts to say no if somebody told you they had a way for you to become measurably more successful than you are right now. All you have to do is something that may or may not be a little bit illegal."

Besides, as Lyons, who has said he believes Bonds, Roger Clemens and Mark McGwire belong in the Hall of Fame, once noted, "cheating" in the game isn't a new concept. "Guys have been trying to figure out a way to cheat in baseball since the day after it was invented," Lyons said in 2009, bringing up the old adage "If you ain't cheatin', you ain't tryin'" as a way of life in sports. "And I don't want to hear from the so-called 'baseball purists' who say the game has changed for the worse," added Lyons. "If the game hadn't changed, there would still only be six teams riding trains to and fro, with no players of color to be found anywhere."

J. P. Hoornstra addresses the temptation of performance-enhancing drugs vs. the use of offensive language around female reporters this way: "I think that [PEDs are] a temptation that—and I truly believe this—most people in the shoes of Bonds, Clemens, or Alex Rodriguez or Manny Ramirez would choose [not to resist]. If you have performance-enhancing drugs available to you, I think most of us would actually use them if we're not being tested for those drugs in our systems. But players using deliberately offensive language around women because they can, when those women are trying to do their jobs and report on what they're doing, I don't think most of us would do that. So, I do consider that to be kind of its own category of evaluating a baseball player's character.

"Now, to that end, I've probably heard all the stories [that are out there] as far as how Barry interacted with the media, [and] I would tend to believe [them]. Probably some of those things might bother me more than his steroid use. Having said that, if you were a player who didn't take steroids and you were trying to compete against Barry Bonds and everybody else who was on steroids, and you chose not to use available performance-enhancing drugs because that violated your sense of right and wrong, I could absolutely sympathize with your point of view that this was a player who cheated, who cheated the system, who cheated his fellow players. You wouldn't want to see him in the Hall of Fame. I get that. I would probably agree with you. But I do think that the way Bonds treated the media has to be sort of evaluated under its own separate paradigm of ethics and character from performance-enhancing drugs and using the performance-enhancing drugs that he did."

The reality, though, is that Hall of Fame voters have often cited the so-called "character clause" in refusing to vote for players who have been linked to performance-enhancing drugs because of the way they "tarnished the game"—but haven't extended that clause to cover candidates who, say, are known to have treated women disrespectfully. In the years that Morris, Bonds and Roger Clemens were on the ballot at the same time, for instance, in 2013 and 2014—the long-time Tigers right-hander was on the ballot between 2000 and 2014, while Bonds and Clemens were first eligible for Cooperstown in 2013—Morris appeared on 67.7% and 61.5% of the ballots. Bonds, meanwhile, received 36.2% and 34.7% of the votes, while the numbers for Clemens were 37.6% and 35.4%.

Additionally, the so-called "character clause"—one of BBWAA's rules for election to the Hall states "voting shall be based upon the player's record, playing ability, integrity, sportsmanship, character and contributions to the team(s) on which the player played"—also doesn't seem to apply when it came to racists, domestic abusers and thugs. In Joe Morgan's 2017 email sent to all Hall of Fame voters to urge them to keep steroid users out of Cooperstown, the former Reds second baseman added the following postscript: "P.S. Families come to Cooperstown because they know it's special. To parents, it's a place they can take their kids for an uplifting, feel-good visit. It's a place where kids can see what true greatness is all about." But are the stories of Kenesaw Mountain Landis and Cap Anson, who played important roles in keeping Black players out of Major League Baseball but have plaques in Cooperstown, supposed to be uplifting? Character and integrity are supposed to matter when contemplating whether someone belongs in the Hall, but what about the stories of plenty of other bad characters—ill-mannered racist Ty Cobb, for instance—already in the Hall?

When one brings up "integrity," a word mentioned in the character clause, Rob Parker, formerly a sports journalist with *The Detroit News* and a Hall of Fame voter, would question whether it even exists by pointing to the fact that baseball kept African-Americans out of the game for decades. "I'm not bothered by the steroids issue and because there were no rules on the books before December 2003, it's impossible to go back in time and penalize people. Would I rather people not use steroids? Sure. People talk about integrity in baseball, but there is no integrity. This is the same sport that kept Blacks out of until 1947. If you want to talk about asterisks, let's go back and do that prior to 1947. It's the most ridiculous witch hunt I've ever heard of. If we got past the omission of Blacks in baseball, we can get past this."

As for performance-enhancing drugs themselves as they relate to the Hall of Fame, the subject isn't that black and white, either. While long-time Red Sox slugger Manny Ramirez, who debuted on the writers' ballot for Cooperstown in 2017, was suspended by MLB for failing drug tests in 2009 and 2011, Bonds never failed a test during his career. Neither did Clemens. For some writers, the gray area gets grayer when Alex Rodriguez and David Ortiz are set to debut on the ballot for Cooperstown in 2022. "Ortiz was supposedly part of the group of players who were tested—but not tested for anything that he could be penalized for taking," Hoornstra says, referring to the long-time Red Sox designated hitter who was one of 104 players who reportedly tested positive for PEDs when Major League Baseball surveyed all of baseball in 2003, results that were supposed to have been anonymous. (Ortiz has said he never knowingly took steroids.) "My inclination would be to vote for them [Hall of Fame-worthy players whose names have been linked to PEDs] simply because I do consider the Hall of Fame to be a museum and not a shrine, and I don't think you can tell the story of Major League Baseball without those guys," Hoornstra explains. "Having said that, I do take the character clause seriously, so I would have to evaluate their failed drug tests on their own merit. Bonds never failed a drug test. Rodriguez did. Ortiz didn't, but maybe he was taking something he shouldn't have. I would consider those to be shades of gray, particularly in the case of Rodriguez, who played during the time when the drug policy was simply different than it was for Bonds—and for Ortiz early in his career."

USA Today's Bob Nightengale, who like others have commented that the Hall already has PED users, says Bonds' name is the first one he checks off on the Hall of Fame ballot every year, and acknowledges he hopes Barry gets in someday. "I sure hope so," Nightengale says. "I think he gets in the last year [on the ballot in 2022]. I think maybe some voters will say, 'You know what? We've punished him and Roger Clemens long enough. Let's let them in.' The bottom line is the Hall of Fame already has guys that used performance-enhancing drugs in there; they just never got caught [and they were] obvious guys. So, it's almost like people are punishing Bonds for being that great, for breaking Hank Aaron's record. Several Hall of Famers have told me if he hadn't broken Hank Aaron's record, he'd probably be in the Hall of Fame already. So, it's almost like he was too good. He was that great. But he was great even before the PED suspicions and everything else. He was the best anyone has seen, unless you've been alive long enough to see Babe Ruth."

Unprompted, Nightengale adds: "In recent years there's all kinds of guys who's in the Hall of Fame with steroid suspicions. Mike Piazza. Jeff Bagwell. [Ivan] 'Pudge' Rodriguez. Why are we keeping out the best? He played in the Steroid Era, and he was certainly the best of the Steroid Era. People are kidding themselves if they think that there's no guys in the Hall of Fame who ever used steroids before."

Former pitcher Tom Candiotti echoes that last point. "There's plenty of guys that were back doing it," the former knuckleball specialist says now. "You know, some of them are in the Hall of Fame, but nothing's ever been said about it because they didn't have, maybe, the recognition or star power or celebrity that Barry carried with him, and his brashness brought attention to himself. Plus, there were just a lot of Barry haters that wanted to take him down. I guess that's one of the problems with being great. If you were just, like, middle of the road, no one really cares, right? But I'll just say this. He was a great player, number one. But he just was trying to keep up with everybody else that was doing it."

* * *

It simply isn't fair to place all the blame of baseball's steroid scandal solely on Bonds. Considering the widespread use of steroids in that era, it's far-fetched to suggest that no current Hall of Famer was a user (and multiple writers, including Nightengale and Hoornstra, have stated they are convinced there already are guys in the Hall who used PEDs). Some players just might have been more fortunate than those who were busted. For some Hall of Fame voters, the thought process is this: How could they, in good faith, not vote for Bonds when they might be voting for other players who had used PEDs? Former *Pittsburgh Post-Gazette* columnist Bob Smizik, who has retired and no longer has a Hall of Fame vote, voted for Bonds and Clemens in the past, without concern about their ties to steroids. As Smizik said in 2020, he believed that Bonds was singled out more than other players—such as Craig Biggio, for instance—because of the dramatic rise in home-run rate Barry enjoyed in the latter stages of his career en route to surpassing Hank Aaron as baseball's all-time home-run king. Speaking to the *Post-Gazette*, Smizik pointed to Biggio having his largest (26) and second-largest (24) home-run totals in 2004 and 2005, when the Houston Astros second baseman was 38 and 39 years old. "What does that sound like?" the long-time columnist was quoted as saying. In Ken Burns' 2010 documentary *Baseball: The Tenth Inning*, meanwhile, columnist Thomas Boswell of *The Washington Post* suggested that Cooperstown already has a steroid user. "There was another player now in the Hall of Fame," Boswell said, "who literally stood with me and mixed something and I said, 'What's that?' And he said, 'It's a Jose Canseco milkshake.' And that year that Hall of Famer hit more home runs than [he] ever hit any other year. So, it wasn't just Canseco, and so one of the reasons that I thought that it was an important subject was that it was spreading. It was already spreading by 1988."

As far as "cheating" is concerned, throughout the history of baseball, players and teams have always been trying to gain an edge. To pretend that the game was somehow pure in one era and impure in another era, many have argued, is disingenuous, as players were already employing shady tactics even prior to the modern era. "If baseball is a business," the 2010 book *The Baseball Codes* noted, "cheating has become little more than a business practice, and, like sign stealing, is generally abided as long as it stops once it's detected. This covers a wide range of endeavors: pitchers applying foreign substances to the ball, and hitters doctoring their bats; outfielders acting as if they've caught balls they actually trapped, and hitters pantomiming pain from balls that didn't hit them." One ballclub known for such tactics was the 1890s Baltimore Orioles, winners of three consecutive NL pennants between 1894 and 1896. Those Orioles were known to interfere with opposing base runners by grabbing their belts. They were known to hide extra balls in the outfield. Orioles catchers were known to throw their masks in the paths of runners racing home—and sometimes even drop pebbles into the shoes of unsuspecting hitters to slow them down—while O's base runners deliberately mashed catchers' feet as they crossed home plate. Baltimore batters writhed on the ground and pinched themselves to fake being hit by a pitch. They also shaved their wooden bats flat on one side, for better bunting, until league officials caught on and banned the practice. As if all of that wasn't enough, base runners even scooted from first base to third when the lone umpire's back was turned. Orioles manager Ned Hanlon, credited with coming up with these tactics, is in the Baseball Hall of Fame.

The spitball was outlawed by baseball in 1920, but banning a practice doesn't stop people from doing it. Use of the pitch grew so pervasive in the 1950s that Commissioner Ford Frick briefly lobbied for its re-legalization. "Restore the spitter?" Dodgers shortstop Pee Wee Reese is said to have asked rhetorically. "When did they stop throwing it?"

Even Hall of Famers cheat; they just keep doing whatever they're not supposed to do as long as they don't get caught. Whitey Ford, who pitched for 11 pennant-winning Yankees teams during his 16-year career and fired a World Series-record 33 consecutive scoreless innings between 1960 and 1962, was one Hall of Famer who'd admit to cheating after his playing days were over. He'd use his wedding ring, his belt buckle or catcher Elston Howard's shinguard to scuff the ball, as well as a "gunk" composed of baby oil, turpentine and resin. Don Sutton and Gaylord Perry, both 300-game winners and members of the Hall of Fame, are also famous for doctoring baseballs. "He had been thrown out of a game in 1978 for scuffing," the book *The Baseball Codes* noted of Sutton, adding that by 1987 he "was already among the most discussed ball-doctors in the game."

Google "cheating pitchers MLB" and you might even see the name Orel Hershiser, the Dodgers' 1988 World Series hero and one of the premier postseason pitchers of his generation. During the 1997 ALCS between Cleveland and Baltimore, the Orioles complained that

Hershiser, then pitching for the Indians, was doctoring the baseball. The Orioles claimed he was repeatedly moistening the ball by going to his mouth and neck, a violation of the rules. Indians hurler Chad Ogea stunned reporters when he said, "I've known Orel for three years. He cheats. And just about everybody else does. Why not?... He showed me how to cheat but said I can't do it until I'm 35." A day later, Ogea revealed he was joking. "Chad just made a mistake," Hershiser said when asked to address Ogea's claim. "I don't want kids to think one of their heroes, if I am, is a cheater, because I don't cheat... That's the only thing I would be depressed about."

Gaylord Perry's name is the one that some in Bonds' corner bring up when it comes to the Hall of Fame. "Steroid use has nothing to do with my vote," former *Seattle Post-Intelligencer* and ESPN.com writer, and Hall of Fame voter, Jim Caple once said. "Steroids were not banned during the majority of their careers when they [Bonds and Clemens] achieved the vast majority of their accomplishments. All we can go by is what they did on the field. If Gaylord Perry is in the Hall for violating a rule that was in place 40 years before his career began, how can you justify withholding a vote from someone for a rule that wasn't in effect?"

Not everyone shares that view. Journalist Adrian Brijbassi, for one, isn't bothered one bit by the doctoring of baseballs by any pitcher, even those in the Hall of Fame. PEDs, however, are a totally different matter. When Perry's name is mentioned, for instance, Brijbassi insists that what the Hall of Fame pitcher has been accused of isn't even in the same orbit as the use of performance-enhancing drugs by players from the so-called Steroid Era. "I think [with] Gaylord Perry, you're referring to him doctoring the baseball," says Brijbassi, who served as a sports editor at New York *Newsday* when the BALCO case broke. "[But] the [number] of times that a doctored baseball would've ended up in play and not getting picked up by an umpire or an opposing player, that's very rare compared to Barry Bonds every time he's up at-bat for season upon season upon season. He's [allegedly] doing it with an unfair advantage over a large majority of the other players. I think trying to compare a doctored baseball to taking performance-enhancing drugs, those are two completely different sets of standards that you're looking at there."

New York Daily News writer Michael O'Keeffe summed up the

Perry vs. Bonds discussion in 2006 this way: "Many apologists say it is not fair to bar Bonds [from Cooperstown] because cheaters such as spitballer Gaylord Perry have already been inducted. That's like saying a lie about sex with a White House intern is the same as a lie about weapons of mass destruction: Although both are fibs, only one led to shattered lives and needless deaths. Don't the apologists have a sense of context? Perry's legacy was greasy catcher's mitts and a boost in Vaseline sales. Bonds' cheating, meanwhile, contributed to a fundamental shift in American culture—kids, after all, emulate sports heroes. Many young ballplayers now believe performance-enhancing drugs are necessary to reach the top of their game, even if it puts them at risk for liver disease, sexual dysfunction, 'roid rage and other health problems. Some kids who have experimented with steroids have committed suicide. Others will die more slowly."

When discussing PED usage specifically, it should be noted that while Oakland A's "Bash Brothers" Mark McGwire and Jose Canseco might have begun baseball's popularization of steroids in the late 1980s, long-time pitching coach Tom House once told a reporter that those drugs were widespread in the game in the 1960s and 1970s. "We were doing steroids they wouldn't give to horses," House was quoted as saying, adding that six or seven pitchers per team were experimenting with steroids or human growth hormone in that era. (Indeed, steroids were already available by the 1960s. Pro football's San Diego Chargers—in particular the 1963 team, then playing in the old American Football League—have been referred to as that particular sport's first "steroids team.") Even prior to that period, amphetamines became widely available in major-league clubhouses by the late 1940s in the form of "greenies," used to fight fatigue and gain physical and mental edges, with Hall of Famers from Hank Aaron, Mickey Mantle and Willie Mays to Johnny Bench, Mike Schmidt and Willie Stargell being connected to amphetamines.

Wrote baseball columnist Jeff Passan on *Yahoo! Sports* in 2017: "Steroid users took man-made products to change their body and help themselves play the game better. Know who else did? Ralph Kiner. He's in the Hall of Fame. He told me in 2005 that when he returned from World War II, a trainer suggested he try Benzedrine, the first pharmaceutical-grade amphetamine. He used them throughout his career. Willie Mays kept an amphetamine-laden drink called 'red juice' in his locker. He's in the Hall of Fame, too. Clubhouses had two coffee pots: unleaded (without amphetamines) and leaded (with Dexedrines, also known as greenies). Amphetamine use in baseball was widespread from the 1940s until testing started in 2006."

On the topic of "greenies," though, not everybody agrees in terms of how amphetamines compare to steroids and other performance-enhancing drugs. Brijbassi, because of his role as sports editor at *Newsday* when the BALCO scandal broke, considers himself well-versed enough to comment on the subject of PEDs since he had to make judgments on news pieces which were going out to readers. "Whatever they were," Brijbassi says, referring to amphetamines, "whether they were illegal, the drugs in the 1970s are not at all [comparable] to what BALCO was [reported to be] selling to Barry Bonds and what athletes like A-Rod and Clemens were [allegedly] using. Those were extremely advanced drugs that not only were capable of being masked against the majority of testing at that time, but also the ability to help an athlete recover from the overall toil of what was happening to their bodies. That was the largest attribute of BALCO's performance-enhancing drugs, was that they allowed Bonds to recover so much faster than his competitors. So, taking an amphetamine that might give you a short-term boost [isn't really comparable to PEDs], but again I don't know if they were deemed illegal at the time and if they were subsequently banned. That's one thing. But, again, you're looking at 30 years of advancement in technology, and an absolute ruthlessness on Bonds' part [if the allegations are true] to subvert the system and try and get away with what he's doing."

Long-time sports radio personality Ted Sobel, likewise, doesn't see amphetamines as the same as steroids. As far as he is concerned, amphetamines are simply energy boosters. PEDs, on the other hand, are performance enhancers. For one thing, Sobel says, steroids have been said to supply a far greater amount of energy and strength than "greenies," not to mention enhancing vision. The advantage over the competition, he argues, is huge when a player takes PEDs. "[Greenies were] just a body enhancer so that you had enough 'juice' left in your body, so you could play every single day," Sobel begins, referring to the fact that baseball was a demanding sport in that players played 162 games over a six-month period, a schedule which included plenty of cross-country travel and few off-days. "But it didn't make you a better player. [In terms of greenies, it] was almost like putting 10 cups of coffee in you, for caffeine, so you could stay awake."

Sobel pauses to acknowledge that he isn't a doctor—but has read up enough on the topic to make an educated comment about amphetamines. "Nobody added to their stats—except the fact that they played as opposed to not being able to play. That doesn't mean their stats were better. They played and didn't have to sit it out and let someone else potentially 'Wally Pipp' them. [Pipp, of course, is best remembered as the man who lost his starting role to Lou Gehrig in 1925 at the beginning of Gehrig's then-record streak of 2,130 consecutive games.] It's their job. It's their career. You want to play every game if you can. The trainers were giving it to the guys. A lot of them. It's not like they were doing these on the side and they had their own trainers like BALCO and all that crap. This was just to survive. And believe me, if they had greenies in the 1930s and 1940s, those guys would have taken it. Babe Ruth probably would've taken it. Or any of the greats. It's a tough game as a reporter covering them every damn night, and I don't even play! Even for a reporter covering baseball every day, that's tough. But if you have to physically play every single day and you have to perform, and you have to come up with stats that are productive that you're going to win games with, that is a different kind of pressure. [So if you look at] the physical part of it, that's what the greenies were all about. They were not performance enhancers. So, I have no problem with any of that. "

It depends on whom you talk to when it came to the debate about whether amphetamines and steroids are the same. When asked to compare the two, *USA Today*'s Bob Nightengale says, "Steroids are stronger than amphetamines, but they're both performance-enhancing drugs. And if guys use greenies or amphetamines now, [they're] suspended just as [they would be] if [they're] using anabolic steroids. It's just what degree does it help you. Guys are always doing stuff. Guys are doing stuff now and just getting away with it because they can beat the testing program."

For others who don't think Bonds deserves a plaque in Cooperstown, their argument is that Barry's link to PEDs is enough of a reason. "I'm a history buff, and that, of course, impacts my thinking on the idea of Barry Bonds entering the Hall of Fame," author Rick Allen told sports editor Rich Perkins in 2020. "I look back in history and see the difficult roads players like Jackie Robinson, Willie Mays, Frank Robinson, Hank Aaron and many other great players of color had to endure just to play the game, much less excel as they did. Those players had to fight through blatant prejudice, in some cases could not even stay in the same hotels or eat at the same restaurants with their teammates, suffered derisive racist comments from other players—and in some alleged cases, umpires—and death threats from 'fans.' Bonds had it so much easier, and on top of that is very likely to have used performance-enhancing drugs to inflate his statistics. So for me, it's very hard to come to grips with him being placed in the Hall of Fame. He was a great player before the Steroid Era, but how great compared to those in the Hall will forever be legitimately questioned."

Regarding that last comment, however, does it truly matter how great Bonds was compared to others in a different era? Those in favor of Bonds having a plaque in Cooperstown will argue Barry was the greatest player of his own era, and if you're not going to have the best player of his generation in the Hall, why have a Hall of Fame to begin with? "The Hall of Fame is a museum. As such, baseball writers are curators of the sport's history; the majority of them need to take a moment to realize what they are doing," opined *Bleacher Report* writer Alessandro Miglio in 2013. "Take a step back and look at the situation from a bird's eye view. We are talking about entry to a museum designated for the sport's most famous athletes. This isn't the 'Hall of Best Natural Athletes' or 'Hall of Really Good Players with No Blemishes.'"

Miglio is hardly alone when it comes to having that viewpoint. "Did Tyrannosaurus Rex have to be 'elected' into a Dinosaur Hall of Fame?" Joe Janish, a contributor to MetsToday.com, asked rhetorically in 2015. "No, but the beast is seen and learned about by many millions of people who go to the Field Museum of Natural History in Chicago. It can be the same way with the Baseball [Hall of Fame]—a curator or group of curators decide who and what is chronicled in the history of baseball. No more 'Hall of Famers'—it's a dumb concept, anyway, for what is a team game."

Count former *Pittsburgh Post-Gazette* columnist Bob Smizik as another who believes Barry belongs in Cooperstown. "He's one of the greatest players in baseball history. He absolutely should be in,"

Smizik said of Bonds in January 2020. "Gaylord Perry's in, and he admitted to cheating. To me, you have to look past what happened because almost everyone was doing it. Put on his plaque, 'Was widely believed to have used steroids.' But he should be in the Hall of Fame."

Sports radio personality Ted Sobel grimaces when the topic of Barry Bonds comes up, but he acknowledges the all-time home-run king belongs in Cooperstown. For Sobel, the logic is simple: If you were a Hall of Fame player without PEDs, then you belonged. If you were completely a product of the juice, then the answer would be no.

J. P. Hoornstra, a BBWAA member who becomes eligible to vote for the Hall for the first time beginning in the winter of 2021 (for the 2022 ballot), is another writer who considers the Hall of Fame a museum. "My response would be three-fold," Hoornstra begins, referring to how he'd respond to those who label Bonds a "cheater." "Number one, there are people who have 'cheated' similarly already in the Hall of Fame. [You'd know that] if you talked to writers, if you talked to players, teammates of players who are already in the Hall of Fame. There are reputable trustworthy people who will tell you that there are already steroid users in the Hall of Fame. If you read the book *Ball Four*, you'll have to conclude that there are amphetamine users in the Hall of Fame and perhaps there have been Hall of Fame players who have subsequently admitted to amphetamine use. [Second], if you're of the opinion that it's the leadership in Major League Baseball—that is, the commissioner—who didn't institute drug testing to enforce a policy banning the use of certain performance-enhancing drugs, who should be held accountable for that player behavior as much as the players, well, Bud Selig's already in the Hall of Fame. Between all of that, between my personal belief that, [thirdly,] the Hall of Fame is a museum and not a shrine, between the simple reality that we can't retroactively test people to know exactly who was doing what with 100% certainty, I just don't see how you can keep Barry Bonds and Roger Clemens out."

Hoornstra's points, which are shared by multiple Hall of Fame voters, are logical. If the Hall is ultimately a museum, how is it possible to exclude the very best players from an entire era in the sport's history? And if you happen to think it is, how in the world is Selig, the man who presided over that era, already enshrined?

Hoornstra takes his argument further, going back to the "greenies" vs. steroids and other PEDs debate. To him, amphetamines and performance-enhancing drugs may not exactly be on the same level, but they're at least comparable. And finding where to draw the line is complicated. "Let's take it a further step. Performance enhancement in different sports means different things," Hoornstra says. "In the sport of cycling, for example, blood boosting is a huge thing, where if you can get a fresh transfusion of blood over a course of several days of a long cycling race, [that gives you a significant] advantage. And you'd have more oxygen in your blood than a competitor, and that's illegal. You can't do that. You're supposed to compete with only the oxygen that's naturally in your blood.

"Would that be as much of a help in baseball? No, I don't think it would be much of a help at all. But we have to ask ourselves, number one, 'What are each of these drugs doing?' Obviously, number two, are they considered legal or not? I think therein you have a lot of different factors to consider. In the case of amphetamines—or, to really understand the ethics around the use of amphetamines by players—I'd want to know specifically, number one, how did it affect them? Number two, was Major League Baseball testing for this drug? Two A, was there a policy of using the drug? Three, was the drug legal or illegal under United States or specific state rules at the time? Within that, there are a lot of different layers where the player had to make an ethical choice. And you could say whether or not the player did right or wrong under your interpretation as a voter of the Hall of Fame's character clause.

"All those things that I just said about amphetamines would apply to whatever performance-enhancing drugs were available to players during the steroid era, whether that's a specific steroid, human growth hormone, something like androstenedione that was found in Mark McGwire's locker where it wasn't banned by Major League Baseball but it was banned by the National Football League. And just because it's banned by one league and not the other doesn't mean it's bad. But it makes you question whether it would help a football player more than a baseball player, which I think is relevant. You can run down that checklist for yourself and make your own conclusion. I guess my conclusion is that if you weren't testing for it, you basically, as a league—American League, National League,

Major League Baseball at large—didn't have a policy on your books at all. Or you didn't have a policy on your books that you cared to enforce. Again, whether it's amphetamines, steroids, human growth hormones, any drugs. You're not testing for it, or if you don't have a policy for it, it's clearly not a policy that you care to enforce. Then, if it is banned by the government at the time, you as a player are making a choice to take something that the government might not want you to take for some reason."

That last statement is what the anti-Bonds faction has repeatedly brought up; the possession and use of steroids without medical need would be illegal as documented in the Controlled Substances Act. "[Some] say Bonds shouldn't be punished by Hall of Fame voters because baseball didn't have an official steroid policy until 2002," journalist Michael O'Keeffe wrote in the *New York Daily News*. "Huh? In 1991, the federal government classified steroids as a controlled substance, making the sale, distribution and use of steroids without a prescription a criminal act. Two months later, commissioner Fay Vincent issued a memo stating that any player caught using illegal drugs, including steroids, faced expulsion from the game. Maybe that wasn't clear enough for Bonds and his fans in the press?"

Hoornstra acknowledges that particular viewpoint—but circles back to the precedent set with multiple amphetamine users already in Cooperstown. "And Hall of Fame voters should reasonably conclude that that has you in violation, your individual interpretation of the character clause, which is fine. But, by and large, we as the Baseball Writers' Association have decided that the use of amphetamines that may have been banned by the government at the time [was] not in violation of our collective definition of the character clause. And I don't think we've collectively held it against the leadership of Major League Baseball at the time to not enforce any bans on drugs that were outlawed by the government. So, right there, again, I don't see any difference between amphetamines and performance-enhancing drugs that were available during the Steroid Era. Any other differences, I think, are a matter of chemistry, and that's not to dismiss that, but to my knowledge, I don't know of a single Hall of Fame voter who has consulted with chemists to talk to them about how an amphetamine might help or harm a baseball player. Certainly, on its own merits or in comparison to steroids, HGH, androstenedione, etcetera, there's a lot to dig into. I don't think it's a simple 'Oh yeah, they're the same' or 'Oh yeah, they're different.' But, again, we as Hall of Fame voters have collectively decided that amphetamine use doesn't matter to the means by which we evaluate a player's ethics. So, I think that is relevant to the precedent of whether or not we should evaluate steroid use or HGH use—or androstenedione use or the use of any other drugs that we might find out players were taking during the steroid era—to their ethics as a person and as a Hall of Fame candidate."

Those who belong in the anti-Bonds faction have argued against that last line of reasoning. *Chicago Sun-Times* columnist Rick Morrissey, for one, has labeled such arguments in favor of alleged PED users getting into the Hall of Fame as among the "flimsiest" he's heard. "The fatal flaw in [that sort of reasoning] is best summed up by what mothers forever have told their crowd-following kids: Just because everybody's doing it doesn't make it right. Just because people have cheated, are cheating and will continue to cheat in baseball doesn't make it right. And it certainly doesn't mean the rest of us should shrug, capitulate and ultimately celebrate these people."

And so, the debate—whether Barry Bonds is worthy of the sport's greatest honor—continues.

Barry: Mr. Clutch Down the Stretch; Hard Luck and Near Misses in the Playoffs

Barry brought that swag to the team and it affected everybody. We won 103 games [in 1993 but] came up one game short [of reaching the playoffs]. I don't think there was any team in Major League Baseball that wanted to play us.

—Royce Clayton, as told to the author (2020)

Even though Barry Bonds never won a World Series, an undeniable fact is that his teams simply won a lot of games. From 1993 to 2007, Barry and the Giants would finish first or second in the National League Western division 10 times, reach the postseason four times—in 1997, 2000, 2002 and 2003—and appear in one World Series. (In fact, not counting the final three years of his career, Bonds' Giants finished first or second in 10 of 12 seasons, including the last eight in a row.) If not for the smallest of misfortunes, they easily could have added postseason berths in 1993, 1998, 2001 and 2004—and Bonds might have led San Francisco to World Series glory in one of those seasons. Bonds' Pirates, owners of the fourth-best record in the National League in 1988, weren't a playoff team in an era when only division winners advanced, but would have reached the postseason that season under the current playoff format.

And in some seasons, Bonds simply had no supporting cast. In 1995 and 1996, when *Total Baseball*, the so-called bible of statistics, concluded that Bonds was the best player in the National League both seasons, the Giants had virtually no pitching—finishing with the league's second-worst ERA both times, ahead only of the Colorado Rockies, who played half their games at Coors Field—and had only one other All-Star slugger in their lineup: third baseman Matt Williams, who missed 125 games due to injuries in the two seasons.

Bonds, who missed only four games in the two seasons, averaged 38 home runs and 116 RBIs with 36 stolen bases (only eight caught stealing) and a .301 batting average.

But the Giants simply had too many holes. Lefty Terry Mulholland, the Giants' Opening Day starter in 1995, would briefly be sent to the bullpen in August and finish with a 5-13 record. Mark Leiter, a journeyman, led the team with 10 wins in 1995 but ended the year with a losing record. William VanLandingham, a 24-year-old and probably the best pitcher on that staff, would be out of the majors by 1997. And while opposing teams feared Bonds, they knew they could beat the Giants if they didn't let Barry beat them. Late in the season, for instance, the Dodgers walked Bonds four times one night, three times intentionally, and manager Tommy Lasorda ordered Barry to be walked with two outs and the bases empty in the eighth inning of a tie game (a contest which the Giants wound up losing in extra innings).

In 1996, only one Giants starting pitcher (Mark Gardner, 12-7) posted a winning record among those who made more than 10 starts. "The San Francisco Giants came to town Tuesday night," the *Los Angeles Times'* Mike Downey wrote during a Giants-Dodgers series in late September 1996, "with their lineup of Barry Bonds and eight other guys wearing caps." The Giants, in that series, had Allen Watson and Mark Dewey on the mound, Desi Wilson at first base, Wilson Delgado at short, Kim Batiste at third and Jay Canizaro at second. Jacob Cruz and Dave McCarty, a pair of light-hitting youngsters, had at-bats in the series. It was a lineup more suited for a split-squad game in Scottsdale, Arizona, than in Los Angeles. "I didn't recognize any of them," continued Downey, referring to the team as Bonds and the "No-Name" Giants. "I think… these were eight dudes San Francisco found at the last minute, who bought their jerseys at Foot Locker."

With that lineup and mediocre pitching staff in 1995 and 1996, not even Babe Ruth would have carried the Giants to the postseason.

Had he played on more talented teams? It could have happened, as the Braves and Pirates discussed a trade prior to the 1992 season that would have sent Bonds to Atlanta. Braves third baseman Terry Pendleton, who edged Bonds for the 1991 MVP and would be the runner-up to him for the award in 1992, recalled in 2020 that then-general manager John Schuerholz approached him in spring training in 1992 and asked what he thought about the idea of acquiring Bonds and whether he'd be a good fit in the Atlanta clubhouse. "He came to me early in spring training and said to me, 'Listen, we've got an opportunity to probably get Barry Bonds. I'm just concerned with his attitude in the clubhouse and how he's going to rub people,'" Pendleton, the unofficial captain of the Braves then, recalled. "And I looked at him and said, 'John, just get him and let me worry about that.' The bottom line, I said, 'We got this. If you can get him, trust me, it ain't going to be an issue.'"

No deal happened, as it turned out. But had Bonds really become a Brave, Pendleton believed, Atlanta—which captured the World Series in 1995 but lost the Series in 1991, 1992, 1996 and 1999— would have won more titles during its run of 14 consecutive division titles, a stretch which began in 1991. "Barry would have made a difference," opined Pendleton. "We probably would have won a few more than we lost going in the playoffs or World Series, because he can definitely change the game, we know that."

* * *

Pendleton and the Braves eliminated Bonds' Pirates in the 1991 and 1992 NL playoffs, with Atlanta capturing both series in seven games before falling short in the World Series each time.

Those two NL playoff series between Bonds and the Braves were just a warm-up to the epic, well-documented Bonds vs. Atlanta battle in the National League West race in 1993, after Barry had signed with the Giants in December 1992. In the final season before Major League Baseball's wild-card era—when each league's playoff field consisted of only two teams, the Eastern and Western divisions champions—San Francisco won 103 games, a total which, in any other year, would have been good enough for a berth in the postseason. But the Giants, despite owning the second-best record in all of baseball, were eliminated on the season's final day when the Braves, then one of the seven clubs which made up the NL West, won their 104th game and San Francisco, having run out of pitching at the end, lost its regular season finale hours later.

And Bonds—who batted .449 with five homers, five doubles and 15 RBIs in 13 games against the Braves that year (with four of those round-trippers coming at Atlanta-Fulton County Stadium, where he batted .417 in six games)—certainly couldn't be faulted for the Giants' second-place finish. (Bonds, in fact, gave the Braves' Hall of Fame trio of Greg Maddux, Tom Glavine and John Smoltz fits all season. He batted .700—.700!!— with two homers in 10 at-bats off Maddux in 1993, .500 with a homer and two doubles off Glavine and .400 off Smoltz. He also homered off 18-game winner Steve Avery and fifth starter Pete Smith, hitting .273 off the former and going 2-for-2 off the latter.)

Entering play on September 17, San Francisco was actually four games out of first place, as the Braves, winners in 29 of their last 35 games, were looking to run away with the division. From that date until the end of September, though, Bonds batted .326 with four homers and 14 RBIs in 14 games as the Giants went 12-2 and made up four full games in the standings. In Game No. 160 on October 1 at Dodger Stadium, with the Giants tied with Atlanta atop the NL West, Bonds had a game for the ages. On a night when 21-game winner John Burkett struggled on the mound, the Dodgers struck for four runs in the first two innings and looked to cruise to an easy victory. Bonds, though, took center stage. With the Giants already having plated a run in the third to cut the deficit to 4-1, Bonds blasted a three-run homer to deep center off Dodger ace Ramon Martinez to even the score. Two innings later, he greeted left-hander Omar Daal, who'd just entered the game moments earlier, with another three-run shot to put the Giants ahead for good. In the seventh, Bonds greeted lefty Steve Wilson with a double, driving in Will Clark from first and giving him seven RBIs on the night. He'd driven in seven of the last eight Giants runs, and San Francisco hung on for an 8-7 victory. (Who said he couldn't deliver when the calendar turned from September to October?) The performance was all the more remarkable when one considers the fact Bonds had faced knuckleball specialist Tom Candiotti the night before. "Barry used to tell me that he hated facing a knuckleball pitcher like me," Candiotti says now. "He said I'd mess his swing and put him in a slump for the next week." But obviously not that time.

And that September performance was nothing new for Bonds, who a year earlier had batted .392 with 10 doubles, 11 homers and 27 RBIs from September 1 onwards to help Pittsburgh capture its third consecutive division title, as the Pirates, holding just a slim three-game lead atop the NL East over Montreal entering the season's final month, went 22-10 over the final 32 contests to easily outdistance the

Expos by nine games. There was also 1990, when he homered eight times over a 13-game stretch in September, batting .370 in that span, as Pittsburgh held off the heavily-favored—and star-studded—Mets to win its first NL East flag in 11 years.

The 1994 season was the year of the players' strike, and had that season been played out, things might have been different. At least as far as Giants center fielder Darren Lewis was concerned. "If you look at the standings," Lewis once said years later, "we were just three games out. That's when we were really starting to pick things up. We just got Darryl Strawberry. With him in the lineup behind Barry and Matt Williams, we were on our way to something special. We just ran out of time." Although John Burkett and Bill Swift—who'd won 22 and 21 games, respectively, just a year earlier—faltered in 1994, going 6-8 and 8-7, respectively, the Giants stayed in contention thanks mainly to the contributions of Bonds and Williams, along with the addition of Strawberry, whose arrival in San Francisco in early July helped slice their deficit from 9.5 games behind first-place Los Angeles to just 3.5 when the strike hit.

It was, for Bonds, yet another missed opportunity. Things would be vastly different when baseball restarted in 1995. Between the 1993-94 off-season and the end of the 1996 season, the Peter Magowan-led ownership group made many roster moves, which included the departures of Will Clark, Darren Lewis, Royce Clayton, Swift and Burkett, among others. Strawberry, whose arrival led to a 9-0 run by the Giants in his first nine games and 16-4 in the first 20, also wasn't brought back. The Giants weren't relevant again until the team's surprise division title in 1997.

And it was Bonds who carried the no-name Giants in September of 1997, when San Francisco and Los Angeles battled down the stretch for the NL West division crown. (With the Florida Marlins, the second-place team behind Atlanta in the NL East, having a better record than both the Giants and Dodgers, the lone NL wild-card spot was not a fall-back option for the club that would finish as the NL West runner-up.) Barry batted .303 in the season's final month, with a team-best nine homers and 19 RBIs. In fact, he homered in seven of San Francisco's last 11 regular season games, batting .344. Against the Dodgers during the course of the season, he had seven round-trippers and 13 RBIs in 12 games, and he certainly delivered again when it mattered. On September

17, Bonds' 426-foot two-run home run off L.A. right-hander Chan Ho Park gave the Giants a 2-1 win, and pulled San Francisco within one game of the Dodgers. The following day, the Giants won again to pull into a tie with the Dodgers in the standings, with Bonds smacking another homer and a triple. The Dodgers, heavy favorites to win the division, never recovered, and the Giants, who were expected to finish last, went on to capture the NL West title. Although the Giants were swept by the Marlins in the Division Series, it was hardly Bonds' fault. In the first two games, he went 3-for-8 (.375) with two doubles, two RBIs and, according to *The San Francisco Chronicle*, "some sterling plays in the outfield"—but Florida won both contests in the bottom of the ninth en route to the series sweep. "So far, Bonds has erased any doubts that he has a tendency to fall short in the postseason," added the *Chronicle* the morning of Game Three.

But that 1997 NLDS could have gone the Giants' way if San Francisco had gotten some breaks. In the opener, Bill Mueller took Marlins ace Kevin Brown's second pitch of the seventh inning out of the ballpark to put the Giants ahead 1-0, and Bonds, the next hitter, just missed his own homer when his high fly ball bounced off the top of the left-center field wall—nicknamed the Teal Tower—at Pro Player Stadium. With Bonds standing on second with none out, however, J. T. Snow, Jeff Kent and Stan Javier all failed to cash him in, and the Marlins rallied for the 2-1 victory. But what if Bonds' drive to left center had gone out? What if he wasn't left stranded in scoring position?

While there are those who criticize Bonds for the Giants' 1998 loss in the National League wild-card tie-breaker game against Sammy Sosa's Chicago Cubs—twice in the final three innings he came up as the potential tying run with the bases loaded, but couldn't get a hit either time in the 5-3 defeat—it's important to remember that San Francisco wouldn't even have gotten to that one-game showdown if not for Barry's heroics down the stretch. In the final week of the regular season, while the baseball world was focusing on the home-run exploits of Sosa and Mark McGwire, Bonds was a one-man show carrying the Giants on his back. In that final week, Bonds hit .462 with three doubles, two triples, four walks and a pair of home runs in seven games. The Giants won the first six before dropping the regular season finale 9-8 in Colorado, forcing the one-game playoff with Chicago for the NL's lone wild-card berth.

And San Francisco needed to win those games just to get to that point. On September 24 against Pittsburgh, Bonds homered in the first inning to put the Giants on the scoreboard, doubled in his next at-bat and scored two runs on the night, as San Francisco won 6-2. Two days later in Colorado, Bonds walked and scored on a double in the first inning, and then doubled to open the fourth inning, which led to a five-run frame that put the Giants ahead for good. He finished with three hits on the afternoon in the Giants' 8-4 victory. In the regular season finale, the Giants jumped out to a 7-0 lead in the fifth—thanks to Bonds' RBI double to open the scoring in the third and his leadoff triple in the fifth which led to a four-run inning—and San Francisco looked to be on the way to clinching the wild-card berth. Alas—shades of the 1993 season finale—the Giants' pitching collapsed over the final four frames, and Neifi Perez's homer off San Francisco relief ace Robb Nen leading off the bottom of the ninth gave the Rockies a stunning 9-8 victory. (Perez, who'd later play for the Giants in 2003-04 and be widely criticized because of his mediocre career on-base percentage of .297 over his 12 major-league seasons, was labeled "one of the worst offensive players in baseball history" by a Chicago sportswriter in 2008.)

Bonds couldn't be faulted for the collapse. He'd been clutch throughout September, hitting .407 with seven homers and 18 extra-base hits with 21 RBIs in 24 games—and certainly came through in the season's final week.

Barry again delivered down the stretch in 2000, when the Arizona Diamondbacks, who'd bolstered their starting rotation in late July with the acquisition of right-hander Curt Schilling from Philadelphia, looked poised to overtake the division-leading Giants. Arizona, with the fearsome one-two punch of Schilling and Randy Johnson in its rotation, entered the month of September only three games behind San Francisco, but Bonds helped keep the Giants in first place with a career-best 14-game hitting streak between September 4 and September 20— they won 11 of those games—batting .426 (20-for-47) with nine homers and 22 RBIs during the streak. San Francisco cruised to the division title, capturing the NL West crown by a remarkable 11 games and finishing with baseball's best record at 97-65.

Had there been two wild-card berths in the early 2000s— baseball's current expanded playoff format, which includes a wild-card play-in game, wasn't introduced until 2012—the Giants would have returned to the postseason in 2001. In what turned out to be Bonds' record-setting 73-homer season, San Francisco finished two games back of NL West champion Arizona and missed the playoffs, but with their 90 victories the Giants would have qualified for the play-in game under the current expanded wild-card format as the NL's second wild-card team.

For Dustan Mohr, the division crown was there for the taking in 2004, a season which ultimately saw the Giants finish two games behind L.A. in the NL West and just one game back of Houston for the NL's lone wild-card berth. "We were swept by the Pirates early that year," he laments, "and you shouldn't get swept by a team [that's lower in the standings like Pittsburgh]. And that cost us." The pennant race came down to the season's final weekend, with the Giants, trailing L.A. by two games in the standings, taking a 3-0 lead into the bottom of the ninth at Dodger Stadium in the penultimate game. Get those last three outs, and then send ace Jason Schmidt—second on the team in WAR only to Bonds in 2004 and who'd finish 18-7 with a 3.20 ERA and 251 strikeouts—out to the mound against the Dodgers the next afternoon to close out the season. With Schmidt going in Game No. 162, the Giants would have a shot to tie L.A. for first place, forcing a one-game playoff for the division crown. Or, at the very least, somehow finish ahead of Houston for the wild card.

But hang on. The Dodgers rallied for seven runs in that final inning in Game No. 161 thanks to three walks, a crucial error by defensive replacement Cody Ransom at shortstop and Steve Finley's game-ending, NL West-clinching grand slam. "We knew we were going to win the final game of the season with Schmidt going," Mohr continues, adding that the decision to replace starting shortstop Deivi Cruz with Ransom might have changed the final inning's momentum. "I'm not second-guessing [manager] Felipe [Alou] putting Cody into the game, but at times he wanted to play his veterans." Ransom, for instance, was a homegrown player in the Giants organization, having been drafted in 1998, while Cruz, who'd already played for Detroit, San Diego and Baltimore, was a newcomer in 2004. "I'm not blaming Cody," Mohr adds, matter-of-factly, "because it's tough to come in and play defense when you've been on the bench the whole game. You go back and look at the last inning, how that unraveled. Then Finley hit the grand slam. It was tough."

The Giants' division-title hopes were dashed with that loss, and so were their wild-card dreams the next day when Houston punched its ticket to the playoffs with a 5-3 win over Colorado. Schmidt and the Giants bullpen blanked the Dodgers 10-0 to give San Francisco its 91st victory of the year, good for fifth overall in the NL, but not good enough for the playoffs in an era which saw only four teams per league reach the postseason. But what if Bonds, Schmidt and the rest of the Giants had gotten a shot in the playoffs that year?

* * *

Even when Bonds reached the playoffs, it wasn't always his struggles at the plate that doomed his teams. Other teammates couldn't get the clutch hits. Opposing pitchers just pitched better while pitchers on his own team were the ones giving up big hits. Opposing teams simply made the plays in the field while Bonds' teams made key errors at inopportune times.

San Francisco's 1997 NL Division Series loss was briefly discussed earlier. As for Bonds' NL Championship Series struggles with Pittsburgh from 1990 to 1992? People forget he faced tough left-handed pitchers against both Cincinnati and Atlanta. In the 1990 playoffs, the Reds sent out left-handers Tom Browning and Danny Jackson against the Pirates. Cincinnati right-hander Jose Rijo, meanwhile, was virtually untouchable that October en route to capturing World Series MVP honors. In the 1991 and 1992 postseasons, the Braves trotted out lefties Tom Glavine, Steve Avery and Charlie Leibrandt. In the 1991 NLCS in particular, Avery was practically unhittable. "Believe me when I tell you this," Jim Leyland said prior to the 1992 playoffs. "The way Avery pitched a couple of games last year, you could find practically every team in the National and American Leagues who weren't going to hit him. Whether it was Barry Bonds or Wade Boggs or George Brett or anybody else."

As well, in baseball one superstar hitter isn't enough to carry his team on his own. "We're here because we're a team," Leyland added, referring to the Pirates' third straight playoff appearance in 1992. "We executed as a team. I feel Barry Bonds is the best player in baseball. Does that necessarily mean that he's supposed to come in here and tear up in the playoffs? No. That just means that hopefully he'll have a good series along with the rest of our ballclub. Sure, we need Barry to perform pretty well. But we need our entire team to perform pretty well." Bonds himself echoed that last statement during the 1992 playoffs. "Maybe they should just let my team go on vacation and let me pitch and catch and play all the positions," he was quoted as saying. "I guess then the media would get what they wanted. But you see, it's not a Barry Bonds show out there; it's a team effort."

During the Pirates' three-year run, one of the reasons they were so successful is virtually every player on the roster contributed. In 1990, for instance, 19 different pitchers won at least one game, 13 started at least once and nine different relievers recorded at least one save. While Bonds, Bobby Bonilla and Andy Van Slyke were the stars, Sid Bream clubbed 15 homers and Jeff King contributed 14 more. (Yes, THAT same Sid Bream. He played for the Pirates for five years before signing as a free agent with Atlanta following the 1990 season.) Veterans Don Slaught and Mike LaValliere shared the catching duties and handled a pitching staff that finished with the league's third-best ERA. In 1991, when Bonds started out hitting .170 through mid-May, Pittsburgh was still in first place. In 1992, following the departures of Bonilla and 20-game winner John Smiley, mid-season acquisition Alex Cole filled in adequately in right field and atop the Pirates' batting order, while Randy Tomlin and rookie call-up Tim Wakefield combined for 22 wins.

Much has been made about Barry's performance in those three consecutive NL Championship Series losses by the Pirates. But what isn't remembered is the fact that even when he wasn't hitting, he was still contributing in other ways. In the Pirates' 4-3 win over Cincinnati in the 1990 NLCS opener, for instance, Bonds walked with two outs in the fourth and provoked half a dozen pickoff throws from Jose Rijo before Bream smacked a pitch into the seats for a two-run homer and a 3-3 tie. In Game Six, Bonds walked and scored on Carmelo Martinez's double in the fifth (the Pirates' only hit of the night) to tie the game 1-1. But there were some bad breaks for Pittsburgh, too. Bonds, again on first base via another walk in the ninth inning of that same sixth game, was the possible tying run with Pittsburgh trailing 2-1, and Martinez hit a long fly ball to right—only to see the Reds' Glenn Braggs, who was playing deep, leap above the right-field fence to take a home run away. "My wrist was over the wall," Braggs recalled of his game-saving catch years later. "I thought it was gone. I went back on the wall. It was right there. I jumped up and caught it." One out later, the Pirates' season was over.

It's just as important to note—John Cangelosi, one of Pittsburgh's reserve outfielders on that 1990 team, reminds readers now—that the Pirates' other starts also didn't fare well, with Bonilla hitting .190 and Van Slyke batting .208 for that Reds series. The trio of Bonds, Bonilla and Van Slyke combined for three extra-base hits in 63 series at-bats. But what if Carmelo Martinez's drive to right hadn't been caught and the series had gone to a seventh game? "Seven inches from Game Seven," as Martinez later said.

Cangelosi, for one, doesn't believe it's fair to blame the Pirates' 1990-92 postseason failures on Barry Bonds. "I think [in that first year in 1990] it was just that we were young and we were excited to be there. Barry wasn't the only one who struggled. Our whole offense struggled. He, Andy Van Slyke and Bobby Bonilla [combined to hit .190 in 63 at-bats] in the series. We didn't get run production from our main three guys that we got all year. We got decent pitching. I just think that [after the NLCS loss to Cincinnati in 1990,] the guys were trying to win really hard for Jimmy Leyland [in 1991 and 1992]," reflects Cangelosi today. "[It became a situation where] you put a little too much pressure on yourself, and then [when] you do that, you're swinging at pitches that you normally wouldn't swing at. I think we were just pressing to try to do too much." Jim Leyland has admitted as much. "Right now, I think Barry Bonds is trying to hit a five-run home run," the Pirates manager said during the 1992 NL Championship Series. "He's trying to make an unbelievable play; he's pressing a little bit. Really, that's not what we want him to do. We impressed upon him that he doesn't have to carry the team, he just needs to be part of the team and make some contributions."

In 1991, despite Barry's .150 average through five games, Pittsburgh took a 3-2 series lead against Atlanta, with Games Six and Seven back at Three Rivers Stadium. "People seem to forget I was 17-for-100 [in mid-May] and we were in first place," Bonds pointed out before Game Six. "If you're waiting for me to hit, then you're missing the aspects of the game. We're 25 guys. I hope we win this and I can do it in the World Series." Blanked through eight innings in Game Six by the virtually untouchable Steve Avery, the Pirates had one last shot against reliever Alejandro Pena, when Gary Varsho led off the ninth with a single and advanced to second on a sacrifice bunt. But Jay Bell lined out to right on the first pitch and, after Varsho moved to third on a wild pitch, Van Slyke—who'd bat .160 for the series—took a called strike three. Pittsburgh lost 1-0 and never scored again the rest of the series.

But had Bell or Van Slyke cashed in Varsho in Game Six, who knows what might have happened?

Avery worked 16.1 shutout innings in the series and won a pair of 1-0 games, but the Pirates could have broken through in his other start, Game Two. In the eighth inning that night, Gary Redus and Bell singled off Avery with two outs to put runners on first and third. Van Slyke, however, grounded into a force-out at second. In the ninth, Bonilla led off with a double and moved to third on a wild pitch with one out. But with the tying run on third, neither Steve Buechele nor pinch-hitter Curt Wilkerson could come through. (Hey, if the Braves could have the likes of little-known Mark Lemke, in 1991, and Francisco Cabrera, in 1992, coming up with big postseason hits, why not Wilkerson, the unheralded reserve infielder for the Pirates, too?)

Had the Pirates somehow pushed across that run to force extra innings in either Avery start, perhaps the series outcome might have been different, and with a World Series berth, Bonds' postseason legacy with Pittsburgh might have been looked at differently?

In San Francisco, meanwhile, Bonds' Giants were plagued by hard luck, misplays, and questionable managerial decisions in the postseason. In 2000, the Giants were poised to defeat the New York Mets in the Division Series, only to drop consecutive extra-inning heartbreakers before being eliminated on a one-hitter by Bobby Jones, the Mets' fourth starter. For Bonds, his teams had now gone 0-for-5 in first-round playoff series while he batted .196 in 97 at-bats with a home run and six RBIs. But the series' turning point came in Game Two, when Giants reliever Felix Rodriguez was allowed to stay in the contest despite having already given up a ninth-inning home run.

With the Giants, already ahead 1-0 in the series (with Bonds' RBI triple driving in the winning run in the 5-1 opening-game victory), trailing Game Two by a 2-1 score in the ninth, the Mets' Edgardo Alfonzo drilled a two-out, two-run homer off Rodriguez to put New York ahead 4-1. In the bottom of the ninth, though, Bonds doubled, Jeff Kent singled and J. T. Snow slugged a pinch-hit, three-run homer off Mets closer Armando Benitez to send the game into extras. Manager Dusty

Baker, inexplicably, sent Rodriguez back out for the 10th inning, and Jay Payton singled home Darryl Hamilton, who'd doubled with two outs, off Rodriguez, and the Mets won 5-4. Why wasn't Giants closer Robb Nen brought in to start the 10th? After all, with no save situation for the home team in an extra-inning game—the contest is immediately over when the home team breaks the tie in extras, meaning you don't need a closer in that situation—why wasn't Nen, the team's stopper and the owner of a microscopic 1.50 ERA during the season, brought into the game? Naturally, when Nen, who racked up 41 saves during the year (and had gone 28-for-28 in saves since July 4), did come in when the series shifted to New York, he coughed up the Giants' 2-1 lead in the eighth inning, and San Francisco lost in the 13th.

Poor managerial decisions with the bullpen and bullpen failures, along with the team's lack of clutch hitting, were reasons for the Giants' series loss, yet fingers are always unfairly pointed toward Bonds when his team couldn't advance—with this 2000 NLDS flameout against the Mets being a prime example. (As a side note, people have forgotten that the 2000 Mets, whose roster included veteran stars Mike Piazza, Todd Zeile, Robin Ventura, Al Leiter and John Franco, were a very strong ballclub; entering the month of September, the Mets—not the Yankees, Braves or Giants—were, along with the White Sox, the co-owners of baseball's best record. When the season ended, the Mets' 94 wins were only three fewer than the Giants' 97.)

San Francisco's four-game Division Series rout at the hands of Florida in 2003, meanwhile, could have turned out differently had the supporting cast done its job. One of the series' key moments came in the 11th inning of Game Three, when Giants Gold Glove right fielder Jose Cruz, Jr., who'd made only two errors all season, inexplicably dropped a routine flyball by Jeff Conine. It proved to be a key error, as the Marlins, one strike away from defeat moments later, rallied for the win when Ivan Rodriguez singled home the tying and winning runs off right-hander Tim Worrell, who'd taken over that season as the Giants' closer with Robb Nen out for the year with a torn rotator cuff. (Nen, as it turned out, would never pitch again.) "I dropped it," Cruz later said of his error. "That's it… It was a flyball into my glove, and it fell out. I gave what I had and I didn't catch it." The following day, it was about how Giants catcher Yorvit Torrealba dropped the ball at the plate while Rodriguez, his counterpart on the

Marlins, didn't. With the game tied, Miguel Cabrera smacked an eighth-inning single with two runners on, and Cruz's throw from right field was up the line a few feet. Torrealba tried to grab the ball and tag Rodriguez, who was chugging home from second. They collided, the ball popped loose, and Rodriguez scored. As the ball scooted away, a second run scored to give the Marlins a 7-5 lead. In the ninth, with the Giants down by a run and J. T. Snow on second (San Francisco was out of position players and couldn't replace the slow-footed first baseman with a pinch-runner), Jeffrey Hammonds delivered a base hit to shallow left field, and Snow headed home. But Conine, playing left field, made a perfect throw to Rodriguez, who easily tagged Snow out. Series over.

Although Bonds hit just .222 in the series, he also wasn't given a lot of opportunities as the Marlins, refusing to let Barry win the series, walked him eight times in four games. In this 2003 series, it was misplays by Cruz and Torrealba that hurt the Giants. It was the pitching failures of starters Sidney Ponson (Game Two) and Jerome Williams (Game Four), and relievers Worrell and Joe Nathan, that doomed the club. It was ace Jason Schmidt's inability to start Game Four on short rest. Second-guessers will also point out that had the Giants placed speedy second baseman Eric Young on the postseason roster, he could've run for Snow and easily would've scored the tying run—but the team had decided instead to take two left-handed relievers (Jason Christiansen and Scott Eyre, who combined to pitch one-third of an inning in the series). And in what turned out to be Barry's last appearance in the postseason, San Francisco faltered at the most inopportune time, allowing the Marlins to be only the second team in 2003 to beat them three times in a row with Bonds in the lineup.

Bonds' only World Series appearance came in 2002, which the Giants lost in seven games to the Anaheim Angels. Although he had a Series for the ages—Barry batted .471 with four home runs, two doubles and 13 walks—San Francisco, with a chance to clinch its first championship since the franchise relocated from New York in 1958, blew a 5-0 lead with eight outs remaining in a stunning Game Six collapse before losing the seventh game 4-1.

But Bonds, who batted .384 against left-handers and .363 against right-handers during the 2002 regular season, came through in nearly every spot throughout that entire campaign. For those who like to quote the famous Stan Musial trivia about how the Cardinals Hall of Famer collected 1,815 career hits at home and 1,815 career hits on the road, how about Bonds' numbers in 2002? No matter what the conditions, if teams pitched to him, Barry always hit. He batted .376 when nobody was on base and .376 when there were runners in scoring position. He came through in nearly every spot during the entire postseason run. In the Division Series, he finally won a playoff series against his long-time nemesis, the Atlanta Braves. His three home runs and .294 average for the series helped the Giants defeat the favored Braves three games to two, with Bonds homering in the series finale as San Francisco won 3-1 at Turner Field.

In the Giants' surprising five-game series victory over St. Louis in the NL Championship Series, Bonds batted .273 with a triple, a homer and five runs scored. With the Giants ahead 2-1 in the series in Game Four, the teams were tied 2-2 with two outs in the eighth and nobody on when the Cardinals, not wanting Bonds to beat them, chose to intentionally walk him to willingly put the go-ahead runner on base. Benito Santiago, the next hitter, promptly hit a home run to give San Francisco a commanding three-games-to-one lead. "He adds dimensions to managing that don't enter into the picture with any other club you manage against," Dodgers manager Jim Tracy later said in defending the Cardinals' decision to intentionally walk Bonds. "You sit there with the card in your hand, looking at each inning, wondering if he's six hitters away. You think, if he's the sixth hitter and the bases are loaded with two outs, he's the hitter. That actually crosses your mind. And then what do you do with your bullpen?... But just the thought of him coming up gives you something you have to think about." In the series clincher, Bonds delivered a bases-loaded sacrifice fly off Cardinals ace Matt Morris in the bottom of the eighth to tie the game 1-1, before the Giants enjoyed a walk-off victory the following inning.

And then there was the Fall Classic against the Angels. In his first World Series at-bat, facing left-hander Jarrod Washburn at Edison International Field, he homered to put the Giants on the scoreboard en route to San Francisco's 4-3 victory. The following night, he became the first player since 1982 (and fourth overall) to hit a home run in his first two World Series games, although the Giants' pitching staff faltered in an 11-10 loss. With San Francisco ahead three games to two—the Giants took two of three when the Series shifted to Pac Bell Park—Bonds homered off Angels rookie sensation Francisco Rodriguez in the sixth inning to give the Giants a 4-0 lead in Game Six. Unfortunately for San Francisco fans, it was Felix Rodriguez, Tim Worrell and Robb Nen failing in relief over the next two innings—with the Angels' Scott Spiezio thumping a three-run homer and Troy Glaus slugging a two-run double—to thwart the Giants. Although Bonds did his part, it ultimately wasn't enough as it was the Angels celebrating the World Series championship one night later.

* * *

Some believed that by simply taking the Giants to the World Series in 2002, Bonds could say that his career was complete. *San Francisco Chronicle* writer John Shea was among those who felt that way following the Giants' NL Championship Series victory over St. Louis which sent San Francisco into the Fall Classic against the Angels. Reaching the World Series in the first place, after all, was a difficult task in itself. The Giants, following their move from New York to the Bay Area in 1958, had won just two National League pennants, in 1962 and 1989. And now, following a 13-year absence, Bonds had taken them back to the Fall Classic. "He doesn't think so, but Barry Bonds' career is complete," Shea opined after the Giants eliminated the Cardinals in the NLCS, with Bonds hitting .286 and contributing four homers and 10 RBIs in the first two postseason rounds. "He could quit the game later this month, and there would be no more 'ifs' and 'buts' or 'what about Sid Bream?' He could retire and never be accused of establishing a Hall of Fame career without the missing link."

Shea also argued that reaching a Series was always a bigger challenge than winning one, listing the names of Hall of Famers Ernie Banks, Ralph Kiner and Billy Williams, those who never played in a World Series. "History is kinder to Ted Williams, Harmon Killebrew and Willie McCovey, Hall of Famers who got to the World Series but didn't win," the *Chronicle* scribe added. Bonds' father, Bobby, never played in one. Willie Mays, meanwhile, appeared in just one World Series in his 14 full seasons in San Francisco. As for Williams, his 1946 Red Sox lost Games Six and Seven to the Cardinals in his only appearance in the Series over a 19-year career. Killebrew, who appeared in only one Series in his 22 seasons in the big leagues, saw his Twins blow a two-games-to-one lead and lose in seven games to the L.A. Dodgers in the 1965 Classic.

Winning a World Series, obviously, isn't an easy feat, either. Just ask the Atlanta Braves. The Braves, forever Bonds' nemesis until Barry finally got a measure of revenge when the Giants knocked them out in the 2002 NL Division Series, won a major-league record 14 consecutive division crowns between 1991 and 2005 (the strike year of 1994 is excluded in the streak)—yet captured only one World Series title in that stretch.

Furthermore, not every superstar player shines in October baseball—although most didn't receive nearly as many criticisms as Barry Bonds did. Most weren't ridiculed as much as he was. Or received as much media scrutiny as him. The Braves' best pitcher during their run (and arguably the game's top pitcher of his era), Hall of Fame right-hander Greg Maddux, didn't perform well in his first few postseason appearances, either, posting a 6.62 ERA over his first six postseason starts. (When he was pitching in Game One of the 1995 World Series, in fact, a graphic on The Baseball Network/ABC telecast indicated that the right-hander owned the highest career postseason ERA entering that start.) In his first postseason series in 1989, Maddux, then pitching for the Cubs, was lit up by the Giants for a 13.50 ERA in two starts, giving up 12 runs (11 earned) in 7.1 innings including a grand slam to Will Clark. He failed to go beyond four innings in either start, and Chicago lost the series in five games. Maddux's next postseason series came in October of 1993, when his Braves were eliminated in the NLCS as he was pounded for six runs over 5.2 innings in Game Six in Philadelphia.

In October of 1996, Maddux gave up a grand slam to the Cardinals' Gary Gaetti and was rocked for eight runs in an NLCS start against St. Louis. Although he regrouped later in that series—as Atlanta reached the World Series for the second straight year—he proved human in an elimination game against the Yankees in Game Six of the Fall Classic. He was outpitched by Jimmy Key and the Yankees bullpen as the heavily-favored Braves were eliminated, which launched a dynasty by the Bronx Bombers. For his postseason career, Maddux would be a pedestrian 11-14 in his postseason career with a respectable—but un-Maddux-like—3.27 ERA in 35 appearances, including a 5.91 ERA on short rest (starting on three days' rest in postseason play). But his un-Maddux-like performances in October baseball have virtually been forgotten.

Pedro Martinez, also in the discussion about who the best pitcher was in the 1990s and 2000s, entered postseason baseball lore for his dominance against Cleveland in the 1999 American League Division Series and won a World Series ring with Boston in 2004. But his meltdown in Game Seven of the 2003 AL Championship Series— Martinez coughed up a three-run, eighth-inning lead with the Red Sox only five outs away from capturing the pennant—saw Boston lose in excruciating fashion as the franchise's World Series drought extended to an 85th year. (That meltdown, by the way, came five days after Martinez was outpitched by Roger Clemens in a Game Three loss at Fenway Park and made headlines by throwing Don Zimmer to the ground after the 72-year-old Yankees bench coach came charging at him when a separate alternation broke out on the field. Why weren't fans or media members pointing the finger at Pedro for losing Game Three, when a victory in that contest might have altered the course of that series?) Yet it was Pedro's manager, Grady Little, who was widely blamed for that series loss, and the Red Sox decided not to pick up Little's option to manage in 2004.

Looking strictly at hitters, the annals of postseason baseball are also replete with big names with poor October stats, from Ted Williams to Frank Thomas and Willie Mays to Jeff Bagwell. These examples are provided to highlight the fact that even the greatest players in history—or in some cases, the best players at their positions in their own eras—didn't always fare well on the game's biggest stage. These players, like Bonds, often didn't hit as well as everybody expected. It happens. Even to the best.

Williams, in his only career postseason appearance, batted .200 with only five hits—all singles—and one RBI in the 1946 World Series as the Red Sox lost in seven games to the St. Louis Cardinals. That particular Fall Classic is remembered for the Cardinals' Enos Slaughter scoring the Series winning run from first base on a play called the "Mad Dash," as he ran all the way home on Harry Walker's two-out, eighth-inning hit to left-center (the hit was officially scored a double but could have been scored a single) and beat Boston shortstop Johnny Pesky's relay throw to the plate. For decades, Pesky, whose name was forever linked with those of Fred Merkle, Mickey Owen and other famous "goats" of baseball history, was blamed for holding the ball and making a delayed throw home—that Series wasn't televised so there are no video replays, but the official game film taken from the stands seems to suggest he didn't hold the ball—to allow Slaughter to score the decisive run. Long forgotten is the fact that Ted Williams, batting with two outs in the top of that inning and the potential go-ahead run on second base, hit a pop fly to second for the third out. It was his last World Series at-bat. It could be argued that Johnny Pesky was unfairly labeled a goat for that loss while Williams, with just one Series RBI and his non-production in the finale, didn't receive enough of the blame himself.

Although Willie Mays made "The Catch" in the 1954 World Series—when he robbed Vic Wertz of an extra-base hit with an over-the-shoulder catch of the Cleveland slugger's 420-foot drive at the Polo Grounds—he didn't fare well with the stick in postseason play. In 20 World Series games, Mays batted .239 with three extra-base hits—no home runs—and six RBIs. In 25 postseason games overall, the numbers were .247, one homer, and 10 RBIs with 12 runs scored. His Giants won the Series in 1954, but lost in 1951 and 1962. In the division play era, his Giants lost the NL Championship Series to Pittsburgh in 1971. In his final appearance in the postseason, his Mets in 1973 reached the World Series but lost in seven games to Oakland. And there was also the image of Mays, in the second game of that 1973 Series, stumbling on the base paths and even falling down in the outfield in the ninth inning during a play where he was hindered by the glare of the sun, an error that allowed the A's to tie the game and force extra innings.

Edgar Martinez, remembered for his dramatic series-winning double against the Yankees in the 1995 AL Division Series, followed that up by batting .087 in the AL Championship Series against Cleveland as the Mariners fell in six games. He hit .188 in the Mariners' next postseason appearance in 1997, a four-game loss to Baltimore in the Division Series. In Seattle's postseason rematch against the Yankees in the 2000 ALCS, he batted .238 in the Mariners' six-game loss. The following October, after the Mariners had won 116 regular season games—tied for the most ever in major-league history—Martinez hit a disappointing .150 as Seattle lost in five games to the Yanks in the AL Championship Series. Although he hit well overall in Division Series play (.375 in 17 games over four separate ALDS), Martinez, who never played in a World Series, batted .156 with just one home run and four RBIs in his 17 career ALCS games.

Ken Griffey, Jr., who never reached the World Series either, performed well in his first taste of postseason play in 1995—"The Kid" belted five homers in five games against the Yankees in the Division Series—but struggled over the final three games of that year's AL Championship Series. With the Mariners ahead 2-1 in that series against Cleveland, Griffey hit just .111 over the final three games and could only look on as the Indians captured the American League pennant in Game Six at the Kingdome. He also struggled in his next two trips to the playoffs. In 1997, he batted .133 with no extra-base hits (and a .188 on-base percentage) in his Mariners' four-game series loss to Baltimore in the ALDS. He didn't return to the postseason again until 2008, when his White Sox fell to Tampa Bay in the Division Series. In his three games in that series, he batted .200 with no extra-base hits and no RBIs. He never played in another postseason series after 2008, and he hit only .147 with three RBIs—and five walks, none intentional—over the final 10 playoff games of his career. His teams lost eight of those contests, yet Griffey, arguably Bonds' greatest competition for the title of the game's best player during the 1990s, is rarely criticized for those failures.

Frank Thomas batted .224 over 16 career postseason games, and he was limited to just 34 games in 2005—the year his White Sox became World Series champions—after beginning the year on the disabled list and then fracturing a bone in his foot. Because of his injury, Thomas was unable to play in the postseason that year—he wasn't even on the postseason roster—as the White Sox finally won the World Series for the first time since 1917. In 2000, "The Big Hurt" went hitless in the Division Series as the White Sox, the AL's top team, were swept 3-0 by the Mariners. With Oakland in 2006, he was hitless in the AL Championship Series as the Athletics were swept 4-0 by the Tigers.

There are also the Killer B's in Houston, Jeff Bagwell and Craig Biggio. In nine different career postseason series, Bagwell batted .226 with two homers and 13 RBIs over 33 games, including a combined .128 in the 1997, 1998 and 1999 playoffs as the Astros lost three consecutive NL Division Series (to Atlanta, San Diego and then Atlanta again). In those three series, Bagwell drove in only four runs without collecting any extra-base hits, and the Astros lost nine of those 11 games. Houston, in fact, lost in the first playoff round in its first four trips to the postseason in the Killer B's era (with the fourth one in 2001, also against the Braves) before finally winning a postseason series in its fifth try in 2004.

As for Biggio, the second baseman batted .234 in those same nine career postseason series, with two home runs and 11 RBIs in 40 games. In his first three trips to the playoffs—the aforementioned 1997, 1998 and 1999 postseasons—Biggio batted .083, .182 and .105. In those first three playoff years, Biggio hit a combined .119 with one extra-base hit and a .260 on-base percentage. (It was easy to see why the Astros lost in the first playoff round in all three years, when both Bagwell and Biggio struggled the way Bonds, Bonilla and Van Slyke did in Pittsburgh in the early 1990s.) As for the 2001 postseason, he hit .167. By the time Biggio finally broke out with a three-hit performance in Game Four of the 2004 NLDS, he'd gone through his first 17 postseason contests with just a .138 batting average, a double and an RBI, with the Astros going 4-13 in that span.

Overall, Bagwell hit .229 in NLDS play, .250 in the NLCS and .125 in the World Series. For Biggio, the numbers were .226, .250 and .222. In the Astros' only World Series appearance in the Killer B's era, Houston was swept in four straight games by the White Sox in 2005. Although the Astros also lost multiple first-round series to the Braves (as Bonds did twice in his Pittsburgh days), with both Bagwell and Biggio struggling mightily against Atlanta, the Killer B's postseason failures somehow weren't as heavily criticized nationally as the postseason losses of Barry Bonds' Pirates and Giants were.

As for Barry Bonds, his critics blame him for the Pirates' three consecutive losses in the NL Championship Series. They blame him for the Giants' postseason defeats. Like quite a few other superstars in the history of the game, Bonds had his moments and his struggles in postseason play. It certainly seems unfair that the other superstars are not criticized as heavily as Bonds was. "I think Bonds shouldered more of the blame for [his teams' postseason failures] than other players," *San Francisco Chronicle* writer Henry Schulman once opined, "because people liked to rag on him and wanted to see him fail."

* * *

While Bonds didn't always talk to the media, he did sometimes share his side of the story regarding his playoff history. And yes, over the years, prior to his 2002 postseason exploits (when he had a Ruthian performance with a .356 average, eight homers, 18 runs and 16 RBIs—and 27 walks with only six strikeouts—in 17 games), even he himself had maintained a sense of humor about his October numbers during his Pittsburgh days. "I didn't suck all of the time," he said one September afternoon in 1999. "Most of the time, though." He did also offer some valid comments about his performance. "I look at it this way. If you look back in baseball history, you tell me how many of the great players have won the World Series for their teams? How many of them have had big numbers for postseason play? You'd be surprised by how little that number is."

Certainly, he had a point. Ryne Sandberg never won the World Series for the Cubs (or even took Chicago there, for that matter). Tony Gwynn never won one for San Diego. The Killer B's, Jeff Bagwell and Craig Biggio, never won one for Houston. Edgar Martinez never won one for Seattle. Ken Griffey, Jr. never won one in Seattle, Cincinnati or Chicago. Cal Ripken, Jr. won one in his second full season, but was then shut out for his final 18 seasons in the big leagues. Although Frank Thomas received a World Series ring from the White Sox in his final year with the club in 2005, he was injured for the majority of that season (and didn't play in that year's postseason) and never, in his 15 other seasons in Chicago, led the team to the Fall Classic. Of course, going a little further back, there was Ernie Banks, who played the majority of his career in the pre-divisional play era, never ever reaching the World Series and Ted Williams hitting .200 in the only Fall Classic he played in.

In 1991, Bonds finished second in the National League MVP balloting to Atlanta third baseman Terry Pendleton, who also didn't come through in that year's NL playoffs. After sitting out on the season's last day to rest for the playoffs (and capturing the batting crown with a .319 average, just ahead of Hal Morris' .318 and Tony Gwynn's .317), Pendleton batted only .167 in the seven-game NL Championship Series, a fact that didn't escape Bonds. "The way I look at it, we're up 3-2 and I ain't hitting," Bonds said after the fifth game. "You all know what I can do; I know what I can do. What's Terry Pendleton doing? He's supposed to be the big hero-star, and he's got one more at-bat and one more hit than me [3-for-20 vs. 4-for-21 up to that point]." The NLCS struggles weren't a one-off for the Braves third baseman (who, it should be noted, was battling a right knee injury during the 1991 playoffs). He would hit .252 lifetime in the postseason for six playoff teams in his career—reaching the playoffs twice with the Cardinals (1985 and 1987) and four times with the Braves (1991, 1992, 1993 and 1996)—without winning a World Series as a player.

More often than not, the players coming through have been non-superstar players. In the 1990 playoffs, it was journeyman outfielder Billy Hatcher collecting seven consecutive hits for Cincinnati in the World Series against Oakland. It was the Reds' Billy Bates, Chris Sabo, Joe Oliver and Herm Winningham delivering clutch hits off Dennis Eckersley and Dave Stewart to help Cincinnati sweep the A's—while the likes of Oakland sluggers Harold Baines, Jose Canseco and Mark McGwire were held in check. In 1991, it was light-hitting second baseman Mark Lemke performing playoff heroics for Atlanta. In the 1995 ALDS, it was the equally light-hitting Joey Cora, another unheralded second baseman, homering off the Yankees' David Cone for Seattle. In 1992, the World Series MVP was a non-descript catcher, Pat Borders. Another catcher, Jim Leyritz, was hitting clutch home runs in six different postseason series between 1995 and 1999 despite never being named to an All-Star team. In 1998, the World Series MVP was not superstar Derek Jeter, but ninth-place hitter Scott Brosius. Go even further back, and you had Mickey Hatcher (Dodgers) and Bucky Dent (Yankees) being the pesky World Series heroes.

"You're facing the No. 1 or No. 2 starter a lot in the playoffs, and if you're facing Randy Johnson possibly three times in the playoffs, what are your chances of success?" Bonds said, referring to the Hall of Fame left-hander as an example. "Sometimes it's that unknown guy [to whom] he makes a mistake pitch and all of a sudden he hits a home run and wins the game for you. I'm a left-handed hitter and Randy's throwing 100 mph, and I'm supposed to win the game for you? You're in a tough situation."

Bonds had a great point. But forget Randy Johnson for a moment. You could insert any other pitcher's name in there (minus the 100 mph) and the comment about unknown guys getting that big hit would still be valid. One fact that's often overlooked is that pitchers pitched differently to Bonds compared to how they pitched to lesser hitters. Weaker hitters might see fatter pitches to hit because pitchers, wanting to go right after them, might throw fastballs right down the middle of the plate. When Bonds was at the plate, those same pitchers, fearing the ball would be hammered out of the ballpark, wouldn't always throw him hittable pitches. What Giants utility infielder Mike Benjamin, a career .229 hitter, once did during a horrid stretch in the summer of 1995 best exemplified that idea. During a three-game stretch that June, Benjamin went 14-for-18 to set a modern record for most hits in three consecutive games. When Bonds told Benjamin, "I can't believe you did that," the utility man replied, "Barry, they aren't going to pitch to you the same way that they're going to pitch to me."

What's also forgotten is Bonds wasn't always in the starting lineup against left-handers early in his career. In his second season, for instance, he platooned with John Cangelosi, a journeyman, in the Pittsburgh outfield, sitting out when a left-handed starter was on the mound. "When we played the Braves at that time [in the early 1990s], when Tom Glavine and Steve Avery pitched, those were the games I sat out during the year," Bonds added. "Lloyd McClendon played those games. Then, all of a sudden, we're in the playoffs and boom! I'm facing Glavine and Avery, but no one knew that."

But for anybody to suggest Bonds never showed up for big games, that's simply untrue.

Barry's Magical Performances

I think he's unbelievable. People dog him and stuff, but I think he's a cool guy. And I think he's the best player in the game. I don't take anything from [Ken] Griffey [Jr.] or Mac [Mark McGwire], but Bonds is the best player, and I'm glad he'll say it. Among players, you hear a lot of respect for him. The ones that don't like him or respect him say he's arrogant. But who doesn't like the limelight? People say he's arrogant, but Michael Jordan's got arrogance, with the way he walks on the court and that look. He's arrogant. So what?

—Cliff Floyd, Florida Marlins outfielder,
as told to *South Florida Sun-Sentinel*'s
David O'Brien (1998)

One quality Barry Bonds possessed as an athlete which set him apart from other superstars of his own era was the fact that he thrived, or so it seemed, when he was portrayed as the villain. It was as though he thrived on controversy and had to be mad to play well.

By the 1990 season, his fifth year in the major leagues, Bonds seemed to perform better, observers noted, when he was criticized by the press and booed by the fans. While other players might not be able to block out all that negativity, Barry appeared to play better when the world was mad at him, when those in the clubhouse or the press box or the stands were angry at something he'd done or said. It was as though he'd developed a way to tap into negative energy and channel it to his advantage, to propel his game to a higher level. By the time he got to San Francisco, people close to him believed he would deliberately say horrible things to the press, hoping to provoke outrage and kick his game up a notch. "He embraced anger like it was his morning meal," sports columnist Bob Padecky once wrote in *The [Santa Rosa, CA] Press Democrat*. "He found agitation to be his friend."

Bonds, who once described himself as "mentally and emotionally drained" from all the negativity received from the press, has actually, through some of his own comments, suggested as much. "Without their [media] negativity, I wouldn't be as good as I am," Barry himself once acknowledged. In another interview, he said, "To me, when people say I have an attitude problem, it give me an edge. It makes me mad, so I play better." And when he saw a 2006 poll which ranked NFL superstar Terrell Owens, then the Dallas Cowboys' star wide receiver, as the most hated athlete in American sports, Barry remarked, "How did T.O. get in front of me? That's B.S. That sucks." Added Padecky: "Bonds breathes in dark clouds like oxygen. Whether it's imagining racism, suffering from an abusive, alcoholic father, butting heads with lofty expectations, recounting those last hours with his dad, believing it's Me Against Them, all of it keeps Bonds, bizarrely, engaged."

Bonds also appeared to play better when dealing with off-the-field distractions that would normally have hampered the performance of most other players. "I like to have my back against the wall," he admitted, "and beat the odds." In the summer of 1994, when Bonds filed for divorce from wife "Sun" Branco after six years of marriage, the split became well publicized in the press. Yet as his private life became daily fodder for the newspapers—the trial dragged on for months and received extensive media coverage—Bonds had another outstanding year on the field, batting .312 with 37 homers and 81 RBIs in 112 games. "Most guys, when they're getting a divorce, it affects them," Giants center fielder Darren Lewis once said. "Their numbers go down, their minds are somewhere else. Not Barry. That wasn't going to stop him. Nothing was going to stop him." During their first two seasons together with the Giants, Bonds and Lewis spent their mornings working out with a trainer at a college in nearby Atherton, California. Several times during the summer of 1994, Lewis would arrive at the scheduled 9:00 a.m. start time, only to find Barry already gone. "He would have these 9:00 a.m. court dates," explained Lewis. "So he'd get there at 6:00 a.m. and run in the dark. Barry refused to let his divorce beat him."

Even when he was constantly surrounded by the steroid talk late in his career—with the press scrutinizing him on a daily basis and the fans in visiting cities taunting him and booing his every move—

Bonds continued to produce, refusing to let all the negativity beat him. By his own admission, his parents had told him at a younger age that the off-the-field problems were going to be there after the game anyway, so during the three hours when the game was happening, just ignore those problems and instead focus on his job on the field. Barry took their advice to heart and had that figured out. "The more they boo him, the more he concentrates," long-time Giants manager Dusty Baker opined.

Bonds' name surfaced in September 2003 as one of six major-leaguers and 21 other athletes connected to the Bay Area Laboratory Co-Operative known as BALCO, which was at the center of a doping scandal involving previously undetectable steroids, and Barry testified in December 2003 before a federal grand jury investigating BALCO. Over the next few months, Bonds was portrayed as a cheater by the press even though he hadn't failed a drug test. He dealt with questions about whether he'd used steroids. He dealt with questions about his personal trainer's drug distribution case. But he soldiered on, capturing his record seventh National League MVP Award in 2004. He also won his second batting title with a .362 average, hitting 45 home runs with 101 RBIs in 147 games while drawing a single-season record of 232 walks. During spring training in 2006, a lengthy excerpt from the book *Game of Shadows* was published in *Sports Illustrated*, detailing Barry's relationship with BALCO. Bonds, though, was unmoved, ignoring all that noise and remaining focused on the field. "I'd already gone through so much negativity in the sport already," he later reflected, "[so] it really kind of, like, was, 'Okay, what else can go wrong? What else are they going to say? What else are they going to do?'"

Despite being repeatedly branded a cheater by the press and the fans, Bonds batted .270 that season with 26 homers and 77 RBIs in 367 at-bats, and his focus and production continued to marvel his teammates. "Everything that's been written, said, yelled at him, said to his face, said behind his back, said by people on TV, I'm sure it takes a toll on him," Giants reliever Jason Christiansen said. "It's been 20 years of that. I couldn't imagine what he goes through on a daily basis, reading some of the outlandish things people say about him." The following year, when he broke Hank Aaron's all-time home-run record, Bonds hit .276 with 28 home runs and 66 RBIs in 340 at-bats. None of the accusations thrown his way was going to slow him down. "Like I tell everybody, you want to be on top, you have to have broad shoulders to be on top," Bonds said in 2004. "Let me tell you that right now, because as fast as you get there is as fast as they try to knock you down. And so I have broad shoulders. I can deal with it."

Bonds simply seemed to perform better when he had, in the words of *USA Today*'s Bob Nightengale, "that chip on his shoulder." Nightengale recalls a time during the 1997 season when Bonds tried to be gentler with the media, but around that same time he went into a slump, one that would last for weeks. He only snapped out of his funk when he again snapped at the media and stopped talking to them. Coincidence or not, it was as though balls fell in for hits only when he wasn't friendly with members of the press. "Tony Gwynn was a very close friend of his," Nightengale remembers. "Tony was, like, the media's best friend. He told Barry, 'Hey, you've gotta be cordial with the media. They'll be a lot easier on you.' Three weeks later, he saw Gwynn. Barry said, 'I tried that, Tony. I can't do it. It just doesn't work for me.' It's almost like he had to have that chip on his shoulder to be a great player." (It might be hard for some to imagine that the late great Gwynn, who had a squeaky-clean image during his Hall of Fame career, was good friends with Bonds, but his son, Tony Gwynn, Jr., has confirmed that fact. "My dad and him always had a really good relationship and they used to love to talk hitting—they used different terminology, which used to have them butting heads, but the funny thing was they were really saying the exact same thing," Gwynn, Jr. once said on NBC Sports Bay Area's "Balk Talk" podcast. "They always had a healthy respect for one another.")

Gene Lamont, Bonds' third-base coach in Pittsburgh from 1986 to 1991, has also acknowledged that Bonds seemed to need that chip on his shoulder. "I almost think Barry thinks he has to have a little bit of an edge about him," Lamont, who also managed in the big leagues from 1992 to 1995 and 1997 to 2000 and is considered a no-nonsense type of coach, reflected in 2020. "But I never saw Barry as a bad guy. He was very respectful."

But he was simply at his best when portrayed as the villain. And when he was angry. There was the series against St. Louis in July 1999, when Mark McGwire and the Cardinals came into San Francisco for a three-game series beginning on a Monday night. Although Bonds was the far better player, virtually all the attention was on McGwire, who'd broken Roger Maris' 37-year-old single-season record of 61 homers a year earlier when he smacked 70 round-trippers. Just as in 1998, everybody wanted to see McGwire take batting practice in every visiting city the Cardinals played in, and whenever St. Louis was in town, some clubs had gotten into the practice of roping off the area around the batting cage to control the crowd of players, coaches and club officials who gathered to watch him hit. And when the Cardinals arrived at Candlestick Park for three games in July, the Giants, too, set up ropes on the field.

Bonds, who'd never seen the ropes on the field before, demanded to know what was going on. "What the fuck is this?" he asked the security guards. When told the ropes were for McGwire, Bonds flew into a rage and began knocking down the ropes. "Not in my house!" Bonds told the guards. Batting .243 entering that series—and in a 6-for-47 slump (.128) since July 4—the frustrated Bonds, perhaps playing with that chip on his shoulder, refused to let McGwire take over his "house." In that first game on Monday night, Bonds hit a two-run homer in the first inning, but after McGwire smacked a three-run homer of his own and the Cardinals jumped out to a 7-2 lead, Barry collected two more hits later in the contest and drove in three more runs— including a game-tying, two-run double—as San Francisco outslugged St. Louis 10-8. "Mainly, it's the desire to be the best," Bonds once said when asked what his driving force was. "If anybody feels they're better than me, that just gives me a bigger edge... You put 18 guys on the field and I want to be the best of all 18."

Dealing with a divorce was one thing, being booed by 50,000 fans on the road was one thing, being constantly scrutinized by the media was one thing, being angry about McGwire taking over Candlestick was one thing and all the other distractions were one thing. But Bonds' otherworldly performance late in the 2003 season, coming during a time of grieving, was simply off the charts. And largely forgotten.

* * *

On December 22, 2003, the day after the death of his father Irvin in Mississippi, a grieving Brett Favre threw for 399 yards and four first-half touchdowns in Oakland as the Green Bay Packers routed the Raiders 41-7 on Monday Night Football in what is considered a legendary performance given the circumstances. Favre's performance that night, in fact, is included among NFL.com's greatest 100 games in league history.

Barry Bonds had experienced his own loss just four months earlier with the death of his own father on August 23—Bobby died after a year of battling lung cancer and a brain tumor at the age of 57—and Barry came through heroically on the field, too. Barry, who admitted he was "spending all [his] time just trying not to have a nervous breakdown," carried the Giants on his back while Bobby was on his deathbed. He took four games off to be with his father, and San Francisco went 0-4. In the first three games of his return (August 19 to 21), he beat the Braves with two 10th-inning, walk-off homers, one of which Bobby made it out to the ballpark to witness, just three days before his death. Barry took a week off after his father's death, and in his first game back (August 30) he went 2-for-2 off the Diamondbacks' Randy Johnson, including his 40th homer, as the Giants triumphed 2-1. He later removed himself from the game due to lightheadedness and an accelerated heartbeat, and spent a day in the hospital. But in his first game back (September 1), he smacked a bases-loaded single in the ninth to give San Francisco a 2-0 win over Arizona in a game started by Curt Schilling. In that emotional stretch, Barry hit .375 with three home runs in six games, with the Giants winning all six. To his teammates, Bonds belonged in a higher league. "He isn't on the [same] planet with us," Giants center fielder Marquis Grissom said. "To stay focused during these bad times is unbelievable."

Yet his performance during those emotional times isn't remembered the way Favre's is. It's virtually forgotten.

J. P. Hoornstra, however, is one who does remember. When asked to recall his experiences in media scrums with Bonds, that emotional week in 2003 is the first thing that Hoornstra brings up. "The one time that I can remember interviewing him—because it was a really important game—it was the game that he first played after [being away for four days to be with his dad]. He hit a home run in extra innings off Ray King. This is his first game back. We're all crowded around him. He was just so distant. His voice was distant from the moment. His eyes were distant from the writers. Everything was like, 'I was present enough to hit this huge home run, and yet I'm so not here in this moment when I'm talking to you.' I can't quite remember doing another interview like that. Under the circumstances, I would not conclude that that was typical of Barry Bonds to act that way. But it was typical in that there were 30 reporters around him with tape recorders trying to hear what he was saying. I think moments of that magnitude were typical for his career just because he hit that many home runs. That memory really stands out."

Those are the types of moments Barry Bonds should be remembered for, coming through in the clutch during that emotional stretch. Late in his career, he also had a knack for coming up huge in front of the home fans. At least that's what he told journalist Joan Ryan in the 2020 book *Intangibles*, suggesting that he was such a genius with the bat that he was able to guarantee his biggest moments came in front of Giants fans. "You either have to know what the hell you're doing or you'd have to be the luckiest son of a bitch on the planet," Bonds told Ryan. "I was the master. My IQ and skill on the baseball field was such that I could do it whenever I wanted to. Whenever I needed to. Didn't matter who was on the mound."

The only time he was going to hit milestone home runs, he added, was in front of the San Francisco crowd. The record books, Ryan pointed out, back Barry's account. Bonds reached his 500th, 600th and 700th round-trippers at home, and also passed Babe Ruth and Hank Aaron, with Nos. 715 and 756, at home. The year he set the single-season home-run record, he hit Nos. 71, 72 and 73 at home to close out the season. The most curious stretch might be the opening month of 2004, when he tied and passed godfather Willie Mays to move into sole possession of third place on the all-time home-run list. He entered that season with 658 home runs, just two shy of "The Say Hey Kid," and he took Roy Oswalt deep on Opening Day in Houston but didn't homer in the final five games of that season-opening road trip. In front of 42,548 fans in San Francisco's home opener versus Milwaukee, though, he hit No. 660 to tie his godfather, who then came out and embraced him in front of the dugout. Bonds passed Mays the following night before another crowd of 42,000-plus fans. "And the only time I was going to do it [hit milestone home runs] was at home in front of my family, and San Francisco is my family," he said.

Former teammate John Cangelosi isn't surprised by anything Bonds could do on the field. Even in the early part of Barry's career, Cangelosi recalls, he could do anything he wanted to. "Barry Bonds was, by far, the best player in baseball. Even before all this black cloud [with the PEDs suspicions] came over him. After the home-run race with McGwire and Sosa, things started following him negatively. [But] by that time he'd already had 400 home runs. He averaged 30 home runs a year, 30 stolen bases a year. He was always flirting with 40-40, but Canseco got there first [with Major League Baseball's first 40-40 season in 1988]. He was probably the last 'five-tool' player. He could do anything on the baseball field. I'd be sitting on the couch with him and he'd say, 'Man, Cangy, I gotta get a couple home runs. I gotta get a couple stolen bases.' He played games with the leaderboards because we used to get stats all the time in our locker room. I mean, that's how good that guy was. He was just, by far, the best player in the game. I think there's not going to be another Barry Bonds, trust me. I know you got the Mike Trouts out there. I'm not saying that there's never gonna be a great player again. But with Barry—and I happened to witness it—he was the best player in the major leagues, period. Bar none. He belongs in the Hall of Fame, just like all the other ones [who have never failed a drug test]. Not naming names, but there are guys in the Hall of Fame that have cheated and done numerous things, and they're still in the Hall of Fame. [If] you let one guy in, I think you let them all in."

* * *

And for anybody to suggest Bonds never showed up for big games, Barry certainly delivered when the spotlight was the greatest when San Francisco played Los Angeles, with the Giants-Dodgers rivalry the West Coast equivalent of Yankees-Red Sox in the East. There was that October 1st game at Dodger Stadium in 1993, when the Giants were battling Atlanta for the NL West title. With the Giants down 4-1, Bonds delivered a three-run homer to tie the game. In his next at-bat, he slugged another three-run shot to give San Francisco the lead. Next time up, he smacked an RBI double. Not quite Reggie Jackson hitting three homers in a single game against the Dodgers in the World Series, but on the night, in the final days of the pennant race, Bonds was 3-for-3 with a pair of homers, seven RBIs, and two walks. The Giants needed each one of those runs, triumphing 8-7. The following afternoon, Bonds walked three more times and scored two runs as the Giants, a 90-loss club which had finished 26 games out just a year earlier, defeated Orel Hershiser and the Dodgers 5-3 to remain tied for first place heading into the regular season's final day.

Entering the two teams' final series of the 1997 season, a two-game set in San Francisco on September 17-18, the Giants trailed the Dodgers by two games in the NL West race. In the opening game, Bonds' first-inning, two-run homer was the difference in the Giants' 2-1 win. The following afternoon, Bonds tripled, hit a three-run homer and scored two runs, as San Francisco won 6-5 in extra innings to pull even with the Dodgers in the standings. The Giants, coming off back-to-back last-place finishes, went on to capture the NL West title, with Bonds hitting .341 with seven homers and 13 RBIs in 12 games against Los Angeles.

In 2001, Bonds helped the Giants stay in contention until the final weekend of the season, and some of his big hits came against Los Angeles. His 500th career homer came in the eighth inning of an April game against the Dodgers, a monstrous two-run shot into McCovey Cove (a section of the San Francisco Bay beyond the right-field wall of the ballpark) which turned a one-run deficit into a Giants' lead on their way to a 3-2 victory at Pac Bell Park. On September 24, Bonds homered in the seventh inning for a 2-1 triumph at Dodger Stadium to move San Francisco to within two games of the NL wild card-leading Cardinals and only 1.5 games back of NL West-leading Arizona. With three games remaining and the Giants one loss away from being eliminated in the pennant chase, Bonds again delivered when the Dodgers came to town for a season-ending series. He homered twice off Chan Ho Park (his record-breaking 71st and 72nd home runs of the year), walked twice and scored three runs—a performance which normally would have been enough for a San Francisco win—but the pitching faltered in the Giants' 11-10 loss.

And Bonds was so dominant in 2001 that the Dodgers once walked him intentionally with runners on first and second in the ninth inning—and a one-run lead. And that was when Jeff Kent, the reigning National League MVP, hit behind him. "So I went to the mound," Dodgers manager Jim Tracy later recalled, "and told [closer] Jeff Shaw,

'You're not going to like this, but… we're going to walk Barry Bonds and take our chances with Kent.' For me to think I'd ever go to the mound and suggest that to my closer was unbelievable. But I did. I walked the winning run into scoring position. Jeff Kent popped up the first pitch. We ended up winning. Then I took a *big* exhale."

In 2002, Bonds and the Giants got the last laugh when San Francisco finished 3.5 games ahead of Tracy's Dodgers for the NL's lone wild-card spot. That season, Bonds batted .400 against Los Angeles with four doubles, six homers, 21 walks and 18 RBIs in 14 games. Out of the 21 walks, nine were intentional, as Tracy didn't want Bonds to beat his ballclub. "We've had 38 games against the Giants the last two years," the Dodgers manager said following that season. "And I've made some decisions against that club in those 38 games I never even considered in seven years managing in the minor leagues—all because of the left fielder. He forces you to do things in certain situations I've never done in any game I ever managed." For instance, two of those nine intentional walks came with runners on first. "We played them in a four-game series in September," Tracy added. "I walked him nine times—in one series." Although he never intentionally walked Bonds with the bases loaded, Tracy admitted he had thought about it, convinced "you could make a good case for it" in certain spots. And when the Dodgers did pitch to him in 2002, Bonds batted .583 with runners in scoring position and struck out only four times.

Critics, however, like to point out those regular season moments and numbers didn't measure up against October playoff moments.

Of course, the most famous series which Bonds' critics point to when discussing his postseason performances is the famous 1992 NL Championship Series, which saw the Braves rally with three runs in the bottom of the ninth in Game Seven against Barry's Pirates in Atlanta. The game's final play, which has been replayed over a million times over the years (the top four most viewed videos on YouTube on either this game or the final inning or play have accumulated over 932,000 views, as of this writing), saw Francisco Cabrera deliver the coup de grace—a two-out single to left field, which brought home Dave Justice with the tying run and slow-footed Sid Bream (who'd already undergone five knee surgeries in his career up to that point) with the pennant-winning run as Bonds' throw to the plate was a little off line. And with that, the Pirates' season was over.

With Bonds and ace Doug Drabek, both free agents, having played their final games with the franchise, Pittsburgh's three-year playoff run was also over.

But the series shouldn't have come down to that play.

And even if you really wanted to point the finger at Bonds—or bring up the 2002 World Series, when Barry bobbled and then dropped a looping single by the Angels' Garret Anderson in the eighth inning of Game Six—and say he didn't come up huge in the game's biggest moment, well, he'd be in pretty good company. It happens even to the best in the business. Babe Ruth, for instance, famously got thrown out trying to steal second base, in a one-run game, to end Game Seven of the 1926 World Series, giving the St. Louis Cardinals their first-ever championship. Even Wayne Gretzky, while playing for the National Hockey League's St. Louis Blues in 1996, had such a moment in playoff competition. In sudden-death overtime in Game Seven of a second-round Stanley Cup playoff series against Detroit, the Great One mishandled the puck in the neutral zone, and the puck found its way to Red Wings captain Steve Yzerman, who rifled home the series-winning goal moments later to eliminate Gretzky and the Blues. Green Bay Packers quarterback Brett Favre was once intercepted a postseason record-tying six times in a National Football League playoff loss, in January 2002, with three of them returned for touchdowns. His costly, game-defining interceptions in the 2007 and 2009 NFC Championship Games for the Packers and the Minnesota Vikings, respectively, are part of his postseason legacy, with each team's season ending one win away from reaching the Super Bowl. Peyton Manning, one of the greatest regular season quarterbacks to ever play the game, went one-and-done in the NFL postseason a record nine times, more than twice as many one-and-dones as any other quarterback in the Super Bowl era. Favored in eight of his nine one-and-dones, Manning was outgunned and one-and-doned by, among others, Mark Sanchez, Chad Pennington and Jay Fiedler.

We could go on and on with more examples, but the point is that it happens. Even to the best in the business.

But the 1992 NL Championship Series shouldn't have come down to that final play.

The 1992 NLCS Revisited

Once again they focused on Barry because he was the star. Barry didn't choke, and I don't think anybody should judge his career by that.

—Jim Leyland, referring to Bonds' performance
in the 1992 NL Championship Series

The 1992 NL playoffs opened with Pittsburgh dropping three of the first four games, with two of them blowout losses in Atlanta. Through four games, Bonds was 1-for-11 and staff ace Doug Drabek (who had won 22 games and captured the NL Cy Young Award only two years earlier) was 0-2 with a 6.00 ERA. In the Pirates' three losses up to that point, the Pittsburgh starting pitchers had a combined 8.44 ERA while the relievers weren't much batter, at 7.54.

In Game Five, though, unheralded veteran right-hander Bob Walk surprised the baseball world by pitching a complete-game three-hitter while the Pirates, who'd been left for dead, erupted for seven runs off Steve Avery and the Atlanta bullpen. Bonds, who went 2-for-5 with two runs scored, doubled home a run as part of a four-run first-inning ambush against Avery. Two nights later, Bonds was at it again with a second consecutive two-hit game. He homered off Tom Glavine to lead off the second inning to put Pittsburgh on the scoreboard, the Pirates plated 13 more runs—and Tim Wakefield threw his second complete game in five days—and the series was extended to a seventh game.

Game Seven is most remembered for Francisco Cabrera's game-winning hit, Bonds' throw to the plate and Sid Bream's slide. What's forgotten are several other circumstances working in the Braves' favor, other key moments that were swept under the rug, moments that could have altered the course of the game—and Bonds' legacy.

For starters, home-plate umpire Randy Marsh, the man who called

225

Bream safe on the game's final play, actually started the game at first base and was only pressed into duty behind the plate when John McSherry, the original home-plate ump, left the contest in the second inning due to severe dizziness. Marsh's move to home plate proved significant in the ninth, as the one-out walk to Damon Berryhill that re-loaded the bases came on a close 3-and-1 pitch that Pirates closer Stan Belinda (and many other observers) thought was in the strike zone. (*The New York Times'* Joe Sexton, for instance, asked rhetorically: "What was the plate umpire, Randy Marsh, watching on that 3-1 Stan Belinda pitch to Damon Berryhill?" Sportswriter John Feinstein, meanwhile, opined in his 1993 book *Play Ball* that the last pitch to Berryhill "was unquestionably strike two." Catcher Mike LaValliere, recalling the pitch in the *Pittsburgh Post-Gazette* years later, remembered grumbling to Marsh: "I like that pitch, Randy. We've got to have that for a strike." As for center fielder Andy Van Slyke: "If John McSherry does not faint, if John stays in the game, I have no doubt that we're moving on.") Would McSherry have called it—not to mention other pitches earlier in the game—the same way? We'll never know.

Meanwhile, Belinda's take was that Marsh's strike zone affected him. His first pitch to Berryhill was either just on or just off the outside corner, and Marsh, known as a hitter-friendly umpire according to the *Pittsburgh Post-Gazette*, called it a ball. "When you come into a game as a relief pitcher," Belinda later said, "you have to figure out an umpire's strike zone pretty quick. You can't afford to not know what a strike is and end up walking a guy. When Randy called that first pitch a ball, it made me uncomfortable. It meant he wasn't giving me any margin for error." In Cabrera's at-bat, which came with the bases loaded, Belinda started with a first-pitch slider. Although it was a close pitch, Marsh called it a ball. When he fell behind in the count, Belinda later said, he had to throw fastballs because he didn't want to walk in the tying run. Cabrera, according to the scouting reports, was a dead fastball hitter.

Another play at the plate an inning earlier, which has virtually been forgotten today, also proved significant. With Pittsburgh ahead 2-0 in the eighth, Bonds singled leading off the frame but was forced at second by Orlando Merced, who was now on first base with one out. (What's worthy of note is that, with the right-handed John Smoltz starting for the Braves on this night, Jim Leyland had gone with his

226

usual platoon lineup against right-hand pitchers that consisted of Merced, Alex Cole, and Mike LaValliere. The Pirates' normal lineup against left-handers—one that consisted of Gary Redus, Lloyd McClendon, and Don Slaught—meanwhile, was on the bench despite being red-hot in the series. The batting averages entering Game Seven: Redus .438, McClendon .727, Slaught: .333; versus Merced .143, Cole .250, LaValliere .167.)

Looking to drive a dagger into the hearts of Braves fans everywhere, Jeff King drove a double into the right-field corner just inside the foul line, with Merced racing around the bases and heading home carrying what would have been Pittsburgh's third run. David Justice, however, fired a perfect throw toward home from right field, a one-hopper right on the money to Berryhill, who tagged Merced to keep it a two-run game. That was a huge out, as was the final out an inning earlier.

In the seventh, with the bases loaded for Andy Van Slyke, left-hander Steve Avery (making only the second relief appearance of his career) came on and coaxed a flyout to center off the bat of the Pirates center fielder. It was one of the four times over the final five innings in which Pittsburgh had at least one runner in scoring position, but the Atlanta bullpen kept the Pirates off the scoreboard over the game's final three frames.

But the ninth inning, with Bonds' throw from left field not beating Bream at home plate still being ridiculed, is the most remembered inning of that game.

* * *

Perhaps what is less remembered about that ninth inning is the fact that, while David Justice had made an outstanding play from right field an inning earlier, the Pirates didn't get one from their right fielder. Yes, right fielder—not left fielder. The red-hot Lloyd McClendon did enter the game as a pinch-hitter in the seventh for Alex Cole, who began the night in right. He walked in his only two plate appearances, including in the top of the ninth with two outs. But two pitches later, McClendon pulled a muscle on the bases advancing on reliever Jeff Reardon's wild pitch—and had to be pinch-run for by Cecil Espy.

227

When the bottom of the ninth began, in right field for Pittsburgh was Espy (who, along with Gary Varsho, was the Pirates' fifth outfielder). The Braves' Terry Pendleton, the reigning National League MVP who brought a .231 playoff average into the game and was 0-for-3 on the night, led off by roping a long fly ball down the right-field line, but Espy, hesitant to make a play on the ball because it appeared it might go foul, let it drop inside the line for a double. Espy, per *The New York Times* report from that night, "allowed indecision to rule and a double to tumble barely inside the foul line." Had either Cole or McClendon had remained in the game, who knows how that fly ball would have been played?

What's less remembered about that ninth inning is that Pirates second baseman Jose Lind, who'd committed only six errors (in 745 fielding chances) all season, muffed a routine ground ball by Justice, putting runners on first and third with none out. "It still haunts me now," Lind, who attempted to backhand Justice's grounder but booted it, recalled in 2012. "If I catch that ball, we probably go to the World Series." Indeed. If he hadn't made that error, perhaps Sid Bream never would have ended up on second base as the potential pennant-winning run.

What's less remembered is a tiring Doug Drabek, who'd already lost twice in the series, was allowed to stay in the game in the ninth. What's less remembered is closer Stan Belinda, who wasn't regarded as an "automatic" stopper (he had yielded eight late-inning home runs while blowing six of his 24 save chances in 1992), was the pitcher who gave up the game-winning hit to Francisco Cabrera. And Belinda's critical comments of manager Jim Leyland after the reliever was dealt to Kansas City has been virtually forgotten.

In other memorable postseason games in which a key error cost the losing team the contest, the "goat" is often remembered (sometimes unfairly). Look in the baseball annals and names such as Bill Buckner, Fred Merkle, Fred Snodgrass and Mickey Owen come up. Yet Lind is merely a footnote to the 1992 NLCS despite his crucial ninth-inning error. In other memorable October games in which a pitcher gave up the "walk-off" game-winning home run or pennant-winning hit, those pitchers are also often remembered (think Ralph Branca, Ralph Terry, Dennis Eckersley and Mitch Williams). Belinda's name, though, isn't remembered.

Those who were on the field that night, though, such as Braves outfielder Ron Gant, certainly remember that entire ninth inning. "After Terry Pendleton led off with a double, their second baseman, Jose Lind, made an error… That was what changed the game," Gant once said. "Jose Lind didn't make errors. He was one of the best in the game. When that happened, it opened the door for us. It gives the other team a little bit of daylight, that we have a chance. When Drabek walked Sid Bream to load the bases, Stan Belinda came in to relieve."

After Gant hit a sacrifice fly to left, the light-hitting Damon Berryhill (who became the Braves' starting catcher only because regular backstop Greg Olson had broken his leg in a home-plate collision in September) walked to reload the bases, and then pinch-hitter Brian Hunter popped out for what should have been the final out. But thanks to the Lind error earlier in the inning, the Pirates needed to get one more out. Next up, pinch-hitter Francisco Cabrera, who hammered Belinda's 2-and-1 offering to left field, scoring Justice from third base. The slow-footed Bream, running from second, came home to score the pennant-winning run to send Atlanta to the World Series. While Bonds is often criticized—and ridiculed—for not being able to throw Bream out to keep the game going, not everybody shares that view.

"Bonds was a Gold Glover, and we didn't have the fastest guy at second base. But Bonds had to go to his left to field the ball," Gant recalled, pointing out a key element of that final play that many seem to have forgotten. "If that ball's hit right at him, he throws Sid out by a mile. But he had to go to his left and then throw across his body."

Gant wasn't the only one who thought so. Lloyd McClendon has said Bonds never should have been blamed for the loss. "I don't think it was Barry's fault," McClendon once told the *Pittsburgh Tribune-Review*. "He didn't throw the pitch. He just fielded the ball and made a hell of a throw to the plate. Yes, it was a good throw. He charged it as good as anybody could have charged it. He got rid of the ball real quickly. I can't see how anyone can say it's Barry's fault." Bonds, added McClendon, had to range to his left for the ball and then throw it across his body, making the play more difficult. "If that ball was hit directly to him, he probably would have thrown the guy out," explained McClendon. "It's a tough play for anyone when the ball isn't coming straight at you, and you're moving away from the plate. I thought it was an outstanding throw."

As for Bonds' side of the story? When discussing the game's final play, he has agreed with McClendon's assessment that it was a good throw. "If I had played any shallower," Bonds once explained, "that ball probably would've gotten past me. I had to come over toward my left, then cross-fire it. You can go back and look at the history of the game of baseball and how many guys have thrown guys out in that situation." As for the oft-cited criticism that he ignored center fielder Andy Van Slyke's signal for him to move in and to his left before Cabrera's hit, Bonds said that Van Slyke, being a center fielder, could roam more, but "if [Cabrera] hits a bullet, that ball's gonna go by me." Barry added, "There were other chances for us to win that had nothing to do with me."

Pirates right-hander Bob Walk, the winning pitcher in Game Five of the series, refuses to blame Bonds for not being able to throw Bream out. In an interview with the author, Walk says, "I know a lot of people look at that last throw that he made in that last game... But one play does not tell you what a guy is all about. He made a throw that was, maybe, five feet off line from left field all the way to the plate, and so that's why people kind of hold that against him. But he was an outstanding left fielder. I couldn't even tell you how many extra-base hits he took away from guys—not just catching the ball and turning them into outs, but also ground balls inside the third-base bag. He was outstanding in just cutting off that ball before it got into the corner and getting it in and holding those guys to a single. So, he was a fantastic defender. He could win a game with his defense."

Third baseman Steve Buechele, who began the 1992 season in Pittsburgh before being traded to the Cubs mid-season, wasn't around for the playoffs, but he echoes Walk's sentiments: "Barry, at that time, was a very, very special player... I know—I don't 'think,' I know—he was a better defensive player than a lot of people gave him credit for." John Cangelosi wasn't a member of the 1992 Pirates—the journeyman outfielder was in Pittsburgh from 1987 to 1990, when Bream was also with the team—but he has seen replays of Bonds' throw from left field. "It was ironic that our ex-teammate, Bream, scored the winning run against Leyland and the guys," Cangelosi says now, scoffing at the notion that Bonds is even blamed for not throwing Bream out. "I mean, it is what it is. It was a close play. Barry made a great throw. Sid Bream just happened to beat the throw. End of story."

As for Bream himself? The Braves first baseman acknowledged years later that he was taking some liberties with his lead from second base (not to mention that with two outs, he was going to be running on contact, another circumstance working in his favor). "I was probably a third of the way between second base and third base," Bream recalled, "and, if Stan Belinda would have just stepped off and thrown back, I would have been out. I think I was saying, 'No way he's going to throw back at this point.' But if he would have, the game would have been over, and I would have been a goat."

To this day, there are still those who pin that loss on Bonds. It can be argued part of the reason they feel that way is because they don't like Bonds. Yet, not as many today blame Stan Belinda, who, like Bonds, didn't leave Pittsburgh on good terms, for the NLCS loss.

Of course, when Jim Leyland, in an obscenity-laced outburst, screamed at Bonds on the field one spring-training day in 1991 after Barry and coach Bill Virdon (the bespectacled center fielder on the Pirates' 1960 World Series team and a former Pittsburgh manager) got into a shouting match, it became a well-publicized incident which was captured on video, replayed on television and made national headlines. After Belinda was traded to Kansas City in July 1993, the former Pittsburgh closer had some harsh words for Leyland and the Pirates organization the following spring, which made headlines both in Pittsburgh and Kansas City but not across the country—and soon became forgotten. Belinda was quoted as saying Leyland and pitching coach Ray Miller didn't teach him to pitch when he was with the Pirates. Leyland, according to him, ignored him after he gave up Cabrera's pennant-winning hit in the 1992 NLCS. "[Leyland] just wanted people to feel sorry for him," Belinda said. "For him not to say anything to me that night shows me that he had no respect for me. I had all winter to sit on it, thinking to myself, 'What is this guy doing to me? Does he want to ruin me?'"

Those who played for Leyland would say he was the ultimate players' manager, one who always protected his players and tried to put them in roles in which they would succeed. Not many former players would ever say anything bad about Leyland, which would appear to make Belinda seem like the villain in this situation. Not many people today, however, would point the finger at Belinda for losing the pennant.

Oakland manager Tony La Russa, whose A's were eliminated in the AL Championship Series in Toronto just hours before Pittsburgh lost Game Seven in Atlanta, is a close friend of Leyland's. As he would point out later, the dagger for the Pirates was that they let themselves get beaten by a *third-string catcher* who'd only been added to the roster August 31. Hunter, a power-hitting first baseman and the hero in Game Seven against Pittsburgh a year earlier (his two-run homer and RBI double were the big hits in Atlanta's 4-0 pennant-clinching victory), was, realistically, the Braves' last, best chance. Cabrera? He'd spent the past three years shuttling between Triple-A and Atlanta, and the book on him was simple: he was a dead fastball hitter and you got him out with breaking pitches. With the count 2-and-1 on Cabrera, though, catcher Mike LaValliere called for a fastball, Belinda obliged and the rest was history. "The killer, to me anyway, was that they *get* Hunter, the guy you're really scared of, and then *Cabrera* beats them," La Russa said.

And Barry Bonds wasn't the one who threw that pitch. More importantly, to paraphrase *The New York Times*, what was Randy Marsh watching on the 3-and-1 pitch to Damon Berryhill? How could Jose Lind have misplayed that grounder? And who the heck was Francisco Cabrera?

* * *

Critics have pointed out that Bonds didn't position himself where Van Slyke told him to when Cabrera came up to bat. But so what? Some of the greatest players in the game, one could argue, didn't always do what was perceived to be best for their team—yet many such examples have been long forgotten.

Consider the case of Ted Williams in the 1946 World Series. In that particular Series, the Cardinals employed a fielding strategy called "the Williams shift" against The Splendid Splinter, moving third baseman Whitey Kurowski to the right of shortstop Marty Marion so that all four of their infielders were bunched up between first and a few feet beyond second base. The outfielders, meanwhile, also moved themselves far to the right, leaving the left side of the field unprotected.

A ballplayer with Williams' sharp eyes and quick hands should have had little trouble adjusting to the shift and taking advantage of the open left side of the field, and even Ty Cobb offered to teach him how to punch hits into left field. Williams, however, could not bring himself to change. He was a slugger, as far as he was concerned, and he was going to get his hits by pulling them where he'd always pulled them, into deep right field. "I hated to go to left field," he later explained, "because I felt it was a mark of weakness." The Red Sox lost in seven games, the first Boston team to lose in a World Series (after the Sox had won their first five appearances in 1903, 1912, 1915, 1916 and 1918). Williams batted .200 for the Series, going 0-for-4 in Boston's one-run defeat in the seventh game, and never played on another pennant-winning club.

Consider, too, Cardinals left fielder Lou Brock in 1968. One of the game's greatest base stealers who helped St. Louis to three pennants and two World Series titles in the 1960s, Brock hit .391 overall with 14 stolen bases and 16 runs scored in 21 Series games. He batted .464 in the 1968 Fall Classic—but also made two damaging mistakes that helped cost St. Louis that Series. In Game Five, with the Cardinals ahead 3-2 in the fifth and leading the Series 3-1, Brock was on second base and seemed certain to score on a single to left. But he never attempted to slide, and the throw from left field arrived in time for the catcher to tag him out. The Tigers were among many who cited that moment as a turning point; Detroit rallied to win that contest and then took the final two in St. Louis. In the seventh game, won 4-1 by the Tigers, Brock had another crucial lapse: He was picked off after leading off the sixth with a single and the game still scoreless.

It happens. Even to the game's greatest. And those examples certainly have long been forgotten.

The Bottom Line

Possibly. But I don't know that. But he's around some really great players as a kid, right? Besides just his dad being a really great player, you have Willie Mays there, you have Willie McCovey—not just Hall of Famers, but elite Hall of Famers—and so obviously Barry wanted to be like them. And Willie Mays is probably one of the top five players in the history of baseball, maybe the best, and he's around all these guys. He wants to be better. He wanted to be better than these guys—and he might have been. But I will say this, though. He is, by far, the best ballplayer I have ever seen. Without a doubt.

—Former major-league pitcher Tom Candiotti,
as told to the author, on his thoughts on whether Bonds
felt extra pressure following in his father's footsteps (2020)

Americans love redemption stories.

Alex Rodriguez, as Royce Clayton alluded to, has risen from the ashes of baseball's steroid scandal—in 2013, MLB suspended him for 211 games for his involvement in the Biogenesis PEDs scandal but the suspension was later reduced to 162 games—to become an adored on-air personality as a baseball analyst on network TV since finishing his playing career in 2016. Referred to as "baseball's most hated player" and "the best paid pariah in the history of sports" during his career, the man known as "A-Rod" tested positive for anabolic steroids in 2003, before penalties were in place, and admitted to using "a banned substance" after the results were leaked in 2009. Two years later, he was caught up in the investigation into the Biogenesis clinic that provided supplements like human growth hormone and testosterone to players. In 2018, MLB chose Rodriguez as its sole representative in London, England, to promote the following summer's games between the Yankees and Red Sox at the London

Stadium, the first regular season MLB games in Europe. Today, A-Rod is widely regarded as a likable analyst on television.

Football star Michael Vick, the former No. 1 draft pick in the NFL, has seen his own redemption story play out. The former NFL quarterback, the first overall pick in the 2001 NFL Draft by the Atlanta Falcons out of Virginia Tech, was released from prison in 2009 after serving almost two years on charges related to his role in a dog-fighting ring. With the Philadelphia Eagles in December 2009, after losing two seasons in the prime of his career, Vick threw and ran for a touchdown in a game in Atlanta—in the city he once ruled—for his first scores since December 2006. A three-time Pro Bowler with the Falcons and one of football's most dynamic players before his stunning downfall for dog-fighting, he went on to play seven more years in the NFL for three different franchises, winning NFL Comeback Player of the Year honors in 2010.

Stories of redemption, from A-Rod to Vick, just to name a couple, are seen all the time in sports. All over baseball, players whose names were linked to PEDs have found forgiveness. To wit, Jason Giambi was named the AL Comeback Player of the Year in 2005 and interviewed for the Rockies' managerial job eight years later. Matt Williams, cited in the Mitchell Report in 2007, became the Washington Nationals' manager seven years later. If others have been forgiven, why not Barry Bonds? Say, have Barry finally enshrined in Cooperstown, where he belongs?

For Royce Clayton, Bonds is already in his own personal Hall of Fame. "He was a difference maker in my life, that's for sure. I love that dude. I played with the best player who ever played the game," says the former major-league shortstop. Former big-league outfielder Ryan Klesko, another ex-teammate, has called Bonds "probably the best player I've ever seen play the game" and added Barry should be in the Hall of Fame. "Whether he did steroids or not, before or after, whatever, I personally don't know. I wasn't there," Klesko told Atlanta-based reporter Tyler Redmond in 2019. "But that dude can hit. He was the most feared hitter in the game. I think best hitter all-time, ever. I played with him my last year when he was, I think, 40. [He] just [had] lightning hands [and a] great eye."

For John Cangelosi, the question of whether Bonds is a Hall of Famer is a no-brainer. "Is he deserving to be in the Hall of Fame?

Absolutely. One hundred percent. I don't have any doubt in my mind," says the former outfielder. "There are guys in the Hall of Fame that cheated. There are pitchers out there that cheat all the time. There are position players that took advantage of certain things in our era. As far as talent-wise and what he accomplished even before what was going on, he is 100% deserving of the Hall of Fame. That's not even a question."

It doesn't work like that with Hall of Fame voters, according to long-time sports radio personality Ted Sobel. "Look, Barry Bonds burned bridges with every media person I've ever known except for one. The media is the one who votes for the Hall of Fame. If I was in your family, and I treated everybody in your family poorly, all the time, every day, you knew about it, they knew about it, nobody liked me, and then at the end when I have five minutes to live, are you going to send me the greatest flowers? I mean, it's life. You treat people poorly, you get what you pay for. It's no different. It's very simple." Sobel, who's not a writer and doesn't vote for the Hall of Fame, does believe Bonds should be in Cooperstown, though—and so should Pete Rose, for that matter—because he believes players should be judged based on their numbers on the field. But he makes it clear he's not a fan of either Bonds or Rose.

When asked if he's surprised Bonds, as of this writing, still isn't in the Hall of Fame, Sobel says, "Hell, no! I'm surprised that anybody cares! The guy was a cheater." He then repeats the argument that some in the anti-Bonds faction often bring up: If you "cheated," you pay the price. But what about other "cheaters" who are already in the Hall? "It doesn't matter. He cheated. We know he cheated. It doesn't matter who else cheated," Sobel continues. "If you cheat, you pay for it. I'm not saying he won't get in. I believe, truly, there should be a special wing in the Hall of Fame for the Steroid Era. Sammy Sosa would not be in, because Sammy Sosa was not a Hall of Fame player until he was doing whatever he was doing. Barry Bonds was a Hall of Fame player. Roger Clemens was a Hall of Fame player. They just extended their careers and got ridiculous video-game numbers because of what they did afterwards, in the latter stages—or the second half, however you want to word it—of their careers. Sammy Sosa doesn't belong in. Mark McGwire doesn't belong in. Those guys weren't Hall of Fame players before that. Bonds and Clemens were. They should have a plaque and it should say they cheated, they broke the law [and] they used stuff that was illegal. But they were incredible players. They should be in a special wing because they were phenomenal players, and they should be here. But we also have to tell the truth.

"The same thing should be with Pete Rose. He should be in the Hall of Fame. How can he not be in the Hall of Fame? He has more hits than any other player in the history of the game. So, he should be in the Hall of Fame with a plaque saying he cheated and lied, [and] he did everything that baseball told him not to do. But he was a great player, so he's here. But he's a piece of crap, and everybody should know it. That's all. He should be in. Just like Bonds should be in. He cheated, but he was a great player. So, he's in. But you need to know what he did. That's all. Very simple. The rest is stupid politics. That's all it is. If they cheated and they deserved to be in anyway, you give him his plaque [with the wording] 'He was found to be a cheater. But he deserves to be here for whatever reason.' It's real simple. But people should know the truth. But people have to make their whole personal agendas over the whole thing. It's just totally stupid."

Adrian Brijbassi, a former New York *Newsday* sports editor, is also surprised that anybody cares whether Bonds has a plaque in Cooperstown. Unlike Sobel, though, he doesn't believe a separate wing is needed in the Hall of Fame. "Cheaters" don't get in, period, a far as he's concerned. "[If you look at the Hall of Fame] going back to the Black Sox days and what they've done with Pete Rose… [And you see that] Mark McGwire isn't in, Roger Clemens isn't in [and] it seems like there's a stain on that generation of players who were caught cheating or caught up in the BALCO scandal [or whose names have been linked to PEDs]," says Brijbassi, a sports editor at *Newsday* when the BALCO steroids case broke.

"The thing is, when Bonds came up, he was a Hall of Fame player before all of the home runs came, right? He was the best offensive left fielder of, absolutely, his generation and possibly right up there with anyone else who's ever played that position. And I think that's the shame of it. He was a Hall of Fame player if he hadn't taken the drugs and gone after the home-run records the way he did. But was he as frightening a hitter, as intimidating a hitter, in the early part of his career versus those years with the Giants? No. But I think he was perfect to watch because he had the ability to come through in the clutch at the plate, and also his speed—and his defensive ability—could turn a game. The thing is, Bonds didn't have to do it, but he cheated, right? If someone cheats in the Olympics and gets caught, they get stripped of their medals. So, I'm not sure what the argument is for Bonds to be in the Hall of Fame knowing that he's been a cheater. I mean, how can you look at his numbers objectively, knowing that he took performance-enhancing drugs to get the most significant [records]? There's been some rigidity with the Baseball Hall of Fame voters through the years against all forms of cheating, and I think obviously [the use of] performance-enhancing drugs is probably a greater violation than what Pete Rose and Shoeless Joe Jackson did. So, if those guys aren't in the Hall of Fame, I don't think Bonds would be deserving."

Ah, yes. Pete Rose. Shoeless Joe Jackson and the Black Sox. Different scandals from different eras.

* * *

The Houston Astros' sign-stealing scheme during their World Series championship season, in which members of the Astros used technological aids to steal signs of opposing teams during the 2017 and 2018 seasons, came to light in November 2019 when Mike Fiers, a pitcher who played for Houston in 2017, told *The Athletic* about the team's illegal sign-stealing tactics. It was revealed that, beginning in 2017, the season Houston won the World Series in seven games over the Dodgers, the Astros had a team employee relay signs to hitters from a dugout hallway by banging on a trash can—all while watching a live feed on a monitor. MLB launched an investigation into the allegations days after Fiers' comments came out, and in January 2020 baseball confirmed that the Astros had, indeed, illegally used a video camera system to steal signs in the 2017 regular season and postseason, and in parts of the 2018 regular season. As a result, the club lost draft picks and faced a maximum fine. Manager A. J. Hinch and general manager Jeff Luhnow, meanwhile, were fired by the ballclub after receiving suspensions from MLB.

On January 7, 2020, *The Athletic* published a report alleging that the Red Sox, the World Series champions in 2018, had also broken MLB rules by using a video replay room during 2018 regular season games to decipher the signs of opposing catchers, according to three unnamed sources who were with the team that year. This news broke while the league was already investigating the Astros. MLB investigated into the matter, and three months later in April, baseball announced that the Red Sox's replay operator had "utilized the game feeds in the replay room" to decode sign sequences but those actions were "limited in scope and impact," as the decoding only happened during some occurrences of the opposing team having a runner on second base and were not known to "then-Manager Alex Cora, the Red Sox coaching staff, the Red Sox front office, or most of the players." The video replay operator was suspended for the 2020 season and the team forfeited their second-round selection in the 2020 MLB draft.

When MLB training camps opened in February 2020, the Astros' sign-stealing scheme was the biggest story in baseball. And with Houston's sign-stealing tactics being exposed, other scandals in the history of the game were revisited. How does the Astros' use of technology to "gain an edge" compare to all those past scandals said to have hurt the game? How does baseball's steroid scandal compare to the sign-stealing scandal?

ESPN conducted a survey of 1,010 adults in January 2020, including 810 MLB fans, asking them such questions. Forty-nine percent of adults said the steroid scandal was more serious than the sign-stealing scandal, while 44% opined the sign-stealing scandal was worse than Pete Rose gambling on his own team. Seventy-six percent of MLB fans, meanwhile, said they believed most teams were using technology to steal signs, but only Houston and Boston were caught. Fifty-four percent of adults said their views of MLB were unchanged by the scandal, though, and 60% of adults said the scandals made no difference in their likelihood to watch MLB games.

Reactions among MLB players, meanwhile, seemed to indicate the sign-stealing scandal was much worse than that involving steroids. Players publicly commented about the scandal during the off-season, and anger towards the Astros from fellow MLB players grew, especially as the scandal wore on. ESPN reported that some Astros players had reached out to other players to assure them that they didn't cheat, but that some of those friendships were fractured and there was a lot of anger towards Astros players after the release of MLB's investigation.

Pitcher Trevor Bauer, who called the Houston players "cheaters" and "hypocrites" who'd "stolen from a lot of other people and the game itself," has opined that the Astros' actions were akin to the 1919 Black Sox scandal, the infamous game-fixing scandal in which eight members of the White Sox were accused of conspiring with gamblers to intentionally lose the World Series against Cincinnati in exchange for money. Writing in *The Players' Tribune* in February 2020, Bauer added, "Personally I think that what's going on in baseball now is up there with the Black Sox scandal, and that it will be talked about forever—more so than steroids. Like the steroid era, you can say what you want about it, but steroids weren't really illegal at the time. The sign-stealing that was going on in Houston, though, was *blatantly* illegal. And with the rules that were implemented last year and the year before—that, by the way, were then still broken—it was very clear."

Two months later, Bauer, who made his big-league debut five years after Bonds played his final game, tweeted: "Barry Bonds is a [H]all of [F]amer." The outspoken Bauer, who'd go on to win the NL Cy Young Award in 2020, later expanded on his thoughts on Twitter. "The Hall of Fame is a shrine to the history of the game," Bauer tweeted. "Regardless of your feelings on this, steroids are part of the game's history. It would be very hard to convince me that no players in the Hall of Fame currently used performance-enhancing drugs. And even if they didn't use what we would consider 'steroids,' substances that are illegal today were legal back then. Greenies, amphetamines, etc., used to be handed out like candy. Players were forced to take them because it was seen as 'not doing everything you could to help the team' if you didn't. Those same substances are illegal today, so by that logic, should every player that took them be disallowed from the Hall of Fame? It would be a hall of empty if that were the case. At some point, the best players of their era have to be enshrined. Period. It's part of our game's history." Then-Dodgers left-hander Alex Wood, who held the Astros to one hit in 5.2 innings in Game Four of the 2017 World Series in Houston (a sixth-inning homer to George Springer), compared the game's two scandals of the 21st century succinctly in one tweet: "I would rather face a player that was taking steroids than face a player that knew every pitch that was coming."

Doug Glanville, a former outfielder who played nine seasons in the majors for the Phillies, Cubs and Rangers, has offered a different perspective, though. In an ESPN.com column in March 2020, he outlined why he believes ballplayers on PEDs had a much more negative affect on those who played the game clean—than did any players from any sign-stealing ballclubs. "Remember how you get security in this game," wrote Glanville, a major-league center fielder between 1996 and 2004 and current broadcast color analyst. "Every year you survive in the major leagues, you will be compared—directly, to the people inside your organization for a specific job, and indirectly, to others with your seniority and who play your position. This assigns you a value in the marketplace." Any time a player comes to the negotiating table, he's compared to other players based on productivity, service time and position. In the PED era, numbers got juiced, and when enough players juiced up, it raised the bar at any given position. "It shifts the expectations of how that position should produce, artificially. It influences the money an organization will commit to you and it directly influences your opportunity." In Glanville's case specifically, "if eight more center fielders juice up, I have a career advancement problem. I can lose eight job opportunities. All of a sudden, the average center fielder has higher power standards than he did before, and if I stay a singles hitter, my career changes for the worse. I could be relegated to a fourth outfielder (if I am even still on the team). It happens quickly enough without PEDs involved, let alone with them."

As for teams involved in technology-aided sign-stealing schemes? Those ballclubs might benefit as a unit, "but from the perspective of a center fielder who needs to look for work the next season, outside of the cheating club's center fielder hitting well because of the sign-stealing system, it does not elevate the entire position throughout the league. If the season ends and I am compared to one sign-stealing center fielder, it might hurt a little, but not like it would if half the league's center fielders were on PEDs." As Glanville said, in that scenario, he could go to the negotiating table and make the case to treat Astros outfielders as an aberration like he might for Colorado players and the high altitude: an outlier. "One 'clairvoyant' center fielder in Houston probably does not keep me out of the big leagues. Seventeen juiced outfielders does."

Opinions differ depending on whom you talk to. Some will say the home-run chase in 1998 helped save baseball. PEDs, they'll argue, didn't prevent the sport from gaining a wider audience. Steroids, they'll say, didn't prevent fans from being entertained.

Others will insist that they were turned off as fans because of PED use by players, shooting down the notion that steroids were just "a part of baseball culture" back then.

Adrian Brijbassi is one who "got turned off" because of that so-called culture. When asked to rank the different scandals in the history of baseball, the former New York *Newsday* sports editor says, "You can compare them in the sense that they're all forms of cheating. It's the extent to which an individual or a team takes their nefarious behavior and how long they perpetrated it. The Astros committed it at the highest level, really—the moment that baseball is built for: the World Series. They cheated the game that way. They had an unfair advantage [but] they have been punished—I think, rightly, with the [suspensions and subsequent] firings [of general manager Jeff Luhnow and manager A. J. Hinch]. That's been dealt with. With the Black Sox scandal and the Pete Rose scandal, I think those were so long ago that, in the case of [Shoeless Joe Jackson] in particular, it's difficult to prove that his performance on the field was impacted by the [fix in the 1919 World Series]. The performance-enhancing drugs [scandal], I think, is at a different level because of how pervasive it was and how much it hampered players who weren't taking those drugs, how much it hurt their careers, and that Bonds, Clemens, McGwire, Sosa and whoever else was caught [or linked to PEDs], they were also being unfair to their own teammates as well. There are all kinds of stories of them threatening teammates for saying anything, having their own trainers who'd inject them with the drugs. It just caused a level of scandal that was harder for baseball to get over than, I think, the Houston Astros' [sign-stealing scandal], which was quite an isolated case."

Contrary to Brijbassi's point, though, Bonds has never been known to intimidate teammates for testifying against him, for instance, during his 2011 trial on charges of perjury and obstruction of justice. Bonds, according to columnist Gwen Knapp on Sportsonearth.com in 2013, "didn't even appear to bear a grudge toward the baseball people who testified against him." Former teammate Marvin Benard testified for the prosecution, and he told Knapp that he remembered looking repeatedly at Bonds from the chair, hoping to make eye contact. "Then in between, when the lawyers were changing places, he looked at me," Benard recalled, "we made contact and we just started laughing." Similarly, when former Giants trainer Stan Conte—no relation to Victor Conte, the former founder and owner of BALCO—first saw Bonds after the trial, the two men were waiting for a delayed flight at an airport, and Barry "couldn't have been friendlier." Bonds approached Conte and proceeded to talk for over an hour, with Barry telling the former trainer that he "had no bad feelings toward [Conte] for testifying, and that he understand what [Conte's] position was." Bonds, concluded Knapp, "distinguished himself from Lance Armstrong, the leading villain in the sports world, by not menacing colleagues or their families when they had to give evidence against him." In the case of Armstrong, specifically, stories which came out about the former professional cyclist, wrote Knapp, revealed "a pattern of intimidation far beyond any accusations ever thrown at Bonds."

Brijbassi is among those of the opinion that steroids are illegal, period; players who used them were villains, period. "It's just that it was a criminal activity, right?" he asks rhetorically. "That is different than trying to take technology and push its limits within the field of play. And people have been trying to steal signs since baseball has been around, right? They would have kids out in center field back in the day with shiny objects to tell the batter if it was a fastball or a curveball. But I think what Bonds had [supposedly] done—and those players of that era had done—was try to destroy the reputation of baseball in a way that ruined the game for a number of people. I'm one of those people who loved baseball and really got turned off by the culture that developed around that time within the sport. I think that ultimately the greatest harm of that era is how that level of deceit impacted the audience—the casual fans, at least, if not some hardcore fans who were just fed up with that kind of activity, not knowing that your heroes were actually villains."

Ted Sobel, like Brijbassi, doesn't buy the "that was a part of baseball culture" line of reasoning regarding PEDs. If you used those things, Sobel says, you cheated. "If it's illegal and it does make your eyesight better and your hand-eye coordination better because, for whatever reason, that's the way the drug works, that's not fair. It's not right. And it's cheating." As for the debate about sign-stealing versus the other scandals, Sobel says we first must take "greenies" out of the equation. "No, [greenies are nothing like steroids] and it's not even close. Remember, baseball's the toughest game to play in the [context] that it's every single day. You might have a half a dozen days off in six months, and it just wears on you. Even if you're not playing, it's a wear and tear. And [then there's] the travel, [where] you're gone for 10 days and you're back home. And then the next day you're back at batting practice. You just don't get time to reboot, ever. So, the greenies were something that just sort of kept you going. It wasn't a performance enhancer where it makes you stronger or makes your eyes better. It wasn't like that. It was just like, 'Hey, I'm still awake.' It was more of a pep pill than it was anything like a performance enhancer. If you didn't take them, you'd have to take some days off. And nobody wanted to do that. And you know the name 'Wally Pipp'; nobody wanted to be Wally Pipped because they were tired. So, you did whatever you could to make sure you played every day. And that's the way it worked. So, I don't fault anybody for that.

"The gambling is another issue. The gambling is a credibility issue. [Sports leagues want] to be sure that not one fan out there would ever question whether a game was legit or not," Sobel continues, addressing the Pete Rose gambling scandal. "If you're a manager and you control everything—I don't believe Pete Rose ever bet against his team so, in that respect, no games were fixed or anything, I don't think, but he could've adjusted pitching rotations just for his own purposes—[and you bet on baseball games in which you're directly involved, that's a credibility issue]. There's a legitimacy, a credibility issue with gambling in any sport." Sobel adds that the rule which forbids betting was already in place well before Rose began his playing career and it didn't go away once he was only a manager. It was always there, and there were signs in every clubhouse. "From a gambling standpoint, for as long as I could ever remember—and this has existed since before I was even born—there's a giant sign right in the front of the clubhouse door. 'No gambling, no this, no that… or you'll be reprimanded [and be declared permanently ineligible] by the league.' Those are the rules. So, if you break the rules, you pay for it. So, Pete Rose is paying for it. But it's all about legitimacy. If the fans think, 'Oh, they threw that game?' people are going to stop going to games. You can't do that. All legitimacy is gone if the public finds out about it [if game fixing were to occur].

"You can't compare that to anything. You certainly can't compare that to greenies. You can't compare that to steroids because steroids are a performance enhancer. Greenies were understandable. Gambling isn't. With respect to steroids and gambling, the only thing they have in common, in my mind, [is that steroids] also affect the credibility of the game. Because now you've got guys doing stuff [reaching numbers and milestones] they would never be able to do without [steroids]. Where's the fairness there? It's supposed to be fair competition. That's what sports is. If you cheat, it's not real. Who wants to follow a sport that's not real? Nobody."

Sign stealing, meanwhile, is akin to gambling and steroids, says Sobel. "If you cheat for one win, your credibility is shot. You're a cheater. That's it. It's not a fair win. You can't do that. I covered all the World Series games in L.A., not in Houston, so I didn't hear the trash-can banging and all that [which happened only at Minute Maid Park, the Astros' home ballpark]. It's all about credibility with the fans and the public. If you lose an ounce of credibility, you lose a lot because they'll stop going. It's like, 'Maybe it's fixed today. Maybe it's not.' Who needs that? The bottom line is this: Forget the greenies. I can't fault the guys for taking them. It wasn't considered a performance enhancer. I can't compare that to any of the other things at all. If it's not a performance enhancer, I don't have a problem with it." Everything else, as far as Sobel is concerned, is cheating, which taints and hurts the game.

When asked to compare all of the scandals, former major-league pitcher Tom Candiotti opines gambling would be the worst. "With Pete Rose, if it's true that he gambled on the team that he was managing—on the Reds—if he was gambling to win or to lose, that, to me, is one of the most serious things [you could do]. To me, that's just the worst. But like I said before, in Barry's case with PEDs—and a lot of guys, not just Barry, but a lot of guys [were doing it] at that time—[he was] trying to keep up with the other guys that were doing it. And the sad thing is all the GMs, they all knew it. They all knew it."

* * *

It's time for the final word. For the purposes of the discussion here, we're not talking about the steroid allegations, but who is the real Barry Bonds?

Once you get to know Barry Bonds, those who know him will tell you, he's really a terrific guy with a soft side to him.

Bob Nightengale is one member of the media who has seen that soft side. "We always got along well," the long-time *USA Today* writer says. "He was much better one-on-one with me and with a few other guys, than in a group. I think, in a group, he could come across as arrogant or standoffish, not want to deal with you. But if you sat down and got to know him, you'd realize his intelligence level. Could have been a major-league manager very easily. He could have done anything. He was big on computers and technology, more than anybody I've ever known, as an athlete. You always came away learning more about baseball talking with him. I've seen the other side of him also, but just the one-on-one interactions were very good."

Sports columnist Larry Stone, who covered the Giants when Barry first arrived in town, has acknowledged that Bonds "sometimes seemed intent on belittling" members of the press, but added, "And yet covering Bonds was not all bite and venom. He definitely had his charming side, which he would flash at unexpected moments. Every once in a while, Barry would summon a beat writer and chat amiably, even showing interest in events in their own life. I had told him once that my daughter, Jessica, shared his birthday. Barry remembered to tell me to wish her a happy birthday when she turned eight in 1994." Three months earlier, on Opening Day, Stone was on the field at sold-out Candlestick Park presenting Bonds with the Player of the Year award given by the Bay Area chapter of the Baseball Writers Association of America, only to have Barry give him a limp handshake. After the game, though, as Stone recalled, Bonds sought him out in the clubhouse and told him warmly, "Thanks, man. I appreciate the award."

For Royce Clayton, Bonds isn't just a former teammate; Barry is his big brother. "To this day, Barry and I still have a relationship," Clayton says. "He's shown up to Little League [games] for my kids. As a matter of fact, my wife tells this story of when I was playing in D.C. [for the Washington Nationals in 2006, and] he hadn't seen my triplets. We'd just had the triples. He saw my wife at the mall with the triplets, and people were following him in the mall. He stopped everything and told everybody to back up and he embraced my babies. He's so happy that I have my [own] family. I'm like his little brother. He's embraced my kids, and for him to come out and support my kids in Little League,

247

throwing out first pitches… That's Uncle Barry. Anything that I need, I know that he would be there for my boys, for my daughters, for my family. My mom and his mom, Pat, are very close to this day. Like I said, people are people, but I love this dude. He's shown nothing but love for my family. Like I said, there's a side to him that's beautiful, a very sensitive side. We all grow as humans. Some of that humility that comes with the experience in growing up, [and] we all get there. I'm just happy that he's happy with his life."

Tom Candiotti, who played in the big leagues between 1983 and 1999, was never in the same locker room with Barry Bonds because they were never teammates. "Again, I don't know him as a teammate. I know him as a competitor and no one was better." But the former knuckleball specialist, one of the most easygoing major-leaguers you'll ever meet, got to know Barry off the field in the mid-1990s and, to this day, they remain friends.

As Candiotti, who faced Bonds numerous times as a Dodger as part of the L.A.-San Francisco rivalry, recalls, they first met each other at Candiotti's off-season golf tournament in Northern California in 1986. "Bobby [Bonds] was a coach in Cleveland and we hit it off because we were both from the Bay Area. And I learned an awful lot from Bobby, even though he was a hitting coach. He'd sit sometimes and talk to you, [sharing information about the tendencies of opposing hitters and base runners, like] what this guy's looking for. Or [things like] 'What do you think he's doing? Look at his speed. Look at his hands,' [and] little things and intricacies to the game, and I think he liked the fact that I'd come up and ask him certain questions. So, we just clicked, and in the off-season he always came out to my celebrity golf tournament. One time, he brought Barry to come out, which was awesome, and this is when Barry had just gotten up with the Pirates and so that was really the first time that I met Barry—and he was funny."

Candiotti certainly didn't mind Barry's trash talk, instead viewing it as a challenge from a great player. "He was cocky like his dad, and he goes, 'One of these days, I'm gonna take you deep. You might not invite me to your golf tournament anymore!' I said, 'Oh yeah? We'll see.' I got to the National League after being with the Indians [prior to the advent of interleague play] and I got to face him, so it was kind of fun a little competition that we had, and he was always gracious, always cool, around me."

Following his retirement, Candiotti became a radio analyst for the Arizona Diamondbacks, and he recalls introducing broadcast partner Greg Schulte, the team's radio play-by-play voice, to Barry prior to an Arizona-San Francisco game in 2006. "I brought Greg down to the dugout, and I said, 'Let's go down to talk to Barry.' But Greg goes, 'You can't get to Barry. Nobody can talk to him.' And I go, 'Just come on down.' So, we're just kind of standing by the dugout. And Barry comes out and all the press is hovering around him. Most of the time, Barry might say a word or two or whatever, but other than that, he'd just walk away onto the field or something.

"So, this time, he goes out there, and, all of a sudden, he sees me standing there. All these guys are asking questions, but he just puts his hand out to stop them all. And he comes over and he's just talking with me, and I introduce him to Greg Schulte and we have a 10-minute conversation just catching up. But [the coolest thing is] he stopped the whole media just to come over to say hi. To me, he is great."

To many, Barry Bonds isn't great. Yet to many others, he is great. Perhaps some people will be swayed and believe Barry Bonds belongs in the Hall of Fame. Others will not care and simply cannot be swayed. Some Hall of Fame voters who have backed Bonds will give up their vote and decide not to participate in what they feel is a hypocrisy when it comes to the voting process. That's okay. At the end of the day, everybody is entitled to his or her own opinion. That's what makes a sports debate great.

As Nikolai Bonds, Barry's son, put it in a 2015 interview with writer Jeff Pearlman, Barry Bonds' job as a baseball player was to entertain. That was it. He didn't owe anybody anything other than providing entertainment to baseball fans during his major-league career. He wasn't the nicest person in the world when it came to dealing with members of the media or with teammates and others in the clubhouse, but not everybody is nice every day of his or her life, either. "That's an impossible standard for anybody to ask you to achieve," Nikolai Bonds reasoned.

"My dad is a hard ass," Nikolai continued in that same interview with Pearlman. "Absolutely. He can be one of the biggest jerks in this world. Absolutely. But my dad also has the biggest heart in the world and never has any intentions to hurt anyone. He had to sit and watch as people threw things at his wife, at his daughter. Attack his family.

My family had to stand quiet and tall while people were sending him death threats every single day. *Over baseball.* People threatening his family. So now he has to protect his family. My dad doesn't owe anybody anything. He owed the fans entertainment, and his family a life. Beyond that, he didn't owe anything. If someone threatened your family and a reporter now wants to get into your personal life, where this person now might have access to your family, would you give it? Would you allow people close? It was easy to portray my dad as a villain. He was an easy target. A closed-off athlete. But spend a real day with that man and tell me if he is a bad person. Because he and I have had our differences but I will never say he is a bad person. My dad is a great man. He just isn't perfect, and he tries to protect himself and his family the best way he knows how."

Barry Bonds did what he was supposed to do as a baseball player. He played the game to the best of his ability, and he brought joy to fans in Pittsburgh and San Francisco. He helped revitalize baseball in San Francisco, providing Giants fans with countless memories over his 15 years in the Bay Area. He had an amazing career and he hit more home runs than any other player in Major League Baseball.

All of that should be enough, and what he did on the baseball field was more than enough for enshrinement in Cooperstown.

Bibliography

Books

Banks, Kerry. *Baseball's Top 100: The Game's Greatest Records.* Vancouver, Canada: Greystone Books, 2010.

Bloom, John. *Barry Bonds: A Biography.* Westport, CT: Greenwood Publishing Group, 2004.

Ezra, David. *Asterisk: Home Runs, Steroids and the Rush to Judgment.* Chicago: Triumph Books, 2008.

Fainaru-Wada, Mark and Lance Williams. *Game of Shadows: Barry Bonds, BALCO, and the Steroids Scandal That Rocked Professional Sports.* New York: Gotham Books, 2006.

Feinstein, John. *Play Ball: The Life and Troubled Times of Major League Baseball.* New York: Villard Books, 1993.

Harper, John, and Bob Klapisch. *Champions! The Saga of the 1996 New York Yankees.* New York: Villard Books, 1996.

Pearlman, Jeff. *Love Me, Hate Me: Barry Bonds and the Making of an Antihero.* New York: HarperCollins, 2006.

Ryan, Joan. *Intangibles: Unlocking the Science and Soul of Team Chemistry.* New York: Little, Brown and Company, 2020.

Turbow, Jason, and Michael Duca. *The Baseball Codes: Beanballs, Sign Stealing, and Bench-Clearing Brawls—The Unwritten Rules of America's Pastime.* New York: Random House, 2010.

Turbow, Jason. *They Bled Blue: Fernandomania, Strike-Season Mayhem, and the Weirdest Championship Baseball Had Ever Seen—The 1981 Los Angeles Dodgers.* New York: Houghton Mifflin Harcourt, 2019.

Newspapers, Magazines and Online

Anderson, Dave. "Sports of the Times: The .300-100-100-30-50 Man." *The New York Times*, October 5, 1990.

Axisa, Mike. "David Ortiz Says His Failed PED Test Leaked Because Too Many Yankees Tested Positive." CBSSports.com, May 19, 2017.

Baer, Bill. "Jack Morris Should Not Be in the Hall of Fame." NBCSports.com, December 10, 2017.

Baggarly, Andrew. "Pirates Give Bonds a Warm Reception." *East Bay Times*, August 14, 2007.

"Barry Bonds: I'm a Felon but Not a Steroid User." *New York Daily News*, December 4, 2012.

"Barry Bonds Returns to Pittsburgh." ESPN.com/Associated Press, March 31, 2014.

Bhattacharjee, Riya. "Berkeley High Inagurates (sic) Sports Hall of Fame, *The Berkeley (California) Daily Planet*, June 8, 2007.

"Bonds Cheers Ill Fan." Associated Press, February 13, 1997.

Boswell, Thomas. "Spitball Flap Turns into an Orel Examination." *The Washington Post*, October 19, 1997.

Brisbee, Grant. "Barry Bonds Still Isn't in the Hall of Fame, But It's Getting Harder to Pretend He Remains a Baseball Villain." *The Athletic*, January 21, 2020.

Brown, Daniel. "Royals Star a Bonds Fan." *San Jose Mercury News*, May 19, 2007.

Brown, Daniel. "Who's the Boss Here? Bonds' Status Earns Him Leeway, Perks, Second-Guesses." *San Jose Mercury News*, May 15, 2005.

Calcaterra, Craig. "It's the 40th Anniversary of Aaron's 715th Homer—But Please, Don't Call Him the Home Run King." NBCSports.com, April 8, 2014.

Calcaterra, Craig. "Mike Schmidt is Not Yet Convinced that Barry Bonds and Roger Clemens Took Steroids." NBCSports.com, February 21, 2013.

Callahan, Maureen. "Inside DiMaggio and Monroe's Twisted Love." *New York Post*, June 8, 2014.

Caple, Jim. "A Giant by Any Standard: Bonds Stands Among Baseball's Best Ever." *Seattle Post-Intelligencer*. June 9, 2000.

Chastain, Bill. "Bonds Doesn't Seem Alarmed by Big Swoon." *The Tampa Tribune*, October 8, 1992.

Cook, Ron. "Belinda's Criticism a Punch to the Gut That Angers Leyland." *Pittsburgh Post-Gazette*, March 20, 1994.

Cowlishaw, Tim. "Steroids or Not, They Should Be In." *The Dallas Morning News*, December 6, 2012.

Crouse, Karen. "Positively Still Barry." *The Palm Beach (FL) Post*, July 10, 2001.

Curry, Jack. "Why Bonds Will Never Have to Borrow a Bat." *The New York Times*, July 28, 2007.

Davis, Scott. "The Patriots are Once Again Embroiled in a Cheating Controversy." *Business Insider*, December 12, 2019.

Diamond, Jeff. "Brady, Belichick Should Receive Better Hall of Fame Treatment Than MLB's Alleged Cheaters." SportingNews.com, August 10, 2016.

"Do Mark McGwire and Barry Bonds Belong in the Hall of Fame?" *The (Memphis, TN) Commercial Appeal*, March 27, 2005.

Dongallo, Angelica. "Obituary: Well-Loved Berkeley High Alumnus Dies of Leukemia." *The Daily Californian*/DailyCal.org, November 28, 2006.

Downey, Mike. "No-Name Giants Not the Answer." *Los Angeles Times*, September 26, 1996.

Early, David E. "Bonds on Bonds: Giants Star Says He Plays for the Love of the Game, Not to Cultivate an Image." *San Jose Mercury News*, September 30, 2001.

Epstein, Jori. "Be Like Barry Bonds? Why Dallas Cowboys Coach Jon Kitna is Telling Dak Prescott Just That." *USA Today*, November 6, 2019.

Ezra, David. "Baseball's Steroid Era Was No Surprise, So Hall of Fame Voters Should Accept It." USNews.com, July 21, 2009.

Fialkov, Harvey. "The Book on Barry: Everything You Wanted to Know About the Giants Slugger." *South Florida Sun-Sentinel*, September 30, 2003.

Fletcher, Jeff. "Beyond Brawny: Introducing Brainy Bonds." *The (Santa Rosa, CA) Press Democrat*, April 24, 2001.

Fletcher, Jeff. "Bonds' Fifth MVP Will Transcend Baseball." *The (Santa Rosa, CA) Press Democrat*, November 10, 2002.

Fletcher, Jeff. "Bonds Finally Blasts No. 714 to Tie Ruth." *The (Santa Rosa, CA) Press Democrat*, May 21, 2006.

Fletcher, Jeff. "Bonds Joins Club." *The (Santa Rosa, CA) Press Democrat*, April 18, 2001.

Fletcher, Jeff. "Will Anyone Pitch to Barry?" *The (Santa Rosa, CA)*

Press Democrat, September 7, 2004.

Freeman, Dennis J. "Barry Bonds, Steroids and the Double Standards of Race." News4UsOnline.com, March 20, 2011.

Glanville, Doug. "I Played Clean in the Steroid Era—and PEDs Hurt Players More Than Sign Stealing Does." ESPN.com, March 9, 2020.

Gonzales, Mark. "Pirates Fans Boo Bonds' First Visit." *San Jose Mercury News*, April 10, 1993.

Graeff, Burt. "A Giant Step toward Maturity: Barry Bonds Ready to Sacrifice Personal Stats for Chance to Win Elusive World Series Ring." *The (Cleveland) Plain Dealer*, April 13, 1997.

Graham, Janet. "Most Disliked: Bonds Doesn't Take Notoriety Personally." *The Cincinnati Post*, May 1, 1991.

Grann, David. "Baseball without Metaphor." *The New York Times Magazine*, September 1, 2002.

Graziano, Dan. "Bonds Close to Leyland after Years, Miles Apart." *The Palm Beach Post*, April 20, 1997.

Hayes, Neil. "Ignorance No Defense." *Chicago Sun-Times*, June 21, 2009.

Heath, Thomas. "McGwire's Heroics Driving up Profits." *The Washington Post*, July 8, 1998.

Hunter, Bob. "Pirates Take Third Swing at NL Title." *The Columbus Dispatch*, October 6, 1992.

Jablonski, David. "Braggs Remembers NLCS Catch as 1990 Team Reunites." *Dayton Daily News*, September 23, 2016.

Jaffe, Jay. "A Gripping Saga: 11 Tales of Pitchers Using Spitters, Sandpaper and Scuffing." SI.com, May 3, 2013.

Jaffe, Jay. "It's Time to Stop Worrying and Learn to Love Barry Bonds' Home Run Record." SI.com, August 7, 2017.

Janish, Joe. "Mike Piazza Admitted Taking PEDs." MetsToday.com, January 6, 2015.

Jenkins, Bruce. "Bonds' Return Shakes Up Pittsburgh." *The San Francisco Chronicle*, April 10, 1993.

Jimenez, Teresa. "Baseball Star Shines for Pal: Barry Bonds Visits Agoura High School Team." *Daily News of Los Angeles*, February 13, 1997.

Johnson, Chuck. "Bonds Finds Media Glare Disillusioning." *USA Today*, March 13, 1992.

Jordan, Pat. "Conversations with the Dinosaur." *Men's Journal*, March 1993.

Joshi, Maitreyee. "'He Doesn't Deserve to Eat': When a Ruthless Michael Jordan Starved His Teammate for Not Playing Well." EssentiallySports.com, May 7, 2020.

Kandadai, Saketh. "'I Had a Problem with How He Tried to Motivate Me': Horace Grant Speaks Out Against Michael Jordan." EssentiallySports.com, May 9, 2020.

Kelly, Cathal. "How Should the Baseball Hall of Fame Be Dealing with PED Users?" *The Globe and Mail*, November 21, 2017.

Klingaman, Mike. "In the Rough-and-Tumble Baseball of the 1890s, Baltimore Rose to the Top with Skill and Guile." *The Baltimore Sun*, July 7, 1996.

Knapp, Gwen. "The King in Limbo." Sportsonearth.com, November 20, 2013.

Kurkjian, Tim. "The Best and Worst." *Sports Illustrated*, July 15, 1996.

Kurtenbach, Dieter. "Why the Baseball Hall of Fame is Incomplete without Barry Bonds." *San Jose Mercury News*, January 24, 2018.

Leister, Roger. "Play Ball! ESPN's Jon Miller Previews the New Season." TVguide.com, March 30, 2007.

Lincicome, Bernie. "Joltin' Joe Never Changed, Only the Rest of Us Did." *Chicago Tribune*, March 9, 1999.

Lyons, Steve. "Hall of Fame Should Get Over the Steroid Scandal—Cheating is Common." USNews.com, July 21, 2009.

McCauley, Janie. "Bonds: Best Hitter Ever?" *The (Fort Wayne, IN) Journal Gazette*/Associated Press, April 23, 2004.

McCauley, Janie. "Five-Time MVP Bonds Wants to be Understood." *The (KS) Chanute Tribune*/Associated Press, November 12, 2002.

McCollough, J. Brady. "The Slide: The Moment that Begat a Legacy of Losing for the Pirates." *Pittsburgh Post-Gazette*, April 1, 2012.

Merkin, Scott. "'I Love the Guy': Tales from MJ's White Sox Days." MLB.com, May 9, 2020.

Meyer, Paul. "Van Slyke's Reaction to Bonds' Set-up Charge: 'It's a Lie.'" *Pittsburgh Post-Gazette*, June 13, 1993.

Millson, Larry. "Wells Latest 'Victim' of Writer." *The Globe and Mail*, July 6, 2000.

Morrissey, Rick. "And Stay Out: Hall Right." *Chicago Sun-Times/(IN) Post-Tribune*, January 10, 2013.

Nesbitt, Stephen J. "Pranks, Panic, Power: Tales of Barry Bonds' Magical Years in Pittsburgh." *The Athletic*, September 15, 2020.

Neubeck, Kyle. "Review: 'Imperfect' Explores the Price Roy Halladay Paid to Be a Hall of Fame Pitcher." PhillyVoice.com, May 29, 2020.

Newman, Mark. "Bonds vs. Pendleton: A Playoff Bust." *San Jose Mercury News*, October 16, 1991.

Nightengale, Bob. "Gaylord Perry Says Put Barry Bonds, Not Pete Rose, in Hall of Fame." *USA Today*, January 12, 2017.

Nightengale, Bob. "Manfred Questions David Ortiz's Positive Drug Test, Urges Leniency by Hall Voters." *USA Today*, October 2, 2016.

Nightengale, Bob. "Roy Halladay's Drug Addiction Exposed in ESPN Documentary 'Imperfect: The Roy Halladay Story.'" *USA Today*, May 28, 2020.

O'Brien, David. "No False Modesty: Barry Bonds Knows He's Good and Doesn't Care If You Don't See His More Human Side." *South Florida Sun-Sentinel*, August 23, 1998.

O'Brien, David. "What If Braves Had Gotten Barry Bonds in 1992 Trade Before Pirates Backed Out?" *The Athletic*, May 8, 2020.

O'Keeffe, Michael. "The Score: Scribes Got It Hall Wrong about Bonds and Bad Guys." *New York Daily News*, March 19, 2006.

Olney, Buster. "'I Don't Feel Cheated One Bit': Pitchers Who Gave Up Home Runs to Both McGwire and Sosa in '98 Tell Their Tales." ESPN.com, June 12, 2020.

Olson, Casey. "If Barry Bonds and Roger Clemens Aren't Hall of Famers, Then Who Is?" *Federal Way Mirror (WA)*, December 6, 2012.

Padecky, Bob. "Up Close, Personal." *The (Santa Rosa, CA) Press Democrat*, April 5, 2006.

Page, Clarence. "Athletes Clad in Nothing but Sexism." *Chicago Tribune*, September 30, 1990.

Passan, Jeff. "I Am Giving up My Hall of Fame Vote Because of Joe Morgan's Letter." *Yahoo! Sports*, November 23, 2017.

Pearlman, Jeff. "Nikolai Bonds." JeffPearlman.com, April 21, 2015.

"Pirates Sign Van Slyke to $12.6 Million Extension." *Deseret (Utah) News*, April 7, 1991.

Poole, Monte. "Visit with Lee Franklin was Unforgettable." *(Walnut*

Creek, California) East Bay Times, November 26, 2006.

Posnanski, Joe. "The Baseball 100: No. 3, Barry Bonds." *The Athletic*, April 8, 2020.

Pugliese, Nick. "Bonds in for Early Workouts." *The Tampa Tribune*, February 25, 1992.

Quinn, T. J. "The HOF: Why I Stopped Voting." ESPN.com, December 21, 2012.

"Reaction Positive to 715." *Seattle Post-Intelligencer*/Associated Press, May 28, 2006.

"Red Sox' Ortiz 'Never Knowingly Took Steroids.'" Sportsnet.ca/ Associated Press, March 27, 2015.

"Reds Trevor Bauer Calls Astros Hypocrites and Cheaters." ESPN.com, February 15, 2020.

Reilly, Rick. "Be Like Mike? No Thanks." ESPN.com, September 16, 2009.

Reilly, Rick. "He Loves Himself Barry Much." *Sports Illustrated*, August 27, 2001.

Roderick, Joe. "Bonds is Rapidly Closing in on His 600th Home Run: Milestones are Arriving Quickly for Giants Slugger." *Contra Costa (California) Times*/Associated Press, August 6, 2002.

Rodriguez, Juan C. "Rodriguez Breaks Giants with Two-Out, Two-Run Hit in 11th." *South Florida Sun-Sentinel*, October 4, 2003.

Rosvoglou, Christopher. "MLB Analyst Destroys Tigers Hall of Famer Jack Morris over Incident with Female Reporter." 12up.com, August 6, 2018.

Rubin, Adam. "Bonds on Broadway." *New York Daily News*, June 2, 2006.

Ryan, Bob. "Let's Face It, Baseball Really Has Three Home Run Champs." *Boston Globe*, September 2, 2017.

Ryan, Joan. "A's Outfielder Slowly Alters the Way He Plays." *The San Francisco Chronicle*, May 31, 1995.

Schoenfield, David. "Marlins Could Be Exploiting Market Inefficiency in Hiring Barry Bonds." ESPN.com, December 1, 2015.

Schulman, Henry. "Bobby Says Barry is at Peace." *The San Francisco Chronicle*, October 2, 2001.

Schulman, Henry. "Bonds Can't Shake World Series Absence." *The San Francisco Chronicle*, September 10, 1999.

Schulman, Henry. "Bonds Says There Are Far Worse Things Than

Steroids, Such As Cocaine and Heroin." *The San Francisco Chronicle*, March 5, 2005.

Sexton, Joe. "The Playoffs; A Drama Plays Out in One Classic Inning." *The New York Times*, October 16, 1992.

Shaughnessy, Dan. "McGwire Victimized by Media's Reports." *Boston Globe* (reprinted in *The Memphis, TN, Commercial Appeal*), August 27, 1998.

Shea, John. "A Change of Heart and Vote for Bonds." *San Francisco Chronicle*, January 7, 2016.

Shea, John. "No More Missing Link in Bonds' Career." *Pittsburgh Post-Gazette/San Francisco Chronicle*, October 16, 2002.

Shea, John. "Willie Mays Lobbies for Barry Bonds to Enter Hall of Fame." *Tribune Content Agency News Service/San Francisco Chronicle*, August 12, 2018.

Squatriglia, Chuck. "Last Game for 'Ballpark Marge'; Giants' No. 1 Fan Rarely Missed a Home Game." *SFGate*, June 27, 2003.

Starkey, Joe. "Bummer of '92: Bream's Slide Lives in Infamy." *The Pittsburgh Tribune-Review*, October 14, 2007.

Stephens, Mitch. "Profile: Lee Franklin Fights Leukemia, Shines for Berkeley High on the Field." *SFGate*, October 19, 2001.

Stone, Larry. "Barry & Me: Covering Bonds Equally Frustrating and Amazing." *The Seattle Times*, July 24, 2007.

Van Natta Jr., Don and Seth Wickersham. "Spygate to Deflategate: Inside What Split the NFL and Patriots Apart." ESPN.com, September 7, 2015.

Warren, James. "Stockpiling." *Chicago Tribune*, April 22, 1993.

"Was Barry Bonds Really Able to Save His Biggest Homers at Oracle Park?" NBCSports.com Bay Area, April 30, 2020.

"What Tony Gwynn Jr. Remembers About Barry Bonds' Exchanges with Father." NBCSports.com/bayarea/giants/what-tony-gwynn-jr-remembers-about-barry-bonds-exchanges-father, July 22, 2020.

Wilson, Burt. "Pittsburgh Radio Host Believes Tom Brady One of Worst Cheaters in Sports History." LancasterOnline.com, December 15, 2017.

Wilson, Duff and Michael S. Schmidt. "Steroid Report Cites 'Collective Failure.'" *The New York Times*, December 14, 2007.

Zirin, Dave. "Bonding with the Babe." TheNation.com, May 22, 2006.

Videos and Audio

ESPN. "Chipper Jones Says Barry Bonds Should Be Hall of Famer; The Dan Le Batard Show with Stugotz." YouTube video, January 25, 2018, www.youtube.com/watch?v=xoQmJPDy2GM.

Expos Classics. "Top 5 Reasons You Can't Blame Barry Bonds." YouTube video, May 5, 2018, www.youtube.com/watch?v=xsYYTPPOCj4.

Kpcanadians. "Vancouver Canadians Manager Mondays—Special Edition." YouTube video, August 20, 2012, https://www.youtube.com/watch?v=HaSA87prLNs.

MLB.com. "Episode 8: Barry Bonds." Forever Giants Podcast with Renel Brooks-Moon, January 16, 2019.

MLB.com. "SD@SF: Giants Clinch the 1997 NL West." YouTube video, December 11, 2013, https://www.youtube.com/watch?v=R_InY-Eaq78.

On Deck with Tyler Redmond. "Klesko: Bonds and McGriff are Hall of Famers." YouTube video, May 1, 2020, www.youtube.com/watch?v=zH2Mb7tC6qM.

Secret Base. "Barry Bonds' Beef with Jeff Kent Included Stolen Bus Seats, Motorcycle Mishaps and a Dugout Fight." YouTube video, May 7, 2019, https://www.youtube.com/watch?v=a_3UuLRt6mk.

List of Interviews

Adrian Brijbassi. Telephone interview, February 4, 2020.

Steve Buechele. Telephone interview, April 28, 2020.

Tom Candiotti. Telephone interview, February 1, 2020.

John Cangelosi. Telephone interview, March 9, 2020.

Royce Clayton. Telephone interview, February 25, 2020.

J. P. Hoornstra. Telephone interview, February 7, 2020.

Dustan Mohr. Telephone interview, March 2, 2020.

Bob Nightengale. Telephone interview, February 6, 2020.

John Patterson. Telephone interview, February 25, 2020.

Ted Sobel. Telephone interview, February 4, 2020.

Bob Walk. Telephone interview, April 14, 2020.

Don Slaught. Telephone interview, April 14, 2020.

About the Author

K. P. Wee is the author of several sports books, including *Tom Candiotti: A Life of Knuckleballs* (2014); *The End of the Montreal Jinx: Boston's Short-Lived Glory in the Historic Bruins-Canadiens Rivalry* (2015); *Don't Blame the Knuckleballer: Baseball Legends, Myths, and Stories* (2015); *The 1988 Dodgers: Reliving the Championship Season* (2018); and *The 1993 Canadiens: Seven Magical Weeks, Unlikely Heroes and Canada's Last Stanley Cup Champions* (2020). In addition, he co-authored the biography of *John Cangelosi: The Improbable Baseball Journey of the Undersized Kid from Nowhere to World Series Champion.* He also has a podcast titled "The K. P. Wee Podcast," which can be heard wherever podcasts are available.

Other Riverdale Avenue Books You Might Enjoy

**The 1993 Canadiens: Seven Magical Weeks, Unlikely Heroes
and Canada's Last Stanley Cup Champions**
By K.P. Wee

*John Cangelosi: The Improbable Baseball Journey of the
Undersized Kid from Nowhere to World Series Champion*
By John Cangelosi and K. P. Wee

The 50 Greatest Red Sox Games
By Cecilia Tan and Bill Nowlin

The 50 Greatest Dodger Games of All Time
By J.P. Hoornstra

**Bronx Bummers:
An Unofficial History of the New York Yankees'
Bad Boys, Blunders and Brawls**
By Robert Dominguez and David Hinckley

Bases Loaded: Baseball Erotica
Edited by F. Leonora Solomon

The Hot Streak: A Baseball Romance
By Cecilia Tan

Made in the USA
Monee, IL
17 April 2021